# Sleep Better!

# Sleep Better!

## A Guide to Improving Sleep for Children with Special Needs

by

*V. Mark Durand, Ph.D.*
University at Albany
State University of New York

·P·A·U·L·H·
BROOKES
PUBLISHING CO.®

Baltimore • London • Sydney

**Paul H. Brookes Publishing Co.**
Post Office Box 10624
Baltimore, Maryland 21285-0624
www.brookespublishing.com

Typeset by Barton Matheson Willse & Worthington, Baltimore, Maryland.
Manufactured in the United States of America by Versa Press, East Peoria, Illinois.

Chapter 12, Sleep and Medications, which appears on pages 185–194, provides information about numerous drugs used to treat sleep disorders. This chapter is in no way meant to substitute for a physician's advice or expert opinion; readers should consult a medical practitioner if they are interested in more information.

Permission to adapt the following material is gratefully acknowledged:
Page 146 (Ann case study): From *Abnormal Psychology: An Integrative Approach,* by D.H. Barlow and V.M. Durand. Copyright © 1995 Brooks/Cole Publishing Company, Pacific Grove, CA 93950, a division of International Thomson Publishing Inc. By permission of the publisher.

Fourth printing, May 2003.

**Library of Congress Cataloging-in-Publication Data**

Durand, Vincent Mark.
    Sleep better!  :  a guide to improving sleep for children with special needs  /  by V. Mark Durand.
      p.    cm.
    Includes bibliographical references and index.
    ISBN 1-55766-315-7 (alk. paper)
    1. Sleep disorders in children—Popular works.  2. Children—Sleep.
I. Title.
RJ506.S55D87     1998
618.92'8498—dc21                               97-28102
                                                           CIP

British Library Cataloguing in Publication data are available from the British Library.

# Contents

# About the Author

**V. Mark Durand, Ph.D.,** Professor and Chair, Department of Psychology, University at Albany, State University of New York, Albany, New York 12222

Dr. Durand received his doctoral degree in clinical psychology from the State University of New York at Stony Brook. He has contributed research in the area of self-injurious and disruptive behavior in people with severe disabilities, including autism. He has lectured nationally and internationally and has published in various journals, including the *Journal of Autism and Developmental Disorders,* the *Journal of Applied Behavior Analysis,* and the *Journal of The Association for Persons with Severe Handicaps.* Dr. Durand's best-selling book *Severe Behavior Problems: A Functional Communication Training Approach* (Guilford Press, 1990) outlines the treatments of problem behaviors using communication. He was honored in 1991 with an Excellence in Teaching Award from the State University of New York at Albany for his undergraduate and graduate teaching efforts. Dr. Durand also has co-authored two textbooks with Dr. David Barlow on abnormal psychology. In addition to his other interests, Dr. Durand has spent the past decade working with families and conducting research on sleep problems in children.

# Preface

This book was born out of my personal experiences with sleeping difficulties. To be more exact, it is the direct result of my own son's multiple troubles with sleep, which included problems falling asleep at night, difficulty sleeping through the night, his occasional episodes of sleep terrors (a disturbing sleep disorder that looks like a frightening nightmare but isn't), as well as nightmares, sleeptalking, sleepwalking, and even bruxism—or tooth grinding during sleep. It was his disturbed sleep and my and my wife's efforts to help him and us sleep better that were the early forces that sparked my subsequent research on sleep difficulties and, ultimately, this book.

Over a decade has passed since the worst of my son's sleep problems have been resolved, yet I still can recall many episodes quite vividly. Unless you have experienced it yourself, it is almost impossible to describe the feeling in the pit of your stomach that you experience when you hear your child cry at 12:30 A.M.—one more night of hundreds of such nights. Just as your body and your mind have begun to give up the tensions of the day, the stirring followed by the inevitable crying jolt you into the dreaded realization that it is happening one more time. One more night that your child will have disrupted sleep, and, despite your feeling guilty about thinking this way, you are aware that you too will not get a full and complete night's rest—by now a luxury for which you would be willing to trade much.

But because you are reading this book, you know this feeling all too well. If your child or someone you care for is experiencing sleep problems, then let me reassure you right away—there is reason to feel optimistic. *It is likely that the procedures described in this book will help you and your child sleep better, perhaps within the next few weeks.* This is not a careless statement. These procedures have been tested in scores of studies on people who do not have special needs and in a growing body of exciting new research studies that focus specifically on people who do have special needs. The news from these studies is worthy of our optimism, suggesting that most people who have problems with their sleep can be helped in a meaningful way.

After my experiences with my son's sleep problems, I had a new understanding of what it must be like for other parents. I could now empathize with the feelings of anxiety that result from not knowing what to do with your child who appears so distressed. At the same time, these helpless feelings can turn into depression—a common occurrence for people who feel that they have no control over important aspects of their lives. There often is embarrassment as well. I must be an inadequate parent (especially one who has a Ph.D. in psychology!) if I can't even get my child to go to bed at night.

Couple these feelings—and the stress that goes with them—with the thousands of parents who have children with special needs, and you have an almost intolerable situation. I have worked with children with special needs for more than 20 years and have been privileged also to work with many of their parents. I was alarmed to learn that children with special needs are *more likely* to have sleep difficulties. It is hard to imagine how stressful life must be for these families to deal with the multitude of problems that these children can present—all without having a good night's sleep! This concern led me to examine more closely the unique difficulties posed by the sleep problems of these children. For example, none of the books on sleep talk about how to deal with the little girl who not only wakes up several times each night but also severely bangs her head into the headboard of her bed. Nowhere could I find advice for the boy with attention-deficit/hyperactivity disorder who never seems tired and whose medication for attention difficulties might contribute to his sleep problems. Little advice was available for the parents of the boy with autism who roamed the house each night and who sometimes would climb out his window at 3:30 A.M. It was for these children and the multitudes of others with similar idiosyncratic needs that my colleagues and I decided to embark on a series of studies to evaluate sleep interventions and to write this book describing our successes.

It is important to point out that not all of our efforts were successful initially. Some of the people with whom we work need additional medical attention. I point out some of these situations as the sleep problems and their treatments are examined. Readers should be warned that for severe and/or persistent sleep problems that do not respond to the suggestions in this book, more extensive evaluation may be needed. Throughout the United States and internationally are Sleep Disorders Centers that can conduct these more extensive evaluations, and we provide a list of the U.S. centers in Appendix C of this book. These centers are accredited members of the American Sleep Disorders Association and provide expert evaluation and treatment.

The language adopted in this book bears mentioning. First, I primarily use the phrase "people with special needs" to indicate a range of individuals with varying abilities. In my colleagues and my work, we have helped and consulted with families who have children with labels such as autism, mental retardation, pervasive developmental disabilities, and attention-deficit/hyperactivity disorder. At the same time, other children have not received official labels but have had difficulties learning or may have experienced some traumatic events (e.g., abuse, accidents) that have interfered with their sleep. I hope that readers will not find the use of the phrase "people with special needs" in any way offensive. It clearly is just a literary convenience.

I describe mostly children and adolescents but sometimes discuss the problems of adults as well. Children grow up, and, frequently, parents struggle with the sleep problems of their adult child, so I include a range of issues that are relevant to children, adolescents, and adults.

You will notice that the "voice" of this book usually is referred to as "we," although there is only one author. "We" is used to recognize the group of us who have worked with parents and children on their sleep problems over the last decade. "I" is used when I am relating some personal anecdote—usually about my son's sleep problems.

Finally, you will come across numbered notations in the text. These numbers refer to notes that can be found in the "Endnotes" section at the end of this book.

We begin the book with a discussion of sleep (Chapter 1), followed by a description of a range of sleep problems (Chapter 2), and then a step-by-step interview (Chapter 3) that will help you identify the type of sleep problem that your child is experiencing. As you will learn, there are many reasons why people do not sleep well, and it may be helpful to you to understand the nature of the sleep problem before attempting any treatment. Having said that, readers still can go directly to Chapter 3 for the Sleep Interview and identify the specific sleep problem. The good news is that most of the sleep problems that we experience can be identified easily. Once you have found the type of sleep problem, you can move on to the sections on treatment. The last sections of the book describe the multitude of treatment options available for these sleep difficulties, most of which involve drug-free approaches. I have tried to include a number of actual cases to show you how my colleagues and I have proceeded with the complexities of these treatment plans. If you carefully follow the steps described here, then sleep should be greatly improved soon. We wish you luck.

# Acknowledgments

There are many people to thank for their help in creating this book. Clearly, I owe a great deal to the many families who opened up their lives and their homes to my colleagues and me. Often, it was embarrassing for families to tell strangers how their lives had been turned upside-down as a result of their child's sleep problems. I thank them for their honesty, for their patience, and for their determination to once again help their children in difficult times. Several of my graduate students, both past and present, served as primary therapists for many of the cases described in this book, and their help is greatly appreciated. Among the students who have had the greatest impact on this work are Eileen Mapstone, Kristin Chistodulu, Dr. Peter Gernert-Dott, and Dr. Jodi Mindell. Their efforts and wisdom are woven throughout this book. I also would like to acknowledge the staff of Paul H. Brookes Publishing Co., especially Christa Horan and Jennifer Lazaro Kinard, for their work in getting my words into print. Finally, my thanks and my love to my wife and son—Wendy and Jonathan—for helping me learn about sleep and for being my support whenever I needed it.

To Wendy, for being the perfect partner,

and

to Jonathan, for being the perfect teacher

# Sleep Better!

# I

# The Nature and Problems of Sleep

# 1

# An Overview of Sleep

Sleep has intrigued us for centuries. Authors throughout the ages have written about sleep, quite positively when sleep is good:

*"Oh sleep! it is a gentle thing,*
*Beloved from pole to pole!"*

Samuel Taylor Coleridge,
*The Rime of the Ancient Mariner, Part V*

but often quite negatively as well:

*"Sleep is a death; oh, make me try,*
*By sleeping what it is to die."*

Sir Thomas Browne, *Religio Medici*

Before we begin our exploration into the problems that people experience with sleep, we first will take a look at what sleep is. Some basic understanding of how and why we sleep is necessary to help explain what can go wrong with this important part of our lives. You may, understandably, be anxious for some answers. If you have a child who has had sleep difficulties for many nights, then you may just want to "get on with it" and move ahead to Chapter 3, which helps you identify the specific problems and why they may be occurring.

Knowing what sleep is, however, might prove to be interesting to you, and this knowledge may help you understand when sleep goes wrong.

Sleep refreshes and restores us. Although many people seem to try to cheat sleep, to "burn the candle at both ends" and avoid wasting precious hours unproductively, we actually need sleep as much as we need food and air. Sleep professionals are just at the beginning of the search for knowledge about sleep and how it affects us, but it is becoming clear that sleep serves several essential roles in our lives. For example, sleep seems to be important for learning and for our memory. Somehow during sleep, the brain processes information and makes it accessible to us later. Research[1] has suggested that sleep also may be involved in the body's ability to ward off illness, helping to restore the immune system. And without sleep, we die. Although many believe that there are people who do not sleep at all, going too long without sleep is, in fact, fatal. You can see that sleep is important to our physical well-being. It is essential for our mental well-being as well. Without sleep, we become irritable, our motivation declines, and our ability to concentrate on everyday tasks is diminished. The seriousness of not sleeping is illustrated in the number of traffic-related accidents due to a lack of sleep, estimated by the U.S. National Highway Traffic Safety Administration at as many as 200,000 accidents per year[2]. Lack of sleep mainly was responsible for the crash of the Exxon Valdez oil tanker[3] and is thought to have a role in most nuclear reactor accidents, which usually occur in the very early morning[4]. Sleep is an essential part of our lives, and sleeping well is necessary for the soundness of our bodies and our minds.

Before describing what problem sleep is and how to sleep better, it is important first to examine what "normal" sleep is. You should already be a little uneasy with this term. "Normal" has been misused when it comes to people with special needs, and the same is true for sleep. There are a number of myths about what is good, or normal, sleep, and it is best to take a look at these myths before discussing the problems that people experience when it comes to sleeping. Following is an overview of important information about why and how we sleep and how sleep can be disrupted.

## HOW MUCH SLEEP DO WE NEED?

Most people believe that everyone needs about 8 hours of uninterrupted sleep each night to be rested and alert the next day. For many people, this is true. About two thirds of all adults report sleeping from 7 to 8 hours per night and feeling rested. The "8 hours" of sleep that we all think is ideal, however, really is only an average—which means that some people need less sleep, and some people need more. On the one hand, there are people who sleep as few as 4–5 hours each night and feel rested. On the other hand, others report sleeping 9 or more hours but complain that they do not feel refreshed.

Sleep professionals still do not understand why sleep needs differ so much among people, but our own individual needs seem to be pretty constant. The number of hours that each of us sleeps might differ from night to night depending on changing schedules or stress during the day; but if you compare from week to week or from month to month, then you will notice that we tend to sleep, on average, about the same amount of time each day.

One factor that determines approximately how long people will sleep is age. Figure 1.1 shows how our total sleep time gradually decreases as we age. In the first few days of life, infants will sleep as many as 16 hours in a day. As they grow older, children begin to sleep less, needing only about 12 hours by the age of 2 and about 8 hours by age 13. Remember, these numbers represent an average, so your 2-year-old may sleep more or less than 12 hours but still be rested. Sleep needs continue to decline throughout adulthood so that by age 50, people sleep on average only about 6 hours per day. In addition, older adults frequently experience sleep problems in the form of frequent night waking and often feel that they are not getting enough sleep.

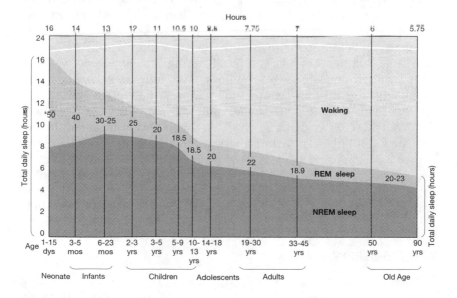

**Figure 1.1.**    Sleep across the life span. (* = percentage of total sleep.) (Reprinted with permission from Roffwarg, H.P., Muzio, J.N., & Dement, W.C. [1966]. Ontogenetic development of the human sleep–dream cycle. *Science, 152,* 604–619. Copyright 1966 American Association for the Advancement of Science.)

## WHEN ARE OWLS AND LARKS NOT BIRDS?

There is one rule in my house that rarely is discussed but that is understood by all: Do not talk to Dad in the morning. Actually, this is not a rule so much as a reminder that if my wife or my son does try to engage me in conversation early in the morning, then she or he will come away quite dissatisfied. Because work forces me to awaken earlier than my body likes, I am often uncommunicative—using mostly grunts to respond to questions—until about an hour after I have awakened. I am one of about 10% of adults who is an owl (or "night owl")—a person whose preferred time to be awake is from late morning until early the next morning. Another 10% of adults are larks—people who relish the early morning. As we will see later, all humans are programmed to sleep in the evening and to be awake during the daylight hours. But there are those of us who push the edges of our nighttime preference for sleep.

Owls' preference for the latter part of the day and evening and larks' preference for early rising have been documented in research studies. In one study[5], owls were found to be at their peak performance on logical reasoning skills at 11:00 A.M., whereas larks were at their best at 8:00 A.M. (By the way, it is 10:30 A.M. as I write this, so I am almost there!) These sleep differences hold up even when these people are kept in the dark and away from normal sleep cues, which means that their different preferences for sleep are more than just a result of their learning different sleep habits. Larks usually exercise in the morning before work, owls in the evening after work. The behaviorist B.F. Skinner was a lark, typically rising at 1:00 A.M. to work for an hour, then sleeping for several hours, and ultimately beginning his day at 5:00 A.M. Famous owls include Socrates, the French philosopher and mathematician René Descartes, and the inventor Thomas Edison.

We will see later that knowing whether a person is one of the minority who is either an owl or a lark sometimes helps to explain presumed problems with sleep. A person's disruption and refusal to go to bed at a particular time may be the result of a clash between a child's owl preference for a later bedtime and a parent's lark preference for an earlier one. Discussed next are sleep itself, what it is, and why we do it.

## WHAT IS SLEEP?

We take sleep for granted because we experience it each day, and most people assume that science long ago unlocked its mysteries. The contrary is true, however; the complete answer to the question "What is sleep?" continues to elude us. Sleep professionals certainly know a great deal about what happens to the brain and the body during sleep, and next we briefly review some of the more important physiological changes that occur while we sleep. But the answer to what sleep is and why we all do it continues to be one of the more fascinating secrets left to explain about human beings.

The first thing to understand about sleep is that it is *not* a time when the brain shuts down for a rest. Despite our being unaware of what is going on around us, the brain is quite active during sleep, as is the body. We go through several stages of sleep that seem to serve different purposes, and these stages are very different from each other. One reason sleep professionals are interested in the different stages of sleep is that each also has its own characteristic sleep problems. We can better understand what is going wrong with sleep if we first understand the way sleep progresses normally.

There are two main phases of sleep—*rapid eye movement* (REM) and *non–rapid eye movement* (NREM, pronounced "non–REM"). The REM phase of sleep is when we dream. The eye movement under closed eyelids during sleep signals the time when people report that they experience the universal phenomenon of dreams. REM sleep was not discovered until 1953 at the University of Chicago by Dr. Nathaniel Kleitman and his graduate student Eugene Aserinsky. These sleep researchers were amazed that everyone whom they studied while asleep had these periods of rapid eye movement, and these episodes began in each person approximately 90 minutes after he or she first fell asleep. Not knowing what these eye movements might mean, they later performed a very simple experiment: They awakened people during these times and asked the participants what they were experiencing. About 80% of the time, the person reported some dream. The discovery of REM sleep revolutionized the field of sleep research because it indicated that there was some order to sleep—regular phases that were common to all people.

Kleitman and Aserinsky observed a period of approximately 90 minutes prior to the onset of REM sleep when the person clearly was asleep but exhibited no apparent eye activity. This phase—NREM—continues to be somewhat of an enigma today. We begin our sleep in NREM sleep and go through several stages. The four stages of NREM sleep roughly correspond to how deeply we sleep. The first stage is "light" sleep, the second stage is a "deeper" sleep, and the third and fourth stages are the "deepest" sleep. During the first stage (creatively referred to as Stage 1), we are in transition between being awake and being asleep. During this stage, people tend to feel that they are awake, although their thoughts begin to drift. Early researchers attempting to study Stage 1 sleep taped open the eyelids of volunteers and found that these people could not later remember pictures shown to them during this time[6].

Following Stage 1, the pattern of brain waves begins to change, and we drift into the deeper stages of sleep (Stages 2 through 4). In the deepest stages of sleep (Stages 3 and 4), it becomes very difficult to awaken someone. I remember that the day when my son was born, I had been up for almost 48 hours (along with my wife, of course). After the birth, I came home to sleep. Approximately 60 minutes after I first fell asleep—which is about the time when we enter the deep stages of sleep—the phone rang numerous times. I was finally awakened and found myself speaking with a friend who was curious about the outcome of my son's birth. My friend was astonished that I could not recall any of the details, including whether it was a boy or a girl! This was not unusual, for although someone can be awakened from these deep stages of sleep with some prodding, it takes a few minutes for the person to become fully alert.

After we cycle through approximately 90 minutes of NREM sleep, we then move into REM sleep. As mentioned previously, this is the time when our eyes move rapidly under our eyelids and people report dreams. What may surprise you about this phase is that although the brain is very active during this time, the body is almost paralyzed (called *atonic*). Did you ever have a dream in which you were trying to run away from someone but felt as though your legs were dragging? Or did you ever dream that something terrible was happening to you, but you could not scream? These are common dream experiences because they correspond to the body's inability to move during this time. Our muscles are almost completely paralyzed, which accounts for the dreams of leg dragging as well as the inability to use your vocal muscles to scream. If you have witnessed someone crying out during a dream, it was probably just as he or she awoke, which signaled the end of REM sleep. This information helps us to understand that several types of sleep problems, such as sleeptalking and sleepwalking (also called *somnambulism*), occur during NREM sleep and probably do *not* represent the acting out of a dream.

We progress through this series of sleep stages several times throughout the night, going through the four stages of NREM sleep, into REM sleep, then back again to NREM. During the transition to NREM sleep after our period of dreaming, we experience a phenomenon known as *partial waking*. This is a brief period (sometimes only a few seconds) when we actually awaken from sleep. You might have had the experience of being in bed next to someone who had been asleep, who sat up and said something, then immediately fell back to sleep. When asked about it the next morning, the person had no memory of the event. This was probably an episode of partial waking, which we all experience as a normal part of sleep. This partial waking is important to understanding the night waking of children. As we will see later, all children experience these partial wakings; however, some children awaken fully from these episodes and then cry out or leave their beds for the comfort of parents. We explore in later chapters why this happens and how to respond to these episodes.

Our dream sleep appears to be extremely important. Although many authors have written quite eloquently about the content of dreams and how to interpret them, the mere act of going through this phase of sleep also seems necessary for our well-being. You may have noticed that when you miss a great deal of sleep, you may sleep a bit longer on subsequent nights, but you usually do not need to make up each hour missed. People who are sleep deprived, however, do make up their missed REM sleep. In other words, the brain seems to compensate for this type of sleep by more quickly moving into REM sleep, even at the expense of NREM sleep. REM sleep is so important because it is involved in memory and in consolidating newly learned information. Looking back at Figure 1.1, you will notice that newborns spend approximately 50% of their sleep in REM sleep, possibly because of their need to make sense of all of the new information that they are exposed to throughout their busy day. The importance of REM sleep in learning and memory, coupled with the relative lack of REM sleep experienced by people with sleep problems, suggests that people with sleep problems may not only become irritable if they continue to go without enough sleep, but they may also experience cognitive impairments as a result[7]. Obviously, for people with special needs who may already have difficulties learning, the added interference with learning and memory caused by their sleeping difficulties is of great concern. A number of research studies[8] show that amounts of REM sleep tend to be lower among individuals with more extensive forms of mental retardation. What is unknown is whether the relative lack of REM sleep further adds to their learning difficulties. This is just one more reason why the sleep of people with special needs is an important area of concern.

## WHAT IS OUR BIOLOGICAL CLOCK?

> *"I know who I was when I got up this morning, but I think I must have changed several times since then."*
>
> Alice, *Alice's Adventures in Wonderland,* by Lewis Carroll

Probably some of the most fascinating information about our bodies and sleep is coming from researchers who sometimes call themselves "chronobiologists." *Chronobiology* is the study of "body time," or how our body's temperature, hormones, and other biological functions fluctuate from day to day and from hour to hour. Like Alice, we all change quite dramatically over the course of the day, and these changes seem to have a profound effect on us. The sleep–wake cycle is considered one of the *circadian rhythms*—the word *circadian* means "about a day."

Deep inside the brain is a little bundle of cells—about the shape and size of this letter "v"—which is called the *superchiasmatic nucleus* (SCN). The SCN is our "biological clock"—the part of the brain that keeps many body rhythms in sync. The SCN is located on top of the main junction of nerve fibers that connects to our eyes, a connection that becomes important, especially for sleep. The SCN seems to signal the brain when it is time to sleep and when it is time to be awake, and this sleep–wake cycle runs through its course over a period of about 24 hours. An unusual thing happens, though, if people literally are kept in the dark and not given information about whether it is day or night. If people are kept away from light cues, then they will fall asleep and awaken on a cycle that runs about 25 hours long. It appears that the increasing light in the morning and the decreasing light at night trigger the SCN to reset itself each day to run through a 24-hour day rather than a 25-hour day.

One group of people for whom this phenomenon is especially important is individuals with severe visual impairments (blindness). Because people with blindness cannot receive light cues from the sun, their sleep–wake cycle sometimes runs through the 25-hour cycle. At first glance, this may not appear to be a serious problem, but consider how their sleep patterns will change over the course of several weeks. If, for example, a person without the benefit of light cues falls asleep at 10:00 P.M. on Sunday evening, then he or she will not be tired and fall asleep until about 11:00 P.M. on Monday (25 hours later). This advances to about midnight on Tuesday, 1:00 A.M. on Wednesday, and by the next Sunday, he or she will be awake all night and not be tired until 5:00 A.M.! This pattern of sleeping during the day and being awake at night will continue the following week, until the pattern gradually comes around again. Parents of children with severe visual impairments often are unaware that their children's sleep is affected in this way. The parents instead report that their children cycle through good and bad times, sometimes seeming to be "in tune" during the day and other times seeming to be "out of it," or irritable and cranky. These children often are referred to sleep professionals for help because they are aggressive during the day, although not every day. Their parents and teachers frequently do not suspect that these mood swings correspond to the synchronousness or lack of synchronousness between the child's sleep–wake cycle and that of everyone else.

Lest you think that the prognosis for people with severe visual impairments and their sleep is all bad, there has been a breakthrough in this area that is beginning to provide relief for these individuals and their families. A certain hormone—melatonin—is partially responsible for transmitting the message to the SCN that it is dark outside. Melatonin primarily is produced in the pineal gland and is secreted in large amounts when the decreasing amount of light at nighttime is detected by the eyes. You may be familiar with melatonin because of the media attention that it has received as not only a natural cure for all sleep problems but also the answer to longer life and any number of ailments. I think that we have become savvy enough to recognize that such dramatic claims often are nothing more than calculated attempts to sell books; however, melatonin does provide some real benefit to the sleep of some groups of individuals. Initial research[9] suggests that small amounts of melatonin, when given prior to the desired bedtime, can stimulate the brain's biological clock to signal the time to sleep. This seems to be very helpful for regulating sleep and wake times, especially for people with blindness. Melatonin is discussed later in more detail along with the group of sleep problems known as *circadian rhythm disorders.*

The discovery of how the sleep–wake cycle naturally leans toward a 25-hour day helped answer several questions about sleep. For example, for most of us, it is easier to stay awake an hour or so later at night than it is to fall asleep earlier. This is because of the body's natural tendency to move toward the 25-hour pattern. This also explains why it is more difficult to adjust to flying eastward across time zones than to flying westward. For example, when you fly from New York to Los Angeles, you "gain" 3 hours because when your body (which is still on New York time) says that it is 11:00 P.M. (your typical bedtime), it is only 8:00 P.M. in Los Angeles. Your body naturally wants to stay awake a bit longer anyway, so it is not difficult to adjust. When you fly from Los Angeles to New York, however, you "lose" 3 hours. Therefore, when you arrive in New York and it is your usual bedtime of 11:00 P.M., your body—which is still on L.A. time—says that it is only 8:00 P.M.—too early to fall asleep. It takes a few days for your body's circadian rhythms to adjust to this new time. Similarly, shift workers find it easier to change schedules ahead from an afternoon to an evening schedule rather than back from an evening to an afternoon shift. Sometimes changes in schedules due to events such as changing time zones or shift changes will have more than a temporary effect. These sleep problems are examined later in the book.

## HOW DOES OUR TEMPERATURE AFFECT SLEEP?

In addition to changes in the hormone melatonin, our body's internal temperature also seems to be involved in how and when we sleep. Our bodies do not maintain a constant temperature of 98.6°F; rather, our internal temperature increases and decreases over the course of the day, making it another circadian rhythm. More recent and accurate measurement of body temperature indicates that the "normal" average temperature is 98.2°F, a little lower than we once thought, and that this ranges from about 97°F at its lowest point to about 99°F at its highest[10]. These changes in temperature during the course of the day seem to closely follow periods of sleep and wakefulness.

Our body temperature is at its lowest in the early hours of the morning (between about 4:00 A.M. and 6:00 A.M.) and begins to rise just before we awaken. This rise in temperature is involved in our alertness, signaling the time to wake up in the morning. Throughout the rest of the day, our body temperature rises gently, with the exception of a slight dip at midday. Our high temperature of about 99°F occurs in the early evening (between 7:00 P.M. and 8:00 P.M.) and then begins its decline. The drop in temperature signals a time of decreased alertness and corresponds to when most people feel the need to sleep. The general rule of thumb is that we are most alert when our natural body temperature is high and least alert when it is low.

Understanding the relationship between body temperature and sleep not only gives us more information about how and why we sleep but also provides us with very helpful information about how our lifestyles will affect sleep. Exercise, for example, raises our internal body temperature. In terms of helping our sleep, the best time to exercise is in the late afternoon, sometime around 4:00 P.M. or 5:00 P.M. The rise in body temperature after we exercise at this point in the day lasts for about 6 hours and then declines, making it optimal for falling asleep in the late evening. You can see that exercising later in the evening just before bedtime may interfere with sleep. Because of the importance of body temperature to sleep, people often wonder whether taking a warm bath or shower at bedtime will actually cause difficulties in falling asleep. This does not seem to be a problem, perhaps because a bath or shower does little to affect our internal body temperature.

## CONCLUSION

Knowing the fundamentals of sleep and how sleep can be affected can help you and your child with special needs sleep better. This introduction to sleep gives you a good knowledge base as we turn our attention to the problems that people can experience with their sleep. Chapter 2 does not provide an exhaustive list of sleep problems (which itself could fill the pages of this book) but rather describes some of the more common sleep problems experienced by people with special needs.

# 2

## Sleep Problems

*O sleep! O gentle sleep!*
*Nature's soft nurse, how have I frighted thee,*
*That thou no more wilt weigh my eyelids down*
*And steep my senses in forgetfulness?*

William Shakespeare, *King Henry IV, Part II*

King Henry IV's longing for sleep seems at odds with modern-day society's desire to wring the most out of a day. Many of us are trying to do more with less sleep. Many more people yearn to sleep better, but, for a variety of reasons, they cannot. Some have difficulty falling asleep or have their sleep disturbed frequently throughout the night. Others feel tired even after what seems to be a full night's sleep. Still others may encounter a number of abnormal sleep experiences, such as frequent and disturbing nightmares, sleep terrors (which at first resemble nightmares but are a very different sleep disturbance), sleepwalking, or sleeptalking. This chapter addresses the many ways in which sleep can be disrupted, along with what is known about the causes of these problems.

## HOW COMMON ARE SLEEP PROBLEMS?

You may be surprised to learn that as many as one of every four other-wise healthy adults experiences significant problems with sleep. At the same time, a similar ratio of children experience sleep problems. What is most alarming is that sleep problems seem to occur *more* often in people with special needs. As if life were not complicated enough, adding a sleep problem on top of all of the other difficulties can make getting through each day a greater challenge for people with special needs as well as for their families and friends.

People with autism may be among the most seriously affected when it comes to sleep problems; some research[1] suggests that almost all of these individuals experience difficulty with sleep at some point in their lives. A survey[2] of children with a range of developmental disabilities found that about 80% of parents reported some problem with their child's sleep and that one in four described the problem as severe. To make matters worse, the parents also indicated that, unlike children without disabilities, their children did not seem to grow out of these sleep problems and that their sleeping difficulties persisted into adulthood. Sleep problems commonly occur among children with a variety of disorders, including Tourette syndrome, Rett syndrome, and cerebral palsy.

Problems with sleep can be a sign of other problems. Nightmares, sleep terrors, and other problems with sleep are commonly reported among children and adults who have been victims of abuse or other traumatic events. Obviously, this does not necessarily mean that a sleep problem is a sign of past or current abuse but simply that these upsetting episodes can increase the likelihood of sleep problems in the affected person. Even something as apparently unrelated as marital discord can disrupt the sleep of the couple's children.

Sleep is often reported as a problem for children with attention-deficit/hyperactivity disorder (ADHD). ADHD affects an estimated 3% of all children[3] and results in difficulties with attention; for many children, it also involves impulsivity and hyperactivity. The most common treatment for these children is a medical one—typically a stimulant medication such as Ritalin. Parents of these children often lament that their children develop sleep problems after being placed on this type of medication. (How to balance the medication needs of these children with their sleep needs is described in Chapter 12.) Research[4] suggests that sleep problems among children with ADHD may be *overreported* by some parents, meaning that they may expect their children to have disturbed sleep because of the medication and therefore inaccurately relate these problems. It is clear, however, that many children with ADHD require assistance with their sleep.

## HOW SERIOUS ARE SLEEP PROBLEMS?

As you can see, many groups of people with special needs experience disturbed sleep. In addition to the sheer number of people who have difficulty with their sleep, the effects of sleep on behavior also contribute to the concern of families and professionals. For example, disturbed sleep has a negative impact on performance during certain tasks—motivation to work decreases, and the ability to concentrate becomes impaired. Similarly, people who have not had enough sleep often report feeling irritable or depressed. What can be said, then, about the effects on people with special needs—especially those who have difficulty learning and carrying out daily tasks?

Unfortunately, research that examines the effects of sleep problems on people with special needs is rare, so there is very little direct knowledge about how they may be affected. Some general conclusions can be made, however, based on research usually conducted on adults without disabilities. It is important to note that one night of disrupted sleep probably will have a minimal effect on a person's ability to carry out daily tasks. That is good news because, occasionally, all of us experience a night when, because of anxiety over a presentation that you have to give, the cup of coffee that you enjoyed too late at night, the excitement over a trip the next day, or even just being anxious about not falling asleep, we sleep very little. Despite being tired, we are able to get through the day relatively well. Should this disturbed sleep persist for more than a day or two, however, noticeable effects are likely. Persistent and chronic sleep disturbances will cause a decline in motivation or concentration as opposed to a loss of ability. As motivation decreases, concentration is impaired, and performance errors increase. People involved in boring, repetitive tasks will show the effects of a poor night's sleep more readily than will those involved in interesting and challenging tasks. Consider this in light of how we tend to treat children and adults with special needs. A person who has difficulty learning new skills (e.g., a person with mental retardation or learning disabilities) is usually given an easier and therefore sometimes boring and repetitive task until he or she is considered "ready" to move on to more challenging work. If the person also experiences sleep problems, then his or her difficulty at work will be made worse by performing the same unchallenging work over and over. You can see that we may mistakenly attribute errors on schoolwork or at a job to the person's cognitive difficulties, when this problem may be a result, in part, of sleep problems and our lack of understanding of its effects on a person's performance.

Sleep also affects our emotional well-being. In research with young children, it has been found that sleeping longer is associated

with adaptability (being able to tolerate changes in routines) and positive mood, whereas sleeping less is associated with children described
as "difficult"—those who get upset when you try to change routines
and who always seem irritable[5]. One young boy with whom I worked
was referred because he lacked motivation in class and was generally
noncompliant of his teacher's requests. The boy had mental retardation requiring extensive supports, and the teacher seemed to assume
that his difficulties were related to his diagnosis. After watching him at
his desk in class for a few minutes, I turned to his mother, who also
was watching, and said, "He doesn't sleep very well, does he?" His
mother was astounded that I knew that without her having told me,
and his teacher was even more astounded because she did not know
herself that the boy slept only 3–4 hours each night. They both looked
at me with awe at my remarkable clinical skills and asked how I knew
this after seeing him for only a few minutes. I ruined the adulation
when I said, "Well, he looks tired!" This story highlights not only how
a lack of sleep can affect mood and behavior (which, fortunately, improved in this boy when his parents and I helped him sleep better—
the full details of which are described in Chapter 3) but also how we
tend to overlook sleep as an important influence on how we think,
feel, and behave.

In some cases, the negative impact of poor sleep can be even more
serious. My colleagues' and my own research on people who display
self-injurious and aggressive behavior—too often observed among
people with autism and other developmental disorders—has revealed
that disrupted sleep can make these behavior problems worse[6]. Not
sleeping well can make some people hit themselves or others more
often. On a positive note, the occurrence of these very disturbing behaviors can be reduced by improving the affected person's sleep.

A final measure of how serious these sleep problems can be is easily seen in the families of people with disrupted sleep. In some cases,
couples' marriages have been threatened because of their child's sleep
problems. Depression among parents—especially mothers—also is
common in these families. The cause of these problems at home can
be traced to several factors. First, a child's disturbed sleep invariably
means that the parents' sleep also will be disrupted. Getting up with
your child each and every night for months and years means that both
you and your child will be sleep deprived. You have just learned that
your ability to concentrate and your mood will be affected in a negative way if you are not sleeping well yourself. In addition, the psychological research literature shows that depression can occur when people feel that they have no control over important parts of their lives[7].
People begin to feel helpless, and they give up trying to improve this

nighttime problem. My colleagues and I worked with one mother whose child awakened and cried each and every night for 7 years. She had long ago given up hope that anything could be done to help them get a good night's sleep and felt guilty that she could not help her child. Obviously, sleep disturbances can have negative consequences for everyone who is in some way touched by this vexing problem. Fortunately, we were able to help this family despite their long history of sleep problems.

## WHEN DOES SLEEP BECOME A PROBLEM?

Chapter 1 mentioned that people have different sleep needs. Some people can sleep for only 3–4 hours per night and feel rested and refreshed. Others can sleep for 9–10 hours and still feel tired the next day. This issue of sleep differences raises an important question: If people have different sleep needs, then how do you know whether a child's inability to sleep more than a few hours per night is a sleep problem or just a normal difference? You might be surprised to learn that sleep experts rely heavily on the subjective impressions of the person with the sleep complaint. In other words, if a person sleeps for only 4 hours per night but is not bothered by this and can carry on daily activities, then it is not considered a sleep problem. Conversely, if a person sleeps for an average of 9 hours per night but is still tired during the day and is concerned about sleep, then it is considered a sleep problem. For children, this often translates into how well they function during the day and how disturbing the sleep difficulty is at night. If a child appears tired and irritable even after 8 hours of sleep, then he or she may have a sleep problem. Similarly, if bedtime is disrupted (e.g., the child cries for 20 minutes or more each night) or night waking is a problem (e.g., screaming out each night), then this too may signal a problem with sleep.

## COMMON SLEEP PROBLEMS

As we turn next to the common sleep problems experienced by people with special needs, bear in mind this subjective quality of sleep. If your child's sleep pattern adversely affects him or her or your family in any important way, then assume that it is significant enough to examine more closely. Keep in mind, too, that there are more than 80 different and distinct sleep problems recognized by sleep professionals—far too many to cover adequately here. Fortunately, only a handful of these problems are commonly experienced by people with special needs. Described next are the most frequently occurring sleep disturbances and some information on their causes.

## Insomnia

What image does your mind conjure up when you think of a person with insomnia? Most people picture a person who never sleeps yet who functions well during the day. This is, however, just one more myth about sleep. It is not possible to go completely without sleep for very long. If you stay awake for more than a day or two, then you will begin having brief periods of sleep that last for several seconds—called *microsleeps*. People with severe insomnia often are unaware that they have these brief sleep episodes and, thus, believe that they never sleep. In addition to experiencing microsleeps, a person who is this sleep deprived will notice significant negative effects on his or her life. Sleep-deprived individuals often have substantial impairments in the quality of their lives and have difficulty getting through even the simplest of life's daily chores. As mentioned in Chapter 1, a complete lack of sleep is catastrophic. One sleep disorder that does involve not sleeping at all is called *fatal familial insomnia*. As the name implies, this progressive sleep disorder ultimately leads to death for those afflicted, but, fortunately, it is an extremely rare problem.

Insomnia is not one problem but encompasses instead a number of different problems with sleep. Sleep professionals break down insomnia into three different and distinct types:

- Difficulty falling asleep at night (called a *difficulty initiating sleep*)
- Waking frequently during the night or waking too early and being unable to go back to sleep (called a *difficulty maintaining sleep*)
- Not feeling rested even after a reasonable number of hours of sleep (called *nonrestorative sleep*)

As with all of the sleep problems described, a person is considered as having insomnia only when the cause of these sleep disturbances cannot be traced to some other medical or psychological problem. If, for example, a person is not sleeping well because he or she is experiencing pain, then this is not technically thought to be primarily a sleep problem. At the same time, a person who is anxious or depressed will often have difficulty sleeping. If the anxiety or depression is the primary cause of the sleep difficulties, then this is where clinical attention is first paid.

Sleep deprivation, whether it is a result of not being able to fall asleep, of waking up too frequently, or of not receiving refreshing sleep, affects about one third of people with special needs and is the most common of the sleep complaints. It also appears that these sleep problems often will not go away on their own. Although many children do seem to grow out of their early sleep difficulties, many do not; and, as we have learned, these sleep problems can upset the lives of everyone in the family. Examining the different types of insomnia is important because it will lead directly to the causes of these problems and ultimately to their treatment.

**Difficulty Initiating Sleep**   One of the symptoms of insomnia is difficulty going to sleep at an acceptable time. As many parents know all too well, this can involve quite emotional outbursts from the child. Some children will scream and cry for hours. Others are more subtle in their efforts to avoid bedtime and concoct elaborate routines that involve the whole family. At one point in my home, for example, my son orchestrated an hour-long parade of events that would begin with reading a story, followed by "just one more" story, then hugs and kisses, followed by back scratching. This was then followed by more hugs and kisses. After a few minutes in bed, there was a need for a glass of water. Then a trip to the bathroom. Then another trip to the bathroom. Then the sheets weren't just right, there was a noise outside, it was too hot or cold. . . . Sound familiar? Still other people will just lie awake in bed, not able to fall asleep. These difficulties can stem from a number of different problems.

For some children, bedtime difficulties stem from the inability or the unwillingness of parents to set limits on their children's bedtime. Many parents report that they become extremely upset when their child cries or screams and that anything is preferable to listening to that kind of gut-wrenching, emotional outburst. They find that going into the child's room to comfort him or her or bringing the child into their own bed will end that evening's battle; but, as we all know, this will just postpone the problem until the next night. Worse yet, repeatedly giving in to a child's tantrums could teach him or her to have a tantrum every night, usually in ever-increasing intensity.

It is important to remember that parents are not completely to blame in this case or in any other case of a childhood sleep problem. Although some parents are quite aware of the pattern that develops at bedtime and recognize their role in the situation, they forget that their child has a role as well. Often, parents have to be reminded that many children fall asleep on their own. In other words, some children's sleep patterns are such that the child has no difficulty falling asleep at night and, in fact, seeks out bedtime. The child who resists bedtime may be one who simply is not tired at the time when most of us sleep. An additional difference is *temperament*. Different children have different personalities or temperaments and will deal with problem situations in their own ways. Some children who are not tired at bedtime may be more easygoing and will therefore do their best to fall asleep after being asked. Other children, however, are more strong willed and feisty, and they put up a fight over most situations. The child who resists being told when to wash up or which clothes to wear may similarly resist your decision about bedtime. If this describes your child, then there is help for you in Chapter 11. Take some solace in knowing that it takes two or more people to create this problem, and there are relatively easy "fixes" that can resolve even the most disturbing bedtime disasters.

Why is it that some people simply are not tired at bedtime? One reason may be what you do, eat, and drink before bedtime. Referred to by sleep experts as *sleep hygiene*, these are daily living practices that influence your ability to fall asleep and stay asleep. Caffeine in coffee and soft drinks is among the biggest offenders because it can increase your arousal; therefore, you do not feel tired enough to go to sleep. What most people do not know is that caffeine stays in the system for up to 6 hours. This means that drinking a cup of coffee or a soft drink at dinner may very well interfere with a person's ability to fall asleep later in the evening. The nicotine found in cigarettes is, like caffeine, a stimulant, and it too can interfere with sleep. Other stimulants, including the medications Ritalin and Cylert, which are often prescribed for people with ADHD, can interfere with sleep as well. As mentioned in Chapter 1, exercising too close to bedtime (3–4 hours before) can also increase arousal and will hinder attempts to fall asleep.

Even where a person sleeps can keep some from falling asleep easily. For one of my cases, the bedtime routine of a young girl was videotaped to see how the family was carrying out recommendations. This little girl did not cry or scream when she was told that it was time to sleep, but she would constantly come out of her room. The videotape was quite revealing because it picked up the family's television programs and all of their conversations even though the camera was in the little girl's room. It was clear that the girl could hear everything going on with the rest of her family because her bedroom was right next to the family room. Her room was much too noisy for her to fall asleep in at night, especially for someone who was already a light sleeper. Relatively minor changes helped her bedtime problems dramatically. In addition to noise, too much light or even an uncomfortable temperature in a bedroom can prevent a smooth bedtime.

Daytime sleeping is a common cause of bedtime disturbances. Many of the children with whom my colleagues and I work take naps during the day, in part because they have not slept well the previous night. Some sleep on the bus to or from school, others sleep during school, and still others will take a nap at home after school. Naps by themselves are not inherently bad. Leonardo da Vinci is reported to have *only* napped, sleeping for 15 minutes every 4 hours throughout the day. In fact, many sleep experts recommend that adults take short naps during the day to make up for the sleep that they lose each night. Our "sleep debt" needs to be paid back, and napping may be just the remedy that many of us need. Unfortunately, for some people, sleeping during the day may also affect attempts to fall asleep the next evening. A nap of more than a few minutes can decrease the likelihood that the person will be tired at his or her usual bedtime. This sets up the beginning of what can become a very vicious cycle. Not being able to fall asleep easily that night will make the person tired again the next day, which in turn will create the desire to nap, and the nap will interfere with bedtime once more. At the root of some children's bedtime problems lies their daytime sleeping habits.

A related problem that sometimes is the cause of a lack of sleepiness at bedtime involves the different patterns, or "phases," of sleep that we prefer. Chapter 1 discussed how some people are larks (those who prefer waking early and going to bed early) and others are owls (those who prefer sleeping late and staying up late). The approximately 10% of people who are owls will not be tired at the usual bedtime because of the differences in their circadian rhythms. For children who are owls, this may result in a resistance to go to bed. Chapter 7 discusses some very intriguing new techniques for helping people shift their sleep phases to more closely match the desired sleep times.

Children's anxiety surrounding bedtime can be a vexing problem for parents. Children often will refuse to go to sleep at night because they are afraid of the dark, because some monster is waiting for them under the bed, or even because they are afraid of having bad dreams. When children cannot talk, parents often wonder whether their resistance to bedtime is a result of fears and anxieties. One of the first challenges for helping a child who reports being afraid of going to sleep is determining how real the anxiety is. Children often are quite creative in figuring out just what to say at bedtime to get the parent into the room. A friend of mine had a great deal of difficulty getting his daughter to go to sleep at night. She complained that monsters might hurt her after the family fell asleep. Using a bit of ingenuity, my friend went to the store and bought a quite elaborate "magic wand" for his daughter. He explained to her that the wand had special powers and that if any monster tried to get her, she could make it disappear with one wave of the wand. This worked well for less than a week. His daughter then began a nightly ritual of asking for water, a back rub, to be tucked in, and so forth. In other words, it appeared that the reports of monsters may have been a conscious or unconscious attempt to get her father into the room; when the wand took away that method, she found a different way. The problem is that because we cannot get inside the head of this little girl, we will never know whether her fears were real and whether she just began the new ritual to allay those fears in a new way or to obtain more of her parents' attention at night.

Children with a history of abuse or who have experienced other trauma often have very frightening dreams, and bedtime can become associated with a great deal of apprehension. Just as many of us associate a physician's office or a hospital with unpleasant events, these children learn that bed and sleep are linked to their bad dreams and are things to be avoided. Children who have problems with bedwetting also may avoid bedtime for the same reason.

Finally, giving medication to children to get them to sleep at night may quickly become the source of a sleep problem. Many parents of children with special needs have at some point been told to give their child some type of sleep-inducing medicine—often the antihistamine Benadryl, which produces sleepiness as a side effect. Pediatricians often will suggest this medication because it can help a child go to sleep quickly at bedtime and can prevent many of the bedtime disturbances just described. The problem with Benadryl and many of the other medications used to induce sleep is that when parents try to stop using it, it can actually make sleep worse than before. The phenomenon of worsening sleep after medication withdrawal is called *rebound insomnia* and is sometimes the cause of nighttime disturbances in children. Medication for sleep, especially among children, typically is not recommended for long-term use, in part because it can make a bad sleep problem worse.

**Difficulty Maintaining Sleep**   I once heard someone say that bedtimes are for parents. Whether a child goes to bed at 8:00, 8:30, or 9:00 P.M. may be less important for the sleep needs of the child than for the mental health of the parents. Parents work hard, and, as much as we love our children, we do need a little break away from them at the end of the day. It is a cruel twist of the natural order of things, then, that just as parents begin to unwind and relax, their child awakens prematurely from sleep. Or worse, just as parents find themselves deep in sleep, the cries of their child snatch them back to reality. This is especially difficult for parents who may have just battled with their child for more than an hour to go to sleep in the first place.

Along with bedtime problems, night waking is among the most common sleep problems experienced by children. Like bedtime disturbances, night waking can be caused by a number of factors. Many times, night waking can be traced to a child's earliest years. Chapter 1 described how all of us go through "partial wakings" throughout the night. These are brief periods in our sleep cycle when we awaken but then immediately go back to sleep and have no memory of them the next day. It is thought that, particularly for children who do not fall asleep on their own at night, children's disruptive night waking originates from these partial wakings. Imagine an infant who is being held in her mother's arms and who falls asleep. The mother places the child in a crib, turns off the light, and leaves the room. An hour later, the infant experiences a partial waking, but instead of being in her mother's arms, she is now in a dark room, alone in a crib. This unfamiliar situation may be disturbing enough to cause the child to cry out. Further imagine that you are the child's parent and that you are a first-time parent or that this child has been ill or has some other problems. Your child's crying will cause you some concern, and you are likely to go into her room to determine whether she is all right. Your child, who may have been only partially awake, is now more fully awake at seeing you in the room. You comfort your child, maybe even hold her in your arms until she falls asleep again, and then you go back to sleep.

What seems to happen in this very common scene is that the child does not learn to fall asleep alone. The child may fall asleep only with a parent in the room or with music playing in the background. When he or she wakes up during the night and the scene has changed dramatically, it can be frightening, and it is more difficult to fall back to sleep. Crying out as a strategy is further reinforced because it brings the parents back into the room. So, instead of learning how to fall back to sleep alone after one of these awakenings, the child learns to get the parent back to re-create the comforting scene that he or she had grown used to. Sadly, many children learn one more stage to this episode. After many nights of this, some parents recognize that they should not be going into their child's room, and they try to ignore the cries. This obviously is upsetting to the child, so she cries longer and louder. At some point, most parents give up because they cannot stand to hear their child so upset. Unfortunately, what the child has now learned is that the next time her parents do not come into her room right away, cry longer and louder because if at first you don't succeed. . . . As you can see, disruptive night wakings can originate from these first experiences with partial wakings.

Early feeding practices also can lead to night wakings in a number of different ways. One reason that this occurs is because, as just described with a parent's presence when the child falls asleep, the child may learn to associate going to sleep with feeding. This often begins in infancy, when the child is fed just before sleep. By the age of about 3 months, children no longer need to be fed at bedtime or at times throughout the night; however, often parents enjoy this closeness as the child goes off to sleep, or their child's occasional awakenings make them feel that the child is hungry. Because of these reasons, bedtime and nighttime feedings frequently will continue well beyond 3 months of age. What can take over is the cycle of awakenings followed by the parents' coming into the room and feeding the child. Nighttime feedings also can disrupt sleep by activating the digestive system at a time when it should be dormant. In addition, consuming liquids can cause the desire to urinate, which can contribute to awakenings. Night waking often results from a combination of being a light sleeper and practicing learned patterns of falling asleep.

In addition to the learning that can go on surrounding these night wakings, certain medical problems also can contribute to nighttime disturbances. Conditions such as colic, urinary tract or middle-ear infections, congestion, or any other condition that is uncomfortable or painful for the child will disrupt sleep. The side effects of certain medications such as antihistamines or antibiotics also can contribute to night waking. On rare occasions, parents will give children a small amount of alcohol at bedtime to induce sleep. Although alcohol will make a person drowsy, it also has a disruptive effect on sleep such that night waking often is increased. These conditions, combined with how parents respond to night wakings, can result in a pattern of chronic nighttime disruption.

**Nonrestorative Sleep**    Some people sleep for what appears to be an acceptable amount of time yet do not feel rested the next day. They may have a very difficult time getting going in the morning and feel tired during the day. Some children will sleep from 8 to 10 hours per night yet still take naps during the day. Usually this is a sign that the child's sleep is being disrupted during the night, even if he or she is unaware of it. A number of medically related conditions can lead to this problem. One of the more common causes involves problems that people experience with breathing as they sleep. In extreme cases, people will stop breathing for several seconds at a time throughout the night in a condition called *sleep apnea*. Less dramatic, many people have obstructed breathing, which can disrupt the normal progression of sleep stages. Like the partial wakings, this sleep disruption brought on by breathing problems often goes unnoticed by the person affected yet can interrupt sleep enough to leave the person feeling unrested the next day. Children may not display excessive sleepiness during the day but may, instead, be more irritable, be hyperactive, or have trouble concentrating. Sleep apnea and related breathing problems are described later in this chapter.

Sleep and seizures (sudden and unpredictable discharges of electrical activity in the brain) are related. Given that both involve electrical activity in the brain, it should not be surprising that sleep can activate certain types of seizures. Seizures during sleep often do not cause the person to awaken fully, but, like breathing problems, they can disrupt sleep enough to cause daytime drowsiness. This condition is further complicated when the person is taking anti-seizure medication because this medication can contribute to daytime drowsiness as well. Medication for asthma symptoms, especially if taken close to bedtime, also can disrupt sleep and be a cause of sleepiness during the day.

### Hypersomnia and Narcolepsy

The word *insomnia* means "not enough or insufficient sleep." We have seen that insomnia covers a variety of problems that all involve not getting enough sleep. *Hypersomnia*, conversely, refers to getting too much sleep. Hypersomnia and a related sleep disorder called *narcolepsy* involve sleeping excessively during the day despite getting sufficient sleep at night. People find themselves falling asleep, sometimes at very inconvenient times, even after a night of 8–10 hours of sleep. Both hypersomnia and narcolepsy are relatively rare—occurring in less than 1% of the general population—but they can be very debilitating to the person afflicted.

Very little is known about what causes hypersomnia. Family history of this sleep problem seems to be common, with about 40% of the people with this problem having a family member who also has hypersomnia[8]. This suggests that one's genetics may be involved in its cause, at least among some of the people who experience this problem. One additional finding about hypersomnia is that a larger proportion of people with this sleep problem than you would expect seem to have a history of having the infectious disease mononucleosis. Unfortunately, it still is not fully understood how genetics or mononucleosis is involved in the development of hypersomnia.

There is more information about narcolepsy, a sleep problem that also involves excessive sleeping during the day. The symptoms of narcolepsy take on a more dramatic quality than those involved in hypersomnia. A person will be awake and alert one minute and slump down to the floor and be fast asleep the next. In addition to falling asleep, people with narcolepsy experience a sudden loss of muscle tone (called *cataplexy*). This loss of muscle tone seems to be caused by the sudden onset of REM sleep. If you remember, REM, or dream, sleep typically begins approximately 60–90 minutes after we fall asleep. This is also a time when we are relatively paralyzed, not able to move any of our major muscles. What appears to happen in people with narcolepsy is that their daytime sleep attacks involve an immediate transition into REM sleep, along with the accompanying paralysis.

Therefore, their head might fall to one side, they may slide down in their chair, or they may even fall to the floor as a result of this immediate transition to REM sleep. Another aspect of these sleep attacks is that people often report that they occur in the middle of some emotional event. People have been known to be watching their favorite sports team on television and, just at a crucial score, fall fast asleep!

Two other unusual events surrounding sleep affect people with narcolepsy. First, these individuals often report experiencing *sleep paralysis,* which is a brief period of time upon awakening when they cannot move or speak. As you can imagine, this feeling of not being able to move or speak can be quite frightening to these individuals. It is important to note that sleep paralysis occurs occasionally to people who do not have narcolepsy, although it is more common among people with this sleep problem. Second, these individuals experience *hypnagogic hallucinations.* These hallucinations are particularly vivid experiences that occur during sleep and are said to be unbelievably realistic because the person experiencing them perceives not only visual stimuli but also the full range of the senses, including touch, hearing, and even the sensation of body movement. People have retold stories, for example, of being in a house on fire and being able to smell the smoke and feel the heat.

Before we examine the causes of narcolepsy, it is intriguing to note that sleep paralysis and hypnagogic hallucinations have been used to explain a most unusual phenomenon—UFO experiences. As you know, people routinely report seeing unidentified flying objects and also more active incidents including being abducted by aliens. In an interesting study[9], researchers questioned people who had had these experiences and separated them into two groups: those with more passive reports, such as just seeing lights in the sky, and those with more active experiences, such as seeing and communicating with aliens. The researchers found that a majority of these experiences occurred at night, and 60% of the more active events were said to have happened during sleep. When you examine their reports, the people with these active experiences describe events that resemble the frightening episodes of sleep paralysis and hypnagogic hallucinations:

> I was lying in bed facing the wall, and suddenly my heart started to race. I could feel the presence of three entities standing beside me. I was unable to move my body but could move my eyes. One of the entities, a male, was laughing at me, not verbally but with his mind. He made me feel stupid. He told me telepathically, "Don't you know by now that you can't do anything unless we let you?"[10]

The realistic and frightening stories of people who have UFO sightings may not be the products of an active imagination or the results of a hoax, but, at least in some cases, they may be a disturbance of sleep. Sleep paralysis and hypnagogic hallucinations do occur in a portion of people without narcolepsy, which may help explain why not everyone with these "otherworldly" experiences has narcolepsy.

Knowledge about the causes of narcolepsy is growing, and it appears that this sleep problem has biological origins. Specifically, it seems clear that narcolepsy is influenced by one's genetics. The first clues about the genetics of narcolepsy came from a most unlikely source—man's best friend. Some years ago, the highly regarded sleep researcher Dr. William Dement was lecturing to a group at the American Academy of Neurology in Boston. In the audience was a veterinarian who commented that he had observed a miniature poodle named Monique who seemed to display the same symptoms of narcolepsy that Dr. Dement was describing about his human patients. Intrigued, Dr. Dement requested that Monique be flown to his sleep laboratory at Stanford University for further study. It was there that he discovered that the dog had a disorder identical to narcolepsy in humans. As a result of this chance encounter, researchers have been able to identify that Doberman pinschers and Labrador retrievers also inherit this disorder and that it may be associated with a cluster of genes on chromosome number 6. Further work with humans is needed to identify the exact cause of this problem, in hope that it leads to more effective treatments.

### Breathing-Related Sleep Problems

Sleepiness during the day that is the result of disrupted sleep at night sometimes is caused by physical problems. A common physical problem that disrupts the sleep of approximately 1%–2% of us involves difficulty breathing during sleep. For all of us, the muscles in our upper airways relax somewhat as we sleep, and this makes breathing a little bit more difficult. Unfortunately, this constriction of breathing is more pronounced in some people, and it can cause very labored breathing during sleep (called *hypoventilation*). As a result of breathing difficulties, these people will experience numerous brief episodes of being awakened during the night, although the person will not be fully awake and probably will not remember the episodes. Because they are not sleeping deeply, however, they do not feel rested the next day even after 8 or 9 hours in bed. In the most extreme cases, some people will have short periods of time during sleep when they stop breathing altogether—sometimes up to 10–30 seconds—which is referred to as *sleep apnea*.

Although immediate signs of breathing difficulty may not be obvious to anyone other than a bed partner, there are other important indications. Loud snoring sometimes is a sign of breathing difficulty. Also, heavy sweating during the night, morning headaches, and episodes of falling asleep during the day may be evidence of breathing problems during sleep. These breathing difficulties occur more often in people who are overweight, perhaps because of increased pressure on the airways. If breathing difficulties are suspected of being the cause of a sleep problem, then a medical evaluation is essential.

## Sleep Schedule Problems

The artist Edward Hopper often painted people at the extremes of the sleep–wake cycle. In *Morning Sun*, a woman is pictured fully dressed anxiously looking out of her window at dawn's light. In sharp contrast is *Nighthawks*, which depicts a couple lingering over their coffee at an all-night diner. What makes our sleep schedules so different? Chapter 1 described how our biological clock informs the brain to help us sleep at night and to help us wake up in the morning and that light from the sun resets this clock each day so that we go through about a 24-hour cycle—known as a circadian rhythm. Unfortunately, sometimes this process is disrupted, and people sleep at times when they want to be awake and are awake at times when they want to be asleep. Unlike with insomnia, whereby people may have trouble sleeping, people with sleep schedule problems may sleep fine but at the wrong times. They may awaken fully alert at 4:00 A.M. and have nothing to do, then fall asleep later that day at 8:00 P.M. despite wanting to be awake. Others cannot fall asleep at night and then cannot get up the next morning. More than just an inconvenience, being "out of sync" can cause these individuals to be tired and have difficulty concentrating during the day when they try to fight their body's desired schedule. These sleep schedules usually do not fit with our typical school or work schedules, and these activities can be seriously disrupted.

You have already experienced what this can be like if you have flown across several time zones in a day and have felt "jet-lagged." People who are jet-lagged usually report difficulty going to sleep at the proper time, as well as feeling fatigued during the day. Certain people seem to be more negatively affected by time zone changes, including older adults, introverts (loners), and early risers (morning people). Repeated travel such as this disrupts the sleep of people so much that they can experience serious and chronic sleeping difficulties.

Another group of people who experience these types of sleep problems are people whose work schedules do not allow them to sleep at night. Many people, such as hospital employees, police, or emergency personnel, must work at night or work irregular hours; as a result, they may have difficulty sleeping or may be excessively sleepy during waking hours. These problems can become more serious, with reports of gastrointestinal symptoms, increased potential for alcohol abuse, low worker morale, and the disruption of family life being more common among these shift workers.

In addition to these self-imposed causes of circadian rhythm sleep problems, there are people who experience the same symptoms because of more internal, although as yet not completely understood, causes. Extreme "night owls," or people who stay up late and sleep late, may have a problem called *delayed sleep phase syndrome,* a type of circadian rhythm disorder. Falling asleep is "delayed," or occurs later, compared with a typical bedtime. At the other extreme, people with an *advanced sleep phase syndrome* are very early to bed and very early to rise; sleep is "advanced" in relation to a typical bedtime. Not going through the 24-hour phase of sleep and wakefulness—called non–24-hour sleep–wake syndrome—disrupts the lives of a significant number of people. For a variety of reasons, individuals with this sleep problem follow a 25-hour phase and are constantly changing the time when they sleep. Recall that we examined how people with severe visual impairments (blindness) often experience this problem and how they go through very difficult phases in which they want to sleep during the day and stay awake at night.

People with delayed sleep phase syndrome (night owls) often seem to develop the difficulty as a child or adolescent, staying up later and later at night and then sleeping late the next morning. Conversely, those with advanced sleep phase syndrome seem to develop the problem later in life, perhaps as part of an acceleration of their biological clocks. Two related causes of these sleep schedule problems are being explored. Chapter 1 described how the brain chemical melatonin seems to be involved in resetting our biological clock. It is believed that for some people who have sleep schedule problems, their production of this hormone may not be sufficient to trigger the brain to begin sleep.

The second area of study for people with sleep schedule problems involves sunlight. Recall that the hormone melatonin, which seems responsible for signaling sleep, is produced deep in the brain by the pineal gland. In some animals, particularly some birds and reptiles, the pineal gland is so close to the top of the skull that it can detect light from the sun directly and transmit this information to other parts of the brain. This ability has earned the pineal gland the label "the third eye" in these animals. Our pineal gland, because it cannot detect light directly, is connected to the nerve fibers in our eyes. As our eyes take in less and less light in the evening, the pineal gland begins producing melatonin, which, in turn, triggers our sleep. If we do not receive sufficient light cues, however, then this elaborate system does not work as it was designed, and our sleep is disrupted. There is one group in which this problem is quite evident: people who live in extreme northern latitudes. The low levels of light to which people are exposed in the winter months seem to interfere with melatonin production and can wreak havoc on sleep schedules. Chapter 7 discusses how bright lights can be used to help "jump start" this light–melatonin mechanism to help someone sleep better.

## Nightmares

The British author Robert Louis Stevenson is said to have suffered greatly from nightmares as a child. Fortunately, he turned this malady into creative success by using one of his nightmares as the basis of his famous book *The Strange Case of Dr. Jekyll and Mr. Hyde* (Stevenson, 1991). We all, from time to time, have had a dream that was frightening or distressful. You dream that someone is about to kill you, that you are running away from some threat but cannot run fast enough, or that you are back in school and cannot find the room where the big final exam is being held. These dreams are so frightening that you awaken feeling very upset and can usually remember at least part of the dream. For some people, these nightmares can impair their ability to carry on daily activities. Recurring nightmares can lead to disrupted sleep, primarily because the person begins to fear bedtime.

 ·"Bad dreams" are almost universal phenomena. Severe and recurrent nightmares also are common, occurring in as many as 20% of children and 5%–10% of adults[11]. As with most of the other sleep problems that have been discussed, there is little information about the frequency of nightmares among people with special needs. One exception is among children with histories of abuse, who do report much higher rates of nightmares than others.

You would expect that because nightmares are so common, a great deal of research would have focused on their causes. Unfortunately, very little is known about why people have nightmares. One study, however, suggests that any form of trauma, even emotional trauma, may contribute to an increase in nightmares[12]. This study looked at how the 1989 earthquake in San Francisco affected people who lived through the event. The researchers compared students from Stanford University and San Jose State University, who experienced but were not hurt by the earthquake, with students from the University of Arizona, who were unaffected by the quake. They found that about 40% of the students who experienced the earthquake reported nightmares, whereas only 5% of the students in Arizona reported having nightmares during the same period of time. One of "nature's experiments" allowed researchers to examine how trauma can directly influence nightmares.

### Sleep Terrors

One evening some years ago, my peaceful and as-yet-uneventful night's sleep was shattered by the blood-curdling screams of my then 3-year-old son. The screaming and crying continued as my wife and I raced to his room. Although it took only a few seconds to reach him, a thousand thoughts of the most horrendous nature went through our minds. Was he being attacked? Was he stricken by some hideous disease that would soon strike him down? What could possibly make him scream like that, a scream that we had never heard from him before? We stumbled into his room to see him sitting up in his bed, still in a panic. My wife and I competed to be the one to hold and comfort him, finally able to rescue him from what then looked like a bad dream. This was different, however. We were not able to comfort him as we had in the past when he had had a nightmare. In fact, we seemed to become the enemy. The unspeakable horror was projected on us as he fought our efforts to soothe him. Minutes seemed like hours until he finally stopped screaming and went back to sleep in his bed. Although my wife and I worried that this was the harbinger of some dreaded affliction, the next morning my son was his same cheery self, seemingly unaware and unscathed from the evening's trauma.

This scenario, which was repeated several more times in my son's early years, describes an experience of *sleep terrors* (sometimes referred to as *night terrors*, although they can occur during daytime naps as well), a sleep problem that is often mistaken for a nightmare. Called *incubus* in adults and *pavor nocturnus* in children, these sleep attacks usually begin with a piercing scream. The person appears extremely upset, often is sweating, and frequently has a rapid heartbeat. Sleep terrors look like nightmares because the child (it most often occurs among young children) cries and appears quite frightened; however, sleep terrors occur during NREM, or nondream, sleep and are therefore *not* instances of frightening dreams. In addition, during sleep terrors children cannot easily be awakened or comforted as is possible during a nightmare. In the case of sleep terrors, children do not remember the incident, despite its often dramatic effect on the onlooking parents.

About 5% of otherwise healthy young children experience sleep terrors at some point in their lives[13], and a small percentage of adults also have these attacks. It is not yet known how often people with special needs endure these types of sleep problems, although my experience has been that they are at least as likely to occur in this population as well.

Very little is known about the cause of sleep terrors. Early thinking was that psychological stress during the day brought on these attacks in some people, although research suggests that this is not a major influence on this sleep problem[14]. Some more medically oriented theories have pointed to things such as enlarged adenoids or an "immature" central nervous system as causing sleep terrors, although today there is very little evidence for any specific cause. Sleep terrors do seem to run in families, although, again, it is too early to speculate about any specific genetic cause. The good news is that for most children—including my son—these sleep problems tend to become less frequent as the child grows older and usually are gone by the teenage years.

## Sleepwalking and Sleeptalking

It might surprise you to learn that sleepwalking (also called *somnambulism*), like sleep terrors, occurs during NREM sleep. This means that when people walk in their sleep, they probably are not acting out a dream. Sleeptalking, which usually is not considered a sleep problem, can occur during either REM or NREM sleep. Occasionally, the muscles that control speech escape the paralysis that goes with REM sleep, and people can talk while they are dreaming. (Both my wife and my son talk in their sleep—an indication of the genetic nature of this behavior—and on rare, special occasions, they talk at the same time in what seems like a dialogue!) Sleepwalking typically will occur during the first few hours of sleep when the person is in the deepest stages of sleep (Stages 3 and 4). Because it occurs when people are in this very deep point in sleep, it is difficult to awaken a person at this time—although, despite the myth, this is not a dangerous thing to do. A second myth about sleepwalking is that the person will never do anything harmful during one of these episodes. People who sleepwalk seem generally aware of their surroundings and tend to avoid harming themselves. There are, however, occasional reports of people hurting themselves or others during sleepwalking, such as the 35-year-old man who was reported to have stabbed another man during an episode of sleepwalking[15].

Sleepwalking primarily is a problem for children, although a small percentage continue to sleepwalk as adults. A relatively large number of children, some 15%–30%, have at least one episode of sleepwalking[16]. Sleepwalking affects less than 1% of adults[17], although, when it does occur, it usually is associated with other psychological problems. As with some of the other sleep problems, it is not known how prevalent sleepwalking is among people with special needs; and it is not clearly understood why some people sleepwalk, although factors such as fatigue, being previously sleep deprived, the use of sleep-inducing drugs such as sedatives or hypnotics, and stress have been suggested[18]. There may also be a role for heredity, given that sleepwalking occurs more often in some families than in others[19].

## Periodic Limb Movements

You probably have had the experience of being next to a person as he or she was falling asleep and seeing his or her body jerk all over. The significance of this whole-body jerk is not understood, but it appears to be unrelated to any sleep or medical problem. There are people whose legs or arms jerk and twitch throughout the night in a condition known as *periodic limb movements.* This twitching lasts for only a few seconds and can occur every few minutes or for several hours. By themselves, these limb movements will not harm the person; however, as with interrupted breathing and apnea, limb movements during sleep can interrupt the person's sleep rhythm. For some, they awaken and are therefore bothered by these frequent night wakings. If they do not fully awaken, then excessive daytime sleepiness may result. Sometimes people report being tired during the day, even after 8–10 hours of sleep, and discover the cause to be these sleep-related body movements. One clue to whether a person has periodic limb movements is the state of his or her bed in the morning. If a person's blankets and sheets are disheveled, then he or she may be experiencing excessive limb movement during sleep. Being on certain medications, such as antidepressants, can cause periodic limb movements, as can trying to stop taking other medications such as tranquilizers or sedatives.

A related sleep problem involves an unsettled feeling in a person's legs, sometimes described as a powerful urge to move. Called *restless legs syndrome,* this feeling in the legs can be most uncomfortable and usually interferes with the ability to fall asleep. Unfortunately, many people with restless legs syndrome also experience periodic limb movements and will feel exhausted during the day. One cause of both of these movement problems may be poor circulation as the result of a lack of exercise. Be warned that an increase of exercise can temporarily increase this problem, although it should resolve itself in a week or two. Too much caffeine also can cause these sleep problems, which is something that easily can be remedied.

## Bedwetting

Bedwetting (also called *enuresis*) is a common problem among children and is surprisingly common among adults as well. Approximately 10% of 5-year-old girls and 15% of 5-year-old boys continue to wet their beds frequently[20]. Among children with special needs, this number generally is higher. Wetting the bed usually is not considered a problem for children when it occurs during the first 4 years of development. By age 5, however, frequent bedwetting—for example, several times per week—can start to interfere with a child's sense of self-worth and self-esteem and probably should be addressed. Bladder control problems can be part of more significant medical problems for some children with special needs, such as those having spina bifida with myelomeningocele (defects in the spinal column producing a fluid-filled sac that is visible from birth).

Some children may go for weeks, months, or even years without bedwetting, then they relapse. Often, this is a sign of some psychological distress; for example, marital problems between their parents frequently lead to bedwetting in some children as does the addition of a new child to the family. It can also signal the presence of a medical problem such as urinary tract infection, diabetes, epilepsy, or a kidney disorder.

## Tooth Grinding

"There it is again!" I told my wife that I had heard a strange noise, and now it was happening again. Being the brave protector, I got out of bed to investigate. Following the noise into my son's room, I found that he was the source. Fast asleep, he was grinding his teeth loud enough to be heard from the other side of the house. More formally referred to as *sleep-related bruxism,* tooth grinding is a little-understood phenomenon that occurs with some frequency among children and adults. The grinding can be related to dental problems and should be brought to the attention of a dentist if it persists. It also is believed that stress can cause tooth grinding, and stress-reduction techniques sometimes are recommended.

## Rhythmic Movement Problems

It is comforting for some children to rock their body or their head back and forth repeatedly just before falling asleep. As with all of the sleep problems, this sleep-related rhythmic movement is not considered a sleep problem unless it is disruptive to sleep or is a source of concern. Children with visual impairments and those with autism and other developmental disorders sometimes may use this as part of their bedtime routine. Unfortunately, this rhythmic movement can become more serious and include injurious forms such as severe head banging. The origins of these rhythmic movements are thought to involve the accidental discovery that rocking can be pleasurable, and, therefore, children incorporate it into bedtime rituals just as you might need to read or watch television before going to sleep each night. Increased stress during the day can cause this rhythmic movement to increase.

## CONCLUSION

We have examined a number of different sleep and sleep-related problems that affect children and adults with special needs. Despite the somewhat lengthy list described here, there are many more—although less common—specific sleep problems. Readers wanting more information about these other sleep problems should refer to the list of additional readings at the end of the book. We next turn to one of the most important sections of the book: how to determine the type of sleep problem that a person has. Before a particular strategy can be recommended for helping a person sleep better, some information must be gathered about the nature of the problem.

# II

# Assessing
# Sleep Problems

# 3

# Identifying the Sleep Problem

If you have read through the first two chapters, then you know that there are many reasons why a child might not go to sleep right away at bedtime, why someone else may wake up repeatedly during the night, or why another person may be tired and disoriented during the day. This chapter walks you through a series of steps that will help you identify the sleep problem and then direct you to one or more strategies that will help. As you gain a better awareness of the specific type of sleep problem, I will direct you to other sections of the book that describe how you can implement your own plan to help solve the sleep problem. Included are descriptions of people with whom my colleagues and I have worked and how we designed plans for them. In most cases, you should be able to carry out your own "diagnosis" and design your own plan. Remember, understanding the sleep problem is the key to successful treatment.

## STEPS TO UNDERSTANDING THE PROBLEM

The first tasks that you would be asked to complete if you were going to any sleep center would be to keep a sleep diary or log for about a week and answer some questions about the type of sleep problem that your child (or you yourself) is experiencing. The sleep diary helps you and the sleep professional get a good picture of things such as how long the child sleeps, what is the pattern of sleep, what happens at problem times, and so forth. You may think that this step is unnecessary because you could describe a typical week easily; you certainly have your hands full already without one more chore to add to the list! The information from such a diary, however, can be extremely important and can save time later. Trying out a plan for several weeks only to discover that it was the wrong one can be extremely frustrating and may be avoided with the right information ahead of time. Sometimes parents find that the problem is worse than they thought once they look closely at the patterns of sleep over a week, and at other times people discover that their child's sleep actually is not as disrupted as they thought. Even if your child's sleep problem requires further consultation with a professional, the information that you collect now will be extremely helpful in discussing the difficulties with someone else. Take the time to monitor your child's sleep for a week. You probably will find that it was worth it.

## SLEEP DIARY

Different sleep professionals use slightly different forms for people to fill out about sleep. My colleagues and I are always looking to collect the most information; at the same time, we know that people are busy and that if the forms are too complicated, then they will not be used. With that in mind, we have changed the forms over the years based on feedback from parents. We actually use two different forms: The first form gives us information on the sleep–wake cycle, and the second form gives us more information about what happens when the child has disruptive behavior either at bedtime or upon awakening during the night. Children with special needs often present two challenges: the sleep problem itself and the difficult behaviors displayed around sleep. Although many children with and without special needs can be disruptive before going to sleep or after waking, often children with special needs exhibit behaviors that are so extreme that they cause additional concern. Chapter 11 examines what are sometimes called "challenging behaviors," which include hitting others (aggression), hitting themselves (self-injurious behavior), and other types of disruptive behavior. Often these behaviors are beyond the expertise of most sleep professionals and sometimes account for why children with special needs are not properly served.

Complete the sleep diary each day. As was done in the sleep diary in Figure 3.1 (see Appendix D for a blank sleep diary), record basic information such as the time when the child was put in bed and at

## SLEEP DIARY

Child: _Michael_                                    Week of: _August 5_

| Day | Time put to bed | Time fell asleep | Nighttime waking (time/how long) | Describe nighttime waking | Time awoke | Describe any naps |
|-----|-----------------|------------------|----------------------------------|---------------------------|------------|-------------------|
| Sun | 9:30 p.m. | Around 11:30 p.m. | — | — | 6:00 a.m. | slept in car for 30 min. |
| Mon | 9:00 p.m. | Around 12:00 a.m. | — | — | 6:00 a.m. | slept in school for 60 min. |
| Tue | 10:00 p.m. | Around 11:30 p.m. | — | — | 6:00 a.m. | slept in school for 60 min. |
| Wed | 9:15 p.m. | Around 12:00 a.m. | — | — | 6:00 a.m. | slept in school for 45 min. |
| Thu | 9:30 p.m. | 11:00 p.m. | — | — | 6:00 a.m. | slept in school and on bus for 60 min. |
| Fri | 11:00 p.m. | 11:30 p.m. | — | — | slept until 9:30 a.m. | slept in school for 50 min. |
| Sat | 11:00 p.m. | 11:30 p.m. | — | — | 10:00 a.m. | no nap |

**Figure 3.1.**   Sleep diary for Michael.

approximately what time the child fell asleep. This reveals approximately how long the child takes to fall asleep each night. Anywhere from 15 to 30 minutes is typical, although some people fall asleep right away. People who fall asleep quickly, even during the day, may have the problem of hypersomnia or narcolepsy; this preliminary information can be used to follow up on this observation. Taking longer than 30 minutes to fall asleep at night could indicate that the child is not tired at bedtime; reasons such as sleep schedule problems would be suspected. There is room on the sleep diary to indicate whether and how many times the child may have awakened during the night; if this happens, then describe the awakening. This information reveals how much the child's sleep is disrupted and the kind of problems that the parents face. If night waking or bedtime is a significant problem, then the parents also would complete a behavior log, which is described in the next section. Finally, information about the time when the child wakes up each morning and naps reveals the total amount of sleep time, any schedule problems (e.g., the child wakes up too early), and the way that sleep is or is not spread out during the day.

Figure 3.1, a page from a sleep diary, describes a week of sleep for Michael, a 6-year-old boy with mental retardation requiring extensive supports. Michael's parents and teacher were concerned because he was tired during the day, and he would be up most of the early evening. You can see from his sleep diary several sleep habits that may have had a negative influence on his sleep. First, notice that Michael had no set bedtime, sometimes being put in bed as early as 9:00 P.M. and sometimes as late as 11:00 P.M. Many children seem to need a stable bedtime and bedtime routine; without it, they may have difficulty falling asleep. Chapter 4 describes how to establish a routine for someone like Michael. Often, this change alone is sufficient to help a child who has difficulty falling asleep at bedtime.

The next thing you notice from Michael's sleep diary is that he took naps during the day. Because he was getting only about 6–6½ hours of sleep each night during the week, it was not surprising that he was tired during the day and that he would nap when he could. Notice too that he napped less during the weekend when he was allowed to sleep as late as he wanted. Based on this information about his sleep, a new sleep schedule was designed for Michael (along the lines of techniques described in Chapter 7) that helped him fall asleep in the evening and not nap at school.

## BEHAVIOR LOG

Michael did not have any bedtime tantrums or night-waking difficulties. Had his parents reported either of these problems, they would have been asked to complete a behavior log (see Appendix D for a blank behavior log) along with the sleep diary. The behavior log reports information about the nature of these problems, such as how many times they occur on a typical night, how long the problem persists, and how the parents respond to their child during one of these episodes. You can see from Figure 3.2, a behavior log for Jodi (an 8-year-old with attention-deficit/hyperactivity disorder [ADHD]), that Jodi would have a tantrum at bedtime as well as sometimes during a night waking. Over the course of 2 weeks, a very distinct pattern emerged both of Jodi's sleep problems and of her parents' reactions. Jodi would resist going to bed each night, and her parents would respond by going into her room and calming her down until she fell asleep. Similarly, when Jodi awoke during the night, her parents would go into her room and stay with her until she fell asleep. As discussed in Chapter 1, some children never learn to fall asleep on their own either at bedtime or after a night waking, and this contributes to their sleep difficulties. Jodi seemed to be a classic case. Her parents were tired of going into her room each time she cried, so they were trying to ignore her. Unfortunately, Jodi would only scream louder or bang her head, and this forced them back into the room. We were concerned that Jodi was learning to escalate her behaviors—making more and more serious efforts to get her parents back into the room—and that she was being reinforced for these more severe outbursts because they worked: Her parents would return. If left unchecked, then Jodi's behaviors could have become even more dangerous. A plan that still let Jodi's parents go into Jodi's room to check on her, which they insisted on for their own peace of mind (see Chapter 5), was designed. Again, the behavior log provides a glimpse into the nighttime world of families who have been struggling with these troublesome problems for years.

## SLEEP INTERVIEW

After information is collected about each night's sleep, a sleep interview is conducted using the Albany Sleep Problems Scale (ASPS) (see Appendix E for a blank form). The ASPS is a form used to help identify the type of sleep problem that a child may be experiencing. Although this is used as a jumping-off point to further explore the nature of the sleep difficulty, the answers to these questions, along with the information from the sleep diary, often reveal just the information needed to begin to design a plan.

Take a few minutes to answer each of the following questions from the ASPS. Questions that seem to point to similar sleep problems have been combined, and descriptions of the implications of your answers to these questions follow. If your answers to one or more of

Name: _Jodi_

BEHAVIOR LOG

| Date | Time | Behavior at bedtime | What did you do to handle the problem? | Behavior during awakenings | What did you do to handle the problem? |
|---|---|---|---|---|---|
| 2/6 | 10:00 p.m. | crying and head banging | went into her room and held her | | |
| 2/7 | 10:15 p.m. | crying and head banging | waited a few minutes but then went in and held her | | |
| 2/7 | 11:45 p.m. | | | crying | sat on her bed until she fell back to sleep |
| 2/7 | 1:00 a.m. | | | crying, screaming! | sat with her until she fell asleep |
| 2/8 | 10:00 p.m. | Screaming, whining, head banging, throwing toys at wall | waited for a few minutes then went in and held her | | |

**Figure 3.2.** Behavior log for Jodi.

44

these questions suggest the source of the problem, then you will be directed to chapters in the next section of the book that will help you design a plan. Think of this interview as a way to brainstorm what may be the problems and what may be contributing to these sleep difficulties. Because most of the recommendations are fairly easy to carry out, in most cases you should try out one or more of the suggestions. In some rare cases—such as with sleep problems related to breathing difficulties—you should seek professional advice immediately.

## Sleep Habits

1.  Does this person have a fairly regular bedtime and time when he or she awakens?
2.  Does this person have a bedtime routine that is the same each evening?

One of the most popular clichés about raising children is that they like structure. Children like predictability and orderliness, despite that they may resist such order at first. There is no time when such routines are more important than at bedtime. Structuring bedtime and time to awaken so that they occur at regular times each day can go a long way toward helping someone with sleep problems. Bedtime problems as well as night waking can be caused by or worsened by unpredictability surrounding sleep. If you answered "no" to either of these questions, then you should implement a bedtime routine and regular sleep–wake cycle (see Chapter 4). This one step alone may fix the problems that you are experiencing.

3.  Does this person work or play in bed, often right up to the time when he or she goes to bed?
4.  Does this person sleep poorly in his or her own bed but better away from it?

One source of difficulty for people who are trying to fall asleep at night is a bad association between the bed or bedroom and sleep. An attorney whom I met once described to me how she could not fall asleep at night. In discussing her problem, she revealed that she used her bedroom as an office and her bed as her desk. She would work on case material until late at night and then try to fall asleep. When she tried to sleep, she found herself consumed with thoughts of work and could not turn them off. Her problem was that her bed became a signal for work and the problems associated with work, and she could not make the transition from work to sleep. In the case of children, often they use their bed to play and then have trouble relaxing in bed when it is time to sleep. Chapter 4 describes what is called *stimulus control,* which in this case involves retraining this connection so that only sleep and sleep-related activities and thoughts are associated with the bed. If you have answered "yes" to either of these questions, then Chapter 4 may be very helpful to you and your child.

5.  Does this person smoke, drink alcohol, or consume caffeine in any form?

The nicotine in cigarettes, the alcohol in certain beverages, and the caffeine in a number of foods and drinks all can disturb your sleep. If you answered "yes" to this question, then turn to Chapter 4 for a discussion of these substances and how to avoid their harmful effects on sleep.

6.  Does this person engage in vigorous activity in the hours before bedtime?

Exercise or even "rough-housing" at the wrong times also can disturb sleep. Chapter 4 provides guidelines for making exercise work *for* better sleep.

### Bedtime and Night Waking

7.  Does this person resist going to bed?
8.  Does this person take more than an hour to fall asleep but does not resist?

Obviously, these questions are designed to identify children who have difficulties at bedtime. The first step is to distinguish those children who fight going to bed from those who are just not able to fall asleep. If falling asleep is accompanied by tantrums, then parents need help dealing with these episodes. As just described, the first step with any bedtime problem is to make sure that there is a regular bedtime routine (see Chapter 4). Sometimes just establishing a predictable routine for a child can be enough to solve these problems. If the problem persists and the child is not resisting bedtime, then turn to interventions for sleep schedule problems (see Chapter 7). If the child is resisting bedtime, then explore several possibilities for a plan (see Chapter 5). Part of what determines the plan is how parents feel about the problem, an issue addressed at the end of this chapter.

9.  Does this person awaken during the night but remain quiet and in bed?
10. Does this person awaken during the night and become disruptive (e.g., tantrums, oppositional)?

You can see that these questions are similar to the previous two questions, but these involve whether the child has night-waking problems. As is the case with bedtime disturbances, managing the night waking differs from child to child. Some children just wake up, and parents find them awake in bed almost by accident. This can signal the presence of a sleep schedule problem (see Chapter 7). If it is accompanied by crying and tantrums, then how to handle the tantrum itself also becomes an issue (see Chapter 5).

11. Does this person take naps during the day?

Napping, by itself, is not a problem. Many people use naps quite successfully to catch up on lost sleep. For some people, however, naps are the problem. They are so tired during the day that it is difficult to keep them awake. Often others report that when a child is not allowed to sleep during part of the day, he or she becomes cranky and is extremely difficult to deal with. Again, a sleep schedule problem may be to blame (see Chapter 7), depending on how long the person sleeps at night. If the child or adult who is napping during the day seems to be sleeping a full night, then a possibility is that he or she has hypersomnia or narcolepsy (see Chapter 9). For someone who seems to be sleeping through the night, naps also may be a sign of a breathing-related sleep problem such as sleep apnea (see Chapter 9), or they may be a sign of a limb movement problem (see Chapter 9), either of which may be disturbing nighttime sleep. One other reason for daytime napping may be related to medication that the person is taking. Medication for seizure problems, antihistamines, asthma medication, and even the use of medication at night to go to sleep may be causing drowsiness during the day (see Chapter 12). Anyone who appears to be getting a full night's sleep but continues to have trouble staying awake during the day should be evaluated at a sleep center (see Appendix C for a list and the address of a center nearest you).

As discussed previously, other people find that naps are not a problem, and they fit naps in well during the day. If these individuals are also having difficulty sleeping at night (either resisting going to bed or waking during the night), however, then the naps may be the cause. A reexamination of their sleep schedule may be needed for these people (see Chapter 7).

12. Does this person often feel exhausted during the day because of lack of sleep?
13. Has this person ever had an accident or near accident because of sleepiness from not being able to sleep the night before?

For many of the same reasons that daytime napping can be a problem, people who are extremely tired during the day despite a full night's rest may be experiencing a variety of difficulties. Sleepiness can be a sign of sleep schedule problems (see Chapter 7), hypersomnia or narcolepsy (see Chapter 9), breathing-related sleep problems such as sleep apnea (see Chapter 9), limb movement problems (see Chapter 9), or the use of certain medications (see Chapter 12). With help from your answers to other questions on this interview, your specific sleep problem can be more closely pinpointed.

14.  Does this person ever use prescription drugs or over-the-counter medications to help him or her sleep?
15.  Has this person found that sleep medication does not work as well as it did when he or she first started taking it?
16.  If this person takes sleep medication, then does he or she find that he or she cannot sleep on nights without it?

Chapter 12 describes the effects of certain medications on sleep. One important factor about using medications to sleep is that it usually is not recommended to use them for more than a few weeks. In most cases, medication is viewed by sleep professionals as a *temporary* measure. One of the concerns with using sleep medication for too long is mirrored in the previous questions. When a person uses medication for too long, his or her body begins to tolerate it so that it needs more of it to be effective. Also, sometimes medication can disrupt sleep after you stop taking it, a phenomenon known as *rebound insomnia*. Chapter 12 describes these issues in more detail and provides guidelines for the safe use of sleep medications.

### Sleep Schedules

17.  Does this person fall asleep early in the evening and awaken too early in the morning?
18.  Does this person have difficulty falling asleep until a very late hour and difficulty awakening early in the morning?

Again, a sleep schedule problem may be the culprit (see Chapter 7). Some children are wide awake at 5:00 A.M., ready to start the day. To attempt to shift the child's sleep to a more acceptable pattern, a close evaluation would need to be conducted of how much time the child spends sleeping and how this sleep is distributed throughout the day. Another concern that these questions may raise is the presence of certain psychological difficulties that may be interfering with sleep. Chapter 10 describes how anxiety and depression can change sleep patterns in this way and also outlines steps to help reduce these problems.

## Nightmares

19.   Does this person wake up in the middle of the night upset?
20.   Is this person relatively easy to comfort from these episodes?

It is important to differentiate nightmares—which are disturbing dreams—from sleep terrors—which do not appear to be bad dreams. If, as these questions suggest, the person is waking up after these episodes and can be calmed and comforted after such a dream, then it is likely that the person is experiencing nightmares. Chapter 8 describes techniques to help people who are negatively affected by nightmares.

## Sleep Terrors

21.   Does this person have episodes during sleep in which he or she screams loudly for several minutes but is not fully awake?
22.   Is this person difficult to comfort during these episodes?

Unlike nightmares, sleep terrors will tend to be more active events that occur despite the fact that the child is still asleep. The child will be very difficult to awaken and comfort. If you answered "yes" to these questions, then turn to Chapter 8 for a new approach to helping children rid themselves of these upsetting sleep disturbances.

## Hypersomnia and Narcolepsy

23.   Does this person experience sleep attacks (falling asleep almost immediately and without warning) during the day?
24.   Does this person experience excessive daytime sleepiness that is not accounted for by an inadequate amount of sleep?

Sleep attacks that occur despite the fact that the person is sleeping for a reasonable amount of time are a sign of possibly serious sleep problems such as hypersomnia or narcolepsy. If you suspect that these are problems, then you should refer to Chapter 9, which describes the various approaches that are used to help these individuals. It is also recommended that a full sleep evaluation be conducted at a sleep center if either of these problems is suspected (see Appendix C).

## Breathing-Related Difficulties

25.   Does this person snore when asleep?
26.   Does this person sometimes stop breathing for a few seconds during sleep?

27.   Does this person have trouble breathing?
28.   Is this person overweight?

If the person is tired during the day despite getting what appears to be a full night's sleep or if the person seems to be restless during sleep, then a breathing problem may be responsible for these difficulties. Answering "yes" to one or more of these questions would suggest that the person's breathing is interfering with sleep. Loud snoring often is a sign of nighttime breathing difficulties. These breathing problems also occur more often in people who are overweight. Chapter 9 describes help for breathing-related sleep problems, and, as recommended with hypersomnia and narcolepsy, any hint that breathing problems may be present should be followed up with an evaluation by a physician or a sleep specialist (see Appendix C).

## Sleepwalking and Sleeptalking
29.   Has this person often walked while asleep?
30.   Does this person talk while asleep?

These sleep phenomena often are not significant problems for most people; however, if they do bother the person affected or if they cause concern for others, then turn to Chapter 8 for a discussion of a variety of ways in which these sleep events can be helped.

## Limb Movement and Rhythmic Movement
31.   Are this person's sheets and blankets in extreme disarray in the morning when he or she wakes up?
32.   Does this person wake up at night because of kicking legs?

Answering "yes" to either of these questions may suggest that periodic limb movements are interfering with sleep. If the person seems tired during the day or if frequent night waking is a problem and limb movements are a suspected cause, then refer to Chapter 9 for a discussion of treatments.

33.   While lying down, does this person ever experience unpleasant sensations in the legs?

This may be a sign that the person has restless legs syndrome, which can cause insomnia in some people. Chapter 9 describes treatments for this troublesome problem.

34.   Does this person rock back and forth or bang a body part (e.g., head) to fall asleep?

These types of rhythmic movements are common, even in some adults. When they begin to cause injury, as with some children who bang their heads, some intervention is recommended. Chapter 9 describes interventions in some of these cases.

### Bedwetting

35.    Does this person wet the bed?

Until the age of about 5 years, bedwetting is not considered a problem. After that age, however, children should be sleeping through the night without accidents. If this is not the case, then refer to Chapter 10 for a discussion of approaches to help with this problem.

### Tooth Grinding

36. Does this person grind his or her teeth at night?

Occasional tooth grinding during sleep is common. If it is a regular occurrence, however, then serious dental problems may result. Refer to Chapter 10 for a discussion of both medical and psychological approaches to helping people with this behavior.

### Anxiety and Depression

37.    Does this person sleep well when it doesn't matter, such as on weekends, but sleep poorly when he or she "must" sleep well, such as when a busy day at school is ahead?
38.    Does this person often have feelings of apprehension, anxiety, or dread when he or she is getting ready for bed?
39.    Does this person worry in bed?
40.    Does this person often have depressing thoughts, or do tomorrow's worries or plans buzz through his or her mind when he or she wants to go to sleep?
41.    Does this person have feelings of frustration when he or she can't sleep?
42.    Has this person experienced a relatively recent change in eating habits?

All of these questions aim to determine problems of anxiety or depression, which can be the cause of sleeping difficulties. If you cannot determine directly whether your child worries or is depressed by asking him or her, then look for other clues. Abrupt changes in eating habits—such as eating too much or too little—may be a sign of depression. Also, if you can pinpoint through your sleep diary certain situations that reliably predict problems with sleep (e.g., difficulties the night before school but not on weekends), then this may suggest that your child is anxious. Chapter 10 discusses these problems, how they may interfere with sleep, and techniques that you can use to help your child deal with these feelings.

## Daytime Behavior Problems

43.    Does this person have behavior problems at times other than bedtime or upon awakening?

Chapter 11 discusses daytime behavior problems. This discussion is important for several reasons. First, getting a handle on daytime behavior problems often can help with bedtime problems. The way you respond to a tantrum at lunchtime, for example, may be similar to your handling of bedtime refusal. Second, daytime behavior problems and sleep problems often are related, and it is important to consider them together. Finally, if parents feel confident in how they deal with a child's daytime behavior problems, then this can help them with the child's sleep problems as well.

## Other Causes

44.    When did this person's primary difficulty with sleep begin?
45.    What was happening in this person's life at that time or a few months before?

These questions can relate to any of the sleep problems discussed. These questions can help identify causes such as illness or disruption of sleep patterns (e.g., vacations) that preceded the current problems. Almost all of the chapters refer to your answers from these questions.

46.    Is this person under a physician's care for any medical condition?

Finally, it is important to know whether medical conditions or the treatments for these problems (e.g., medications) are contributing to the child's sleep difficulties. Chapter 12 describes how certain medications can affect sleep, and many of the other chapters rely on your answer to this question to determine possible causes of sleep problems.


## CONCLUSION

There are few everyday experiences more frustrating than not being able to fall asleep at night. Even worse is the mix of emotions felt by a parent whose sleep is turned inside out by a child's disturbed sleep. You want to help, but you cannot help. You want to scream, but that would make things worse. You want to blame someone, but you end up blaming yourself. And the guilt sometimes prevents you from reaching out to others for help. My colleagues and I have worked with many families who have had serious problems with sleep for many years but have been too ashamed to seek professional help. Still others have looked to pediatricians or other nonsleep professionals for advice but have come away disappointed. It is important to be aware of how your own emotions will or will not affect your ability to carry out a plan. Many times parents cannot bear to listen to their child cry for even a minute, which excludes any plans that involve ignoring these problems. Be realistic about what you can reasonably handle in the interventions described in the following chapters. Do not be afraid to take things slowly. It is better to observe some success initially than to feel that things are hopeless, so look for small signs that things are getting better. Most sleep problems can be helped just by having parents change small things about the way they respond to them. Good luck!

# III

# Strategies for Change

# 4

# Good Sleep Habits

We now know that our sleep can be affected by what and when we eat and drink, when we exercise, the temperature in our bedroom, any noise, and even what we do in bed. Everyday activities that we tend to take for granted can have an impact on how well we go to sleep and whether we stay asleep. Along these lines, there are a number of good sleep habits that should be followed when sleep is disturbed. Remember, what disturbs one person's sleep may not affect another's. You may be able to fall asleep with the television on, but the television in your room may be disturbing the sleep of your child in the next room. Coffee after dinner may not disrupt your friend's sleep but may keep you up long after your typical bedtime. We each react in our own way to many of the foods and activities of the day, so it is important to check the major ones to determine whether they are interfering with a good night's sleep. Before describing some of these good sleep habits, let's first take a look at the case of a child for whom just changing some sleep habits dramatically improved his sleep.

> Harry was a 5-year-old boy with mental retardation who would resist going to bed at night. Harry's mother reported that he usually slept through the night and that he didn't appear tired during the day. Unfortunately for Harry's mother, he didn't appear tired in the evening either. Harry was a very likable kid who seemed to have a great deal of en-

ergy. At bedtime, which his mother decided should be at 9:00 P.M., he would like to wrestle and jump on his bed. At times, his mother would try to get him to lie down, but he would bounce up immediately. On other nights, she thought that maybe she could "tire him out" by letting him be rambunctious. She would wrestle with him, chase him around the house, sit with him to have his evening snack, and, on summer evenings, go for a walk/run. Harry's mother was astonished at her son's ability to remain awake and alert—which seemed to surpass her own ability by far. One night they were up until 2:00 A.M., but Harry showed no signs of letting up.

One of the first things that was obvious to my colleagues and me when we consulted with Harry's mother was his activity at night. Harry was very active right up until bedtime. His mother believed that the more active she allowed her son to be, the more likely Harry would be tired at bedtime. Unfortunately, as discussed before, many times just the opposite is true—exercise can actually interfere with sleep. Letting Harry run around the house, jump up and down on his bed, and go for evening runs may have been raising his internal body temperature, which in turn may have made him less likely to be drowsy at bedtime. Our first recommendation was to curtail Harry's more vigorous activities, at least for the hour before bedtime.

A second factor that may have been interfering with Harry's ability to fall asleep at bedtime was the lack of any stable bedtime routine. When 9:00 came around each evening, his mother would tell Harry that it was time for bed. She would help him wash up, but other than this brief activity, there were no other rituals that would help Harry make the transition from playtime to bedtime. We helped his mother design a calming bedtime routine for the 30 minutes before she wanted him to sleep in order to help Harry get ready for bed.

Another factor that we thought might be interfering with Harry's ability to fall asleep at night was his evening snack. Just before washing up for the night, Harry's mother allowed him to have a snack, which Harry enjoyed because he seemed hungry and which his mother enjoyed because it was one of the few quiet and pleasant times that they shared in the evening. Weight was not a problem for Harry; in fact, he was on the thin side, which concerned his mother, so she allowed Harry to pick his own snack each night. Harry's favorites were Ring Dings and a Coke. The problem with this snack is that both Ring Dings (which are chocolate-covered cakes) and Coke contain caffeine and may have contributed to Harry's late-night energy. Because snacktime seemed to be a positive ritual for both Harry and his mother, we recommended that they keep this activity but substitute milk and nonchocolate cookies for Harry's snack.

One more factor about bedtime may have contributed to Harry's difficulty going to sleep. When he wasn't sleeping, Harry's bed was the wrestling ring. This is where he and his mother would good-naturedly wrestle and fool around each night. The problem with this arrangement is that Harry probably associated his bed more with fooling around than with sleeping. It may have been difficult for him to get into bed at 9:00 P.M. and turn it all off after an evening of fun and excitement. Again, because wrestling was something that Harry and his mother both enjoyed, we recommended that they move their wrestling ring into the living room and reserve Harry's bed for his bedtime story and sleep.

After following these four simple recommendations alone—limiting activity in the hour before bedtime, creating a calming and stable bedtime routine, removing foods and drinks containing caffeine for his evening snack, and limiting activity in his bed to stories and sleep—Harry seemed more tired at bedtime, and he quickly got into the habit of falling asleep within about 15 minutes of being put into his bed. In fact, we were about to present his mother with a more elaborate plan for his bedtime problems when she called excitedly to tell us that Harry was now no trouble at bedtime.

## THE GOOD SLEEP HABITS CHECKLIST

As we saw quite dramatically in the case of Harry, there often are simple things that we can change that will positively affect sleep. Figure 4 1 is a checklist to help you identify things that you or your child may be doing that are interfering with bedtime or causing night waking. Regardless of the sleep problems that you may be experiencing, everyone should check this list to determine whether certain habits have developed that are contributing to the problem. Discussed next are some of the factors that may be at the root of your child's sleep difficulties.

## BEDTIME ROUTINES

As mentioned before, most children seem to thrive on structure and order. Whether this order includes the rules that you make about how to eat at the dinner table, how to behave in public, or sitting in a car seat when traveling, children soon learn what to expect of most situations and accept the structure—if you are consistent. This is especially important at bedtime. There are children who, when their parents say that it is time for bed, kiss their parents goodnight, climb into bed, and fall asleep within minutes. (It's true! I have seen it happen—although not with my son!) Most children, however, need a "wind down" time—a time to help them with the transition to sleep. Any relaxing series of activities that you and your child choose to include can be successful. For example, when my son was younger, we would have

---

THE GOOD SLEEP HABITS CHECKLIST

☐ Establish a set bedtime routine.

☐ Develop a regular bedtime and a regular time to awaken.

☐ Eliminate 6 hours before bedtime all foods and drinks that contain caffeine.

☐ Limit any use of alcohol.

☐ Limit any use of tobacco.

☐ Try drinking milk before bedtime.

☐ Eat a balanced diet, limiting fat.

☐ Do not exercise or participate in vigorous activities in the hours before bedtime.

☐ Do include a weekly program of exercise during the day.

☐ Restrict activities in bed to those that help induce sleep.

☐ Reduce noise in the bedroom.

☐ Reduce light in the bedroom.

☐ Avoid extreme temperature changes in the bedroom (i.e., too hot or too cold).

---

**Figure 4.1.**   The Good Sleep Habits Checklist.

him brush his teeth, wash up, and change into pajamas. Then we would sit on his bed and read to him for 15–20 minutes. This would be followed by back scratching and kisses, and then the words "OK, it's time to sleep. Goodnight." We would do the same things in the same order each night. This type of routine seems to have a calming or sedating effect on most children and helps them to associate this time with sleep. *Everyone* should have some type of bedtime routine, including adults who have difficulty falling asleep at night. Often, just this one change can help someone who previously had a great deal of difficulty falling asleep. Following are some dos and don'ts for bedtime routines:

- Make the last 30 minutes before bedtime a regular routine.
- Include activities such as dressing for sleep, washing, and reading.
- Keep the order and timing of the activities about the same each night.
- Do not include activities that—for your child—could cause conflict (e.g., picking out clothes for school, organizing papers).
- Avoid watching television during this time; it can interfere with sleep.
- Avoid extending the time for the bedtime routine (e.g., "Just one more story? Pleeeease!!").
- Most important—DO WHAT WORKS FOR YOU.

### The "Out of Control" Child

Many parents believe that things are so out of control that there is no way that they can impose a bedtime routine and expect their child to accept it. These are parents who often have a great number of problems with their child and, unfortunately, other parts of their lives and feel powerless to recapture control. These parents often say that their children are "uncontrollable" and that nothing seems to work with them. They often admit—with some guilt—that they have tried punishing their child but that the child seems immune to such punishment.

   With parents who feel that they have no control over what their children do, I usually begin by discussing their children and the things that they do during the day. Often, we can find any number of things that the child does when instructed—an obvious sign that the child is not uncontrollable. In the most difficult cases, I can point out that they, like all parents, get their children to go to school. When I point this out, the parents' demeanor often changes, and they say quite confidently, "Of course he [or she] goes to school each day. There is no way my child is going to miss school." This is the key. If you can get your child to do one thing consistently, then you should be able to make it two things, then three things, and so forth. For many families, the difference between getting a child to go to school and having him or her go to bed is one of personal resolve rather than of ability. Our society has made it very clear that all children go to school. In fact, if a child does not go to school, then the parent is held accountable and, in extreme cases, can be sent to jail. Because parents do not accept any alternatives, the rate of school refusal (the number of children who refuse to go to school) is quite low compared with other problems that children experience. Parents must be taught to have the same resolve for other essential demands that they place on their children, and they must be given the techniques that will help them carry this out. If you feel unable to place this structure on your child because you are concerned that he or she will become too disruptive, then refer to Chapter 11 for some suggestions on how to deal with these problems outside of bedtime.

It also is important to point out that *you* should direct the bedtime routine. This is not to say that your child should not have a say as to what activities should be included in these routines. Your child's input is crucial. If you find, however, that the bedtime routine is becoming longer and longer and more elaborate, then it is time to regroup and take control. This happened to me. My son enjoyed his bedtime routine so much that he often wanted just one more minute of back scratching. Then it became one more round of kisses. He then seemed to build in an extra stop to the bathroom, followed by one more trip to get a glass of "cold water," which had to come from the refrigerator. Our routine, which previously had been about 30 minutes, began to take almost an hour. He obviously wanted to avoid going to sleep at all costs.

If you find your routine taking on more and more activities and becoming longer and longer, then you may need to consider that your child is using this to delay bedtime. If you both enjoy this time and have no problem with a bedtime routine that is longer than 30 minutes, then there is no real need to change things; however, if this extra time is cutting into the amount of time that your child sleeps and is becoming a concern, then you may need to start again with the original routine and make it clear when it starts and ends. There probably will be some initial resistance to this reduction in time; however, your child should adjust within a few days or weeks.

### Bedtime Routines for Children with Autism

One word of caution about bedtime routines should be made for children with autism: It frequently is the case that these children latch on to routines so strongly that they become rituals. For some children with autism, varying their ritual even the slightest bit can result in a major tantrum. One child with whom my colleagues and I worked established his own bedtime routine. He would set up his extensive collection of stuffed animals around the bed, a task that could take 15 minutes given the large number that he had to arrange. Unfortunately, if one of the animals were out of place or missing, then he could not go to sleep. To complicate matters, if he happened to wake up at night and find the animals moved—which sometimes happened because of his moving around in bed during sleep—then he would scream and cry until his mother came into his room to fix things.

There were a number of reasons we did not try immediately to get this boy to give up his ritual. He seemed to like arranging his stuffed animals, and he had few activities that seemed to give him as much joy. We obviously did not want to take away what appeared to be his one pleasure in life. His mother also did not want to take on the challenge of changing this ritual (which would have resulted in weeks of severe disruption), and we all believed that any attempt to do so probably would be unsuccessful. Instead, we first taught him how to rearrange his stuffed animals himself after waking in the middle of the night. We taught his mother to not put back the animals when he awakened screaming but instead to prompt him to do it himself. Although this was at first rather difficult—he would cry longer—after a few weeks, he was doing it with his mother's prompting. Soon the boy was not crying at night at all but was presumably getting up, fixing the toys, and going back to sleep. In addition to this recommendation, we also suggested that his mother encourage new arrangements from time to time to get him to accept new variations. Two months after our initial contact with this mother, she was reporting that her son was going to bed more easily and was not waking up crying as he had for years before. Parents of children with autism should be cautious when introducing new routines and should consider building in variation (e.g., changing the order of the activities each night) from the very beginning.

### Bedtime Routines for Children with Attention-Deficit/Hyperactivity Disorder

Parents of children who have been diagnosed with attention-deficit/hyperactivity disorder (ADHD) often report that one of the sleep problems that their children experience is taking a long time to go to sleep. This may be related to ADHD or to the medication that many of these children take each day (see Chapter 12 for a discussion of medication and sleep). Whatever the cause, bedtime routines may take much longer for these children. One recommendation is to allow a longer-than-usual bedtime routine for children who seem to need more time to wind down. After a few weeks of a 1-hour bedtime routine that the child seems to accept, you can decide whether you want to change the time. Again, if this extra time seems to be interfering with sleep or is difficult to manage, then parents should fade back the routine until it approximates the 30 minutes recommended. This is done slowly by decreasing the routine from 60 to 50 minutes. If after 2 weeks the child has adapted to the 50-minute routine, then cut back the time to 40 minutes, then 30 minutes. Fading back the bedtime routine often prevents fighting at bedtime and lets the child slowly adapt to the restriction. It is important to note that fading routines, as with any of the recommendations made in this book, will need to be individually assessed. For example, if your child is doing well with 60 minutes but becomes difficult to manage when you move it back to 50 minutes, then try 55 minutes instead. Remember that bedtime routines should be a calming time and not a time for fights. If fading the time is too disruptive no matter how you break it down, then consider some other alternatives, such as those described in Chapter 7.

## REGULAR SLEEP TIMES

We are creatures of habit. For the most part, our bodies work best when we have a fairly regular schedule. Having irregular sleep–wake habits can negatively affect some people. One family with whom my colleagues and I worked completed the sleep diary prior to the interview. We found that their 3-year-old daughter sometimes would be put to bed at 10:00 P.M. and other times as late as 2:00 A.M. Bedtime was determined by her parents' schedule rather than by when the little girl seemed tired. In fact, the parents reported that they tried to keep her up late on some nights because they wanted some alone time in the morning and hoped that keeping her awake the night before would make her sleep late the next morning. Other times when they wanted her to go to sleep, she would remain awake and would often awaken in the middle of the night. It seemed pretty clear that the girl's lack of a regular sleep–wake schedule was contributing to her disturbed sleep.

In addition to a consistent bedtime routine, children and adults who have difficulties with their sleep should be sure to have a consistent time when they go to bed and a consistent time when they wake up each day. Providing your child with this structure may help prevent him or her from waking up at night and can help with bedtime problems. We typically help parents design good sleep–wake times by examining the sleep diary and determining how long their child typically sleeps. We then compare that time with what is typical for a child at that age (see Figure 1.1) and approximate how long this child should sleep to be properly rested. Then, we look at the wake time that the child will need for school or if a parent needs the child to be awake for another reason (e.g., child care) and work backward. For example, if we find that 10 hours seems to be about the right amount of sleep time, and the child needs to be awake by 7:00 A.M. for school, then we suggest that bedtime (the time when the bedtime routine ends) should be no later than 9:00 P.M. If bedtime is a problem for this child or if he or she wakes up frequently during the night, then we often suggest sticking to this 9:00 P.M. to 7:00 A.M. schedule each day. Weekends can be varied somewhat (e.g., 10:00 P.M. to 8:00 A.M.), although you want to avoid too dramatic a change. People have difficulty adjusting to new schedules, especially when they require going to bed earlier than usual, so Sunday night may become a problem if your child stays up too late on Friday and Saturday nights. Following are some guidelines for determining a good sleep–wake schedule:

- Use your sleep diary and Figure 1.1 in Chapter 1 to find the number of sleep hours that your child seems to need to be rested (e.g., 10 hours).
- Determine a good wake time that fits with your and your child's schedules (e.g., 7:00 A.M., an hour before she must leave for school).
- Move backward from your desired wake time the number of optimal sleep hours to find the best bedtime (e.g., 7:00 A.M. minus 10 hours equals 9:00 P.M. bedtime).
- Try to stay with this sleep–wake schedule each day.

Although a consistent sleep–wake schedule is recommended for everyone, sometimes parents take this too seriously and become rigid in their scheduling. It is good to have fun. In fact, when life is too boring, this too can interfere with sleep. Try to keep to a regular schedule, but do not be too concerned when you vary from it on occasion.

## CAFFEINE

We all know that coffee contains caffeine. Caffeine is a naturally occurring chemical that acts as a stimulant to the brain. People have used caffeine for centuries to give them more energy. Unfortunately for us, caffeine can also seriously interfere with our ability to fall asleep at night. What most people do not realize is that caffeine stays in our system, acting as a stimulant, for up to 6 hours. This means that the cup of coffee that you drink after dinner at 7:00 P.M. may still be affecting you at midnight. As is the case with most drugs, caffeine affects us all differently. Some are very sensitive to its effects, yet others could fall asleep even after having two cups of coffee.

It is important to be aware of foods and drinks that contain caffeine and to avoid them in the hours prior to bedtime. As you can see in Table 4.1, a number of other common foods and drugs have sufficient caffeine to interfere with sleep. Tea contains less caffeine than drip coffee, but one cup has enough to keep you awake at night. Chocolate, especially the kind used in baking, contains a fair amount of caffeine, which means that eating too many chocolate chip cookies before bed can be the culprit in bedtime problems. Coke and Pepsi have a fair amount of caffeine—probably enough to keep most people awake if they drink 8 ounces or more before bedtime. Other soft

**Table 4.1.**   Common sources of caffeine

| Item | Milligrams of caffeine |
|------|------------------------|
| Coffee (6 fl. oz.) | |
| Brewed | 103 |
| Instant | 57 |
| Decaffeinated | 2 |
| Tea (6 fl. oz.) | |
| Black | 36 |
| Instant | 31 |
| Iced | 11 |
| Chocolate | |
| Chocolate chips, semi-sweet | |
| (6-oz. package) | 105 |
| Baker's semi-sweet chocolate (1 oz.) | 13 |
| Milk chocolate (1.55-oz. bar) | 11 |
| Chocolate milk (8 oz.) | 8 |
| Cocoa beverage (6 oz.) | 4 |
| Selected soft drinks (12 oz.) | |
| Mountain Dew | 54 |
| Coca-Cola | 46 |
| Pepsi-Cola | 38 |
| RC Cola | 18 |
| 7-Up, Sprite | 0+ |
| Nonprescription drugs (standard dose) | |
| Weight control aids | 168 |
| Diuretics | 167 |
| Alertness tablets | 150 |
| Analgesic/pain relief tablets | 41 |
| Cold/allergy remedy | 27 |

From Pennington, J.A.T. (1994). *Bowes' and Church's food values of portions commonly used* (16th ed., pp. 381–383). Philadelphia: Lippincott-Raven Publishers; reprinted by permission.

drinks, such as 7-Up, Sprite, and Fresca, essentially are caffeine free and are therefore good substitutions for people who really enjoy these drinks. Most people are unaware that certain nonprescription drugs contain significant amounts of caffeine. As you can see in Table 4.1, certain over-the-counter weight control drugs, diuretics (drugs designed to increase the discharge of urine), cold and allergy medicines, and even some pain-relief drugs contain significant amounts of caffeine. You should evaluate whether your child is consuming caffeine in significant quantities from anytime up to about 6 hours before bedtime; if so, then try to find caffeine-free substitutions.

## ALCOHOL AND TOBACCO

It is midnight and you are still wound up from a hectic day. You can already tell that you won't be able to fall asleep easily tonight, so you fix yourself a drink. Within a few minutes, the alcohol seems to work its magic—the tensions of the day are fading, and you look forward to getting into bed. You put your head down on the pillow and fall asleep within minutes. This same scenario is played out in thousands of homes each night across the United States and may describe your own occasional sleepless night. The problem is that alcohol is a wolf in sheep's clothing when it comes to sleep. Although it can relax you at bedtime and help drive out thoughts that may interfere with your sleep, alcohol can also disrupt your sleep enough during the night to more than cancel out any helpful effects. This can lead to a particularly vicious cycle for people who worry about their sleep. Consider the person who is concerned that he may not fall asleep soon enough and therefore drinks at bedtime in order to fall asleep at a good time. His sleep will be restless because of the alcohol, waking up many times throughout the night (although he may be unaware of it). The next morning, he will not feel rested. The next evening, he will be even more concerned about his sleep because he is so tired and tense about not being rested. This will only serve to encourage him to drink again that night, which will in turn disrupt his sleep and start the cycle all over again. This vicious cycle is similar to what happens to people who use medications for sleep, sometimes resulting in a dependence. The bottom line is that despite its positive short-term effects on sleep (drowsiness), consuming alcohol within about 2 hours of bedtime can actually worsen your sleep, ultimately causing you to sleep *less*.

Obviously, the use of alcohol is not a problem for the children who are referred for sleep problems; however, alcohol and another drug—the nicotine in tobacco—are used by some of the adults who are referred for assistance. Often, adults with mental retardation live at home with their parents or live in community residences. Sometimes the care providers for these people have to be informed that alcohol should not be used as a sedative. More often, however, these individuals with mental retardation smoke, and the nicotine in the tobacco may be a source of their sleep problems. Just like caffeine, nicotine stimulates the nervous system. Smoking right before bedtime can result in an overstimulation of the brain, which will interfere with sleep. Another problem for people who smoke is that to maintain their "fix" of nicotine, they need to smoke fairly often throughout the day. The problem that this creates with sleep is that they can experience "withdrawal" during the night, and this can disrupt sleep. It is not surprising that many smokers light up almost as soon as they wake up in the morning because their brain is craving nicotine.

Remember that smoking cigarettes is not the only way of ingesting nicotine. Some people chew tobacco, and this too can stimulate the brain enough to disrupt sleep. Following is a description of one of the most intriguing cases for my colleagues and me. It illustrates how nicotine can impair sleep.

Michael was an unusual individual who presented us with some unique challenges, only one of which was his sleep problem. My first contact with Michael was when he first arrived at the residential facility where I was working. He was 18 years old; had never been to school; and, as far as we could tell, had spent a feral, or semi-wild, existence in the rural mountains of Virginia. Both of his parents had some level of mental retardation and let Michael spend his days wandering in the woods. When he came to us, he had never used utensils to eat, was unfamiliar with toilets, and had never slept in a bed. He did not speak, and he appeared quite nervous, which was to be expected given his new and unusual (to him) surroundings.

The staff quickly grew to like Michael, who, despite his background, seemed to have a good sense of humor. The staff spent a great deal of time patiently teaching him the skills that he would need to be more independent. Michael rapidly learned how to feed himself using a fork and a knife, how to use the bathroom, and how to take care of many of his personal needs.

Unfortunately, however, Michael's sleep became quite disrupted shortly after his arrival. He did not seem tired at bedtime, often sitting up in bed until 1:00 or 2:00 A.M., and then was difficult to awaken in the morning. When we questioned his social worker, who had known Michael for a number of years, she indicated that sleep was never a problem for him. At first, we thought that sleeping in a bed or in a strange bedroom might be the problem because his sleeping difficulties seemed to start in the residence, but after several months in which he seemed to adjust to most other routines, his sleep remained disrupted. His physician was about to order chloral hydrate to help him sleep, but this drug can have serious side effects, so we asked for more time to try to find the cause of his difficulties.

One of the habits that Michael was particularly resistant to changing was pica, or the eating of inedible objects. When he lived at home, Michael would pick up twigs or nuts from the ground and hold them in his mouth most of the day. He would also hide some of these small objects in parts of his clothing. At around the time when we became most concerned about Michael's sleep, we had found bits of tobacco in the folds of his pants. We investigated further and found that he was picking up cigarette butts off of the ground outside, sometimes putting the tobacco in his mouth and sometimes saving some in his pants.

It seemed that this tobacco could have been keeping him up at night. We were also concerned that continued ingestion of enough tobacco over time could make him ill, so we set out to get him to stop eating cigarette butts. Unfortunately, Michael's ingenuity got the better of us. He quickly surmised that we did not want him to pick up the cigarettes, so he would wait for some opportune time when we were not looking to bend down, pick one up, and pop it in his mouth. In fact, our efforts at surveillance seemed to make him more interested in cigarettes.

Accepting defeat, we decided to take a more thoughtful approach to this habit. Suppose we gave him chewing tobacco to keep in his pocket so that he could have tobacco whenever he wanted. If this stopped him from picking up cigarettes off of the ground, then it would at least be more sanitary. We found that he stopped reaching for cigarette butts altogether and was not swallowing the tobacco that we gave him. Next we decided to try to reduce the amount of chewing tobacco that we were giving him and replace it with candy or gum. The nicotine gums and patches were not available at this time or we would have tried one of them with Michael. Over the course of several months, we slowly and methodically reduced the chewing tobacco that we were giving him and gave him substitutes. After 3 months, he had only tiny amounts of tobacco and was sleeping on a regular schedule. His sleep seemed to improve as the amount of tobacco that he chewed was reduced.

You should limit drinking alcohol and smoking cigarettes in the hours before bedtime. Perhaps more important for a person's overall health would be to quit—especially smoking—altogether. Be warned: If a person stops smoking completely, then he or she may experience an increase in sleep problems initially. (This is why Michael was weaned off of tobacco slowly, to prevent him from going after cigarettes on the ground again.) Sleep problems can worsen because the body will go through withdrawal symptoms that will interfere with sleep. In the long run, however, sleep should be improved.

## SLEEP AND YOUR DIET

Whether certain foods can help you sleep has been discussed for centuries. You may have your own family remedy—for example, warm milk and cookies—to bring on sleep at night. Fortunately, sleep researchers have investigated the helpful and harmful effects on our sleep of what we eat and drink. One of the long-recommended sleep aids—drinking milk before bedtime—seems to help bring on sleep for many people. Food high in fat may disturb sleep, so it may be helpful to limit it. This does not mean that all fat should be eliminated because fat can create a feeling of being full or satisfied and is necessary for proper hormone development. In addition, eating a well-balanced and healthful diet seems to assist people who have difficulty sleeping. Being healthy in general, which can be helped with a good diet, seems to be related to good sleep.

Certain foods that may bring on an upset stomach or heartburn during the night should be avoided. It is difficult to make specific recommendations because people have their own individual reactions to certain foods. Common problem foods include highly spiced foods, cucumbers and beans (which can cause painful gas later in the evening), and foods with monosodium glutamate (MSG), which can cause difficulties with sleeping. As many of you know, MSG is often used in Chinese food (and is in meat tenderizers), although, increasingly, it is being left out, or the restaurant will leave it out if requested. Experiment with certain foods, and use the sleep diary to determine whether your child seems to respond negatively to anything in specific (e.g., a bad night's sleep after eating Chinese food).

Several years ago, the naturally occurring amino acid L-tryptophan was touted as a cure for insomnia. This amino acid is found in foods that are rich in protein, such as milk, cheese, eggs, beans, and meats. It is believed that L-tryptophan may help sleep because our bodies break down this substance into the brain chemical serotonin, which in turn may help slow down our nervous system. This may be especially important for parents of children with autism because autism has been linked to serotonin production and may account for the high rates of sleep problems in this group (serotonin and sleep also are discussed in Chapter 12). In the late 1980s, synthetic L-tryptophan was sold as a supplement in health food stores. Unfortunately, because of impurities in the manufacture of some brands of the supplements, serious side effects were observed in some people taking this substance (e.g., blood disorders, rashes, aching muscles and joints), and it was removed from the market in 1989. Obviously, you can still receive the benefits of L-tryptophan (which tend to be mild) by eating protein-rich foods, and you may want to try assessing the effects of these foods on sleep.

Finally, certain vitamins and minerals seem to have some limited positive effects on sleep. Vitamins such as $B_3$ (niacin), $B_{12}$, and folic acid (also a B vitamin) appear to help some people sleep better. Taking a B-complex multivitamin supplement each day for at least 1 week may result in some improvements in sleep. It is believed that calcium and magnesium also can serve as sedatives (sleep-inducing substances), and some people have found that supplementing their diets with these minerals has promoted improved sleep.

With all of the diet recommendations discussed here, it is important that you monitor your child's sleep to assess whether and how these foods are affecting sleep. It also is important that your physician be included in any discussions concerning changes in diet, especially if you are using supplements.

## EXERCISE AND ACTIVITY AND THEIR EFFECT ON SLEEP

Timing is everything, especially when it comes to exercise and sleep. If you exercise too close to bedtime, then you may have difficulty falling asleep. If you engage in regular exercise earlier in the day, however, then you may find that sleep is even better. Why would the time of day matter when it comes to exercise? Chapter 1 described how our internal body temperature changes throughout the day and night and how a dip in temperature in the evening seems to be related to our becoming drowsy and a rise in temperature in the early morning is related to our becoming more alert. Exercise or vigorous activity in general is important to this pattern because it can serve to raise our internal body temperature, therefore making us more alert. Such activity right before you want your child to sleep can be counterproductive, keeping him or her awake and alert rather than drowsy and sleepy. Fortunately, you can make exercise work for instead of against your child's sleep. Raising the body's temperature by exercising will cause a kind of temperature "catch up" whereby the body compensates by subsequently lowering its temperature 4–6 hours later. If you time it right and have your child exercise 4–6 hours before bedtime, then his or her body temperature will drop just at the time you want it to—in time for him or her to become drowsy for sleep.

What about exercise that occurs earlier in the day, more than 6 hours before bedtime? Unfortunately, such activity will not have a direct effect on sleep. It does appear, however, that being fit in general is related to better sleep. Research suggests that "couch potatoes" are more likely to have trouble sleeping than are those who engage in regular exercise.[1]

It is recommended that the exercise that you have your child attempt be of the aerobic type in order to have a positive impact on sleep. In other words, the child must raise his or her heartbeat such that there is heavy breathing for at least 20 minutes per day. Obviously, you should not start right into a hefty exercise plan if your child has not been active. Consult with your physician and start slowly. Injuries caused by doing too much too soon can be painful and can themselves disturb sleep.

Added caution must be heeded for some people with special needs. For example, individuals with Down syndrome (a disorder that results from having an extra 21st chromosome and that is accompanied by some level of cognitive impairment) often have cardiac problems and should be extremely careful when engaging in any exercise. Similarly, people with severe physical disabilities, such as those with cerebral palsy, also should have the advice of a physician to determine the type and duration of any exercise. Do not be discouraged if your child is not able, because of physical limitations, to engage in vigorous exercise. As discussed next, any increase in activity may help him or her with sleep.

Often, people are engaged in activities each day, either in school or at work, that are extremely boring. For example, it is all too common for people with mental retardation to be provided with the same repetitious tasks day in and day out. Similarly, many children with learning disabilities are routinely drilled on academic tasks to help them with their basic skills. Unfortunately, these boring tasks can contribute to sleep problems. Research with older adults, for example, suggests that if they lead uneventful daily lives, then they are more likely to have trouble falling asleep and staying asleep[2]. It may be valuable to reexamine the types and flow of activities that your child engages in throughout the day and make some changes if necessary. One 17-year-old young man with mental retardation with whom my colleagues and I worked spent his whole day sitting at the same table working. We suggested that he be allowed to get up from the table to get his own work (previously, his teacher would get it for him) and that he get up to put it away. Even this small change seemed to make him more alert during the day and more tired at bedtime. Following are some suggestions for exercise and activity:

- Establish a daily exercise regime for your child.
- Encourage your child to engage in aerobic exercise 4–6 hours before bedtime.

- Discourage your child from exercising or engaging in vigorous activity right before bedtime.
- Consult with a physician before starting any new exercise programs.
- Look for ways to decrease boredom and increase activity throughout the day.

## THE BED AND THE BEDROOM

Many of us use our bedroom as an office, a family gathering place, a dining room, an entertainment center, and a place to plan the future. For you, this may not be a problem. Many people, however, come to connect their bed or bedroom with activities that interfere with sleeping. Both positive and negative associations with the bed can cause a person to have trouble falling asleep. The beginning of this chapter discussed how Harry may have come to associate his bed with wrestling and fooling around with his mother. It may have been very difficult for him to turn off these exciting times and fall asleep in the same place where minutes before he was so exhilarated. Other people work in bed and find it difficult to stop thinking their anxious thoughts and fall asleep. Because it is difficult to determine whether these types of associations are the problems that are causing sleep difficulties, parents should restrict the child's activities surrounding the bed to only sleeping. This technique is called *stimulus control,* meaning that the bedroom or the bed can trigger behavior that can help or hurt sleep. Previously learned associations, such as "bed = wrestling," are relearned to reflect new associations that are more beneficial to sleep ("bed = sleep").

Sometimes there are practical limitations when trying to follow through on this approach. For example, in smaller homes where the bedroom may be the only place to play, the child should play on the floor, and the bed should be restricted to bedtime stories and sleep. Some people live in one-room apartments where the bed is a couch and the bedroom literally is the living room, the dining room, and so forth. In those cases in which it is impossible to keep the bed as a place only for sleep, the parents must rely heavily on the constant and predictable bedtime routines described in the beginning of this chapter to help the child associate the bed with sleep, at least at night.

Last, when consulting with a family, my colleagues and I often ask parents to "sleep an hour in their children's beds." We do not mean this literally but instead want parents to focus on things in the bedroom that might be interfering with their child's sleep. Is the bedroom noisy? Can you hear conversations in the next room, the television, a dishwasher? Any number of noises at bedtime can keep a light sleeper from falling asleep. It may be necessary for the family to be quieter at night, at least until the child is asleep. Other families have found that they can move their activities into another room that is not as close to their child's bedroom and that this reduces the noise that can be heard. Light can be another problem. A hallway light that is too bright, for example, may be interfering with sleep. On one occasion, my colleagues and I found that a child who was waking up too early in the morning did not have any window coverings in her bedroom, and the early morning light was waking her up. Even something such as a bedroom that is too cold or too warm might be a problem for your child. Spend some time in your child's bedroom at night and determine whether there are any common-sense changes that can help the onset of sleep.

## CONCLUSION

This chapter is recommended for everyone whose child is having trouble sleeping. It began with The Good Sleep Habits Checklist, which everyone should consult before moving on to more specific techniques. These recommendations include many of the suggestions that sleep experts collectively refer to as "sleep hygiene." Just as good physical hygiene helps us to be healthier physically, good sleep hygiene has been found to help people sleep better. The introduction of routines was highlighted first because it can be a powerful sleep technique. Recommendations such as limiting certain foods and drinks have helped people who were unknowingly disrupting their own sleep.

It is important to point out that your child's disturbed sleep probably is causing your own sleep to be disrupted. Unfortunately, even when the child can be helped to sleep better, the parents' sleep continues to be disturbed. This is why the recommendations in this book are applicable to anyone who is having trouble with sleep. It may be helpful, therefore, for you to complete The Good Sleep Habits Checklist for yourself to determine whether you can improve your own sleep as well.

# 5

## Help for Bedtime Problems

You've spent a long day juggling the demands and needs of your active family. Now, as evening approaches, you are looking forward to the all-too-brief time when your child is safely and quietly asleep and when you will have a few precious moments for yourself or to share with your partner. As you begin to get your child ready for bed and the resistance begins, you remember again that tonight, like most nights, will be the "battle at bedtime." For one more night, the way in which your child goes to sleep will resemble combat: a skirmish here, a small victory there, and then the onslaught that characterizes most nights. When the war is over for the night, you are so wound up that sleep will be difficult for you as well.

Bedtime resistance or, in the more extreme case, bedtime tantrums, can be extremely upsetting to a family. Chapter 4 described how important it is for many people to have a quiet transition to sleep. For many households, however, the time before sleep is anything but quiet. Fortunately, there are ways to deal with even the worst bedtime battles, and these techniques can lead to significant improvements in a matter of weeks. Let's begin by looking at one family who had bedtime troubles for many years but who managed to successfully overcome these difficulties.

Dena's parents both were college students and were concerned about their 5-year-old daughter. Dena recently had been diagnosed as having

75

autism, in part because of her delays with language and relative lack of interest in other people. Dena knew and recognized her parents but seemed to interact with them, as her parents described, "on an angle." She would never look straight at them when she approached, and she often took their hands to lead them to things that she wanted. She seemed to enjoy sitting with her parents but would always face away from them and would not share toys with them like other young children do. Dena liked spinning things, especially on the hardwood floors because of the sound they made.

As her parents described, Dena never was a good sleeper but recently was beginning to sleep through the night. Unfortunately, bedtime was still a problem. Their pediatrician had suggested that they give Dena a small dose of Benadryl (the allergy medication) before bedtime to make her sleepy. For a few nights this seemed to help, but she appeared to her parents to fight off the effects of the medication in order to stay up. A typical night would begin with a good bedtime routine that included washing up, dressing for bed, a nighttime story that Dena seemed to pay some attention to, and then a short ritual whereby Dena would arrange the covers of her bed before getting into it. As soon as her parents got up from the bed, however, Dena would be up too and would try to go out into the living room. When they attempted to get her to go back to bed, Dena would fall to the floor and cry. As this continued back and forth, in and out of her room, she would cry more loudly and struggle to be let loose. Her parents had been dealing with this for the past 3 years by having Dena's mother stay in bed with her until Dena fell asleep. Her mother would be in bed with her for 15–30 minutes each night before Dena was asleep. On some nights, Dena would wake up when her mother tried to leave the bed, and this usually prolonged the ritual for an additional 30 minutes.

After Dena's parents completed the assessment procedure, we talked about how they felt about Dena's crying at night. Her mother and father both admitted with some embarrassment that they could not stand to hear her cry. Perhaps because they recognized the problems that she was having learning to speak and develop in a typical fashion, they felt guilty when she was upset, especially when they could prevent her distress by staying in bed with her. They said that it wasn't her fault that she had autism (as if perhaps it were *their* fault), and she shouldn't have to be so miserable over bedtime. I spent some time going over with them some of the research on autism[1], which clearly shows that their early parenting could *not* have caused Dena's current condition. They both confessed to feeling both personally guilty, as if they were responsible, and secret resentment toward the other spouse, feeling that maybe it was the other partner who was to blame. Dena's mother and father appeared greatly relieved to hear that neither one of them was the cause of their beautiful daughter's autism. It was hoped that if this information also made them feel less guilty about letting their daughter cry, then they would be able to ignore her crying at bedtime, at least for a few minutes.

The habit of waiting for her to fall asleep started innocently enough when she was 2 years old and was ill. They stayed in the bed with her on those nights to console her because she was obviously uncomfortable; however, Dena kept them there each night, even after the illness was resolved, by crying plaintively when they left before she fell asleep. They now felt trapped in this pattern and were desperately seeking a solution to this problem.

Before discussing the particular plan that was designed for Dena's parents, let's examine the intervention procedure in general and how it can be used in most cases of bedtime resistance.

## GRADUATED EXTINCTION

Graduated extinction involves spending increasingly longer amounts of time ignoring the cries and protestations of a child at bedtime. It is a variation of the typical approach of simply ignoring the crying, and it is an adaptation that many parents find more acceptable. Most parents who have had children who have put up a struggle at bedtime probably have at some point tried to ignore it. In fact, the most common recommendation made by pediatricians when asked by parents how to respond to bedtime resistance is simply to ignore the crying child. Let the child just "cry it out," and eventually he or she will go to sleep on his or her own. I remember quite distinctly my and my wife's attempts to ignore the crying of our infant son. Because he was our firstborn, we did not know whether his cries meant that he was hungry, thirsty, ill, in pain, wet, lonely, or what. Over the months, we began to feel comfortable that his nightly crying was not due to some horrible plague that only showed itself at night, but we still could not ignore him when he cried. I can recall feeling the pangs of guilt while this poor innocent infant cried as we heartlessly left him alone at night.

Fortunately, my wife and I gathered up our courage and began a plan that has been demonstrated to be quite successful in assisting with bedtime problems as well as night waking (which is discussed more fully in Chapter 6). We implemented a graduated extinction program that involved ignoring his cries but also checking on him periodically in case there really was something wrong with him. The first step in the plan (which we had already completed) was to establish a bedtime routine (described in detail in Chapter 4). My wife and I then had to agree on what was a good bedtime for our son and stick to it. Even if he did not seem tired or, more likely, if we were not ready for the battle, we needed to put him to bed at the same time each night. Then the hard part—how long could we ignore the crying without breaking down and going into his room? We came up with 5 minutes, which seemed like only a brief moment when we discussed it but which felt like an eternity when we actually had to follow through. The first evening of the plan had us putting our son to bed at 8:00 P.M. after about a 30-minute bedtime routine. As usual, he cried when we left the room. We waited the full 5 minutes and then *briefly* went into his room, saw that he was all right, and then told him to go back to bed. Importantly, we did not pick him up as we usually did at these times, nor did we feed him, give him something to drink, or play music. It was in and out in about 15 seconds. We then had to wait another 5 minutes, listening to him cry, before we could go back and repeat the brief checkup. This continued—wait 5 minutes, check on him, wait 5 more minutes—for almost 2 hours on the first night. It was difficult for us, and I remember feeling little confidence in the plan.

Despite our reservations, we extended the time between visits to his room on the second night from 5 minutes to 7 minutes. Everything else was the same—no picking him up, no rocking him, no feeding him—except that now we had to wait longer. On the second night, the crying continued again for about 2 hours until he finally fell asleep. The first sign that something good was about to happen occurred on the third night. That night we again extended the time—this time to 9 minutes between visits—keeping our checkups brief and neutral. On that night, however, he did not cry continuously between the check-ups. There were seconds here and there when he stopped crying briefly. On that night, it took only about an hour for him to fall asleep. On the fourth night, we extended the time a bit more (to 11 minutes) and found that he whimpered more than cried, and he fell asleep in about 45 minutes. After that night, we decided not to go into his room again once we left at bedtime, and he stopped crying in about 20 minutes and presumably fell asleep. Two weeks later, he only fussed a bit at bedtime but would not cry at all after we left the room.

Graduated extinction seems to work by forcing the child to learn how to fall asleep on his or her own. Chapter 2 discussed that many children never learn to fall asleep alone. Often, parents are present when their child falls asleep as an infant because they are feeding the child or just lying next to him or her when he or she falls asleep. There is nothing more special than holding a sleeping infant. If this is the only situation when their child falls asleep, however, then parents run the risk of creating a situation like the one that I found myself in with my son: The child needs someone physically present to sleep. Graduated extinction requires the child to learn to fall asleep alone because you will not be present and because other sleep-inducing factors, such as the music that parents sometimes play, are not available. As cruel as this may feel at the time, children do need to learn how to fall asleep on their own. Fortunately, graduated extinction does allow for periodic checks on the child, which seem to reassure parents that everything is all right. As the time lengthens between visits to the child's room and as these visits bring very little to the child (only brief attention from parents—no holding, no feeding, no music), children learn to comfort themselves. Research using infrared video (so that you can see them in the dark) of children going through graduated extinction shows these children rearranging blankets or pillows, cuddling stuffed animals, and finding their own comfort prior to sleep[2]. Treatment research has shown that many children can benefit from this approach to dealing with bedtime problems[3].

Following are the steps to implementing a graduated extinction procedure:

- Follow the procedures for establishing a bedtime routine.
- Establish and be firm about a bedtime.
- Determine how long you are able to wait before checking on your child.
- Pick the night to begin the plan, assuming that no one will have a good night's sleep that evening—most people begin on a Friday night.
- On the first night, put your child to bed, leave the room, then wait the agreed-on time (e.g., 3 minutes). If after 3 minutes your child is still crying, then go into the room (do not pick up your child, do not give him or her food or a drink, do not engage in extensive conversation), tell him or her to go to bed, then leave. Wait another 3 minutes, and go back into the room if your child is still crying. Continue the pattern until your child is asleep.
- On each subsequent night, extend the time between visits by 2 or 3 minutes. Continue the same procedure when entering the room.

In Dena's case, we designed a plan following these guidelines. As is so often the case, however, a number of factors caused us to modify the plan somewhat. First, her parents broke down on the first night and stayed in bed with her after only the second checkup in her room. The amount of time that they selected (2 minutes) was brief for most families but obviously was too long for them to listen to Dena cry. We then modified the plan to only 30 seconds between visits, increasing the time each night by 15 seconds. Although we were not sure how well this would work, after 2 weeks Dena began having nights when she would fall asleep on her own. Unfortunately, several weeks after having some success, Dena became ill, which included a loud cough, and her parents felt that they needed to be in her bed at bedtime to comfort her. As we expected, after her cough stopped, she again was disruptive at bedtime when her parents left the room. Our suggestion was to start again from the beginning and implement the graduated extinction program starting at 30 seconds. Dena's parents, however, were not emotionally ready for more nights of battling and put the plans on hold for a few months. After about 3 months, they again wanted to help Dena fall asleep on her own. This time, they stuck with the program. After 6 days of the restarted program, Dena would fall asleep with minimal disruption, and after 6 months she continued to have few problems at bedtime.

The problems that Dena's parents experienced were not unique. We often have to modify the basic plan for our interventions to meet the needs of the child, the family, or the situation. We hope that cases such as these give you some ideas as to how to adapt plans such as graduated extinction to fit your own needs. In this spirit, let's look at the case of another child for whom we used graduated extinction and for whom we needed to modify our plan.

Nick was a 12-year-old boy who had received a diagnosis of autism. He lived at home with his parents and a sister and attended a general sixth-grade class at his neighborhood school. Of most concern to his parents and school were his frequent self-injurious behaviors, which mostly involved his poking himself in the eyes. He also frequently would get upset at home and at school, throwing objects and sometimes even breaking windows.

We first had contact with Nick because of his very disruptive and disturbing behaviors. As we talked with his family, we found that he also had difficulty at bedtime and throughout the night, and we suspected that his sleep problems may be contributing to the daytime behavior problems observed at home and at school. One of the major problems surrounding Nick's sleep was his unwillingness to go to bed at night. Often, he would remain awake for up to 4 or 5 hours after he was put to bed for the night. During this time, he frequently would scream, yell, throw things around his room, and bang on the walls with his fists. Unfortunately, this was almost an every-night event.

As happens very often in children with bedtime problems, Nick also sometimes had trouble remaining asleep at night. Several nights each month after he fell asleep, he would awaken, be unable to fall back asleep, and then become disruptive in the middle of the night. Two or three times each month, he would not sleep at all and would have tantrums on and off throughout the night.

Before we had contact with Nick and his family, a physician had prescribed several different medications to try to help him sleep. As is often the case, they tried giving him some Benadryl at bedtime to make him drowsy. Unfortunately, Benadryl seemed to have just the opposite effect on Nick, making him more agitated, and he stayed awake later than ever. For a short time they tried a drug called Inderal—which is used to control high blood pressure and migraine headaches and is also used sometimes to reduce anxiety—but this drug seemed to have no effect on his sleep. A third drug, Mellaril, was prescribed to be given right before bedtime, and this seemed to help Nick fall asleep more easily. The positive effects of using this drug were not without cost, however. During the first 4 months that Nick was taking Mellaril, he gained 40 pounds. One night he somehow got access to the bottle and drank a large amount of the drug and needed emergency treatment. Because of these concerns, Nick's parents were anxious to try a different approach that did not involve the use of medication.

Nick's parents had already established a fairly stable bedtime routine. When we looked at his sleep diaries, we found that, even with the Mellaril, it would take him an average of almost 2 hours each night for him to fall asleep. His parents had selected an 8:00 P.M. bedtime, in part because they wanted him to get more sleep and also because they relished time alone at night for themselves. Our suggestion for a later bedtime (10:00 P.M.), which was probably more appropriate for a child his age, was met with obvious resistance. The compromise that we all agreed to involved continuing to put Nick in his bedroom at 8:00 P.M., but instead of turning out the lights and trying to get him to sleep, he would be allowed to stay up and play in his room until 10:00 P.M.

Each evening, Nick's parents would begin the bedtime routine, which would end with his being in his room at 8:00 P.M. He could keep his light on and play until 10:00 P.M. If he were very disruptive, then the parents could go into his room, but other than these times they were to leave him alone. An alarm clock was set to go off at 10:00 P.M. to signal both Nick and his parents that it was time to sleep. At this time they would enter his room and sit by his side for a few minutes of quiet activity (backrubs, quiet talking). After no more than 15 minutes, his parents were instructed to say goodnight, turn off the light, and leave the room.

The compromise at bedtime dramatically reduced the disruption at night. During most evenings, Nick did not fight bedtime and generally cooperated with going to sleep. There were still one or two nights each week when Nick was disruptive, however, so we designed a graduated extinction plan for these times. On nights when Nick refused to stay in his bed at 10:00 P.M. and go to sleep, his parents were instructed to wait 5 minutes before going into his room. We suggested that they stand by his closed bedroom door so that they could hear him and so that they could respond when he tried to leave his room. If he opened the door and tried to come out, then his parents would lead him back to his bed without saying anything other than, "Go back to bed." On a few nights, they could hear him banging his head, so they calmly entered the room, placed him back into bed, and then left the room. Over the course of several weeks, the problems continued to decline, and Nick's parents were delighted with the changes.

The solution of having Nick stay in his room from 8:00 P.M. until 10:00 P.M. obviously was a compromise that was not without some risk. By letting him spend so much time playing in bed at night, we were concerned that he might associate the bed with play rather than with sleep, and this might interfere with his sleep. Fortunately, this was not the case, and on most nights he fell asleep soon after the alarm went off. Ideally, his parents should have kept him up until 10:00 P.M., but the needs of the family—some "mental health" time together—were important to consider when we designed the plan. Its success was welcomed by the whole family.

Again, Nick's case illustrates the need to tailor these programs for each family. When children present multiple problems surrounding sleep, as Nick did, it is important that you be patient and continue to monitor your child's progress. Parents should complete the sleep diaries throughout the time of the program so that they can see whatever changes are occurring, even if progress is slow. Nick's parents initially were skeptical about the program until we showed them his improvements each week. Seeing that Nick's tantrums were becoming shorter and shorter gave them the motivation to keep going. Remember to keep monitoring your child's progress, and, if you need it, use this information to help you persist.

## BEDTIME FADING

Although graduated extinction can be a very effective plan for children who have tantrums at bedtime, and it certainly is easier for most parents to implement than simply to ignore all cries, this procedure is not for all families. We have many parents who cannot tolerate the crying that occurs when using a technique such as graduated extinction. Sometimes it is because their child's cries make them feel so miserable that it is not worth even this temporary battle. Dena's parents are a good example; they found it very difficult not to respond to their

daughter even after only 30 seconds of crying. Other parents are concerned about neighbors. Living in an apartment often means that you
cannot allow your child to scream for hours each night. In fact, many
parents fall into the trap of being in their child's bed at bedtime not because they cannot handle the crying but because they are concerned
that neighbors or other family members may be too disrupted. One
mother who contacted us for help told us that she slept on the floor
next to her son's bed so that she could respond immediately if he woke
up and so his cries would not awaken her husband and disrupt his
sleep. For 7 years she slept apart from her husband in order to safe-
guard his sleep.

Finally, sometimes children are so disruptive at bedtime that a
parent cannot allow the child to continue the tantrum for too long.
Often this occurs as the child grows older and can inflict more damage
on him- or herself, on others, or on property. One 11-year-old boy who
had attention-deficit/hyperactivity disorder (ADHD) once bragged to
us that he broke his bedroom window five times over the past few
years in fights over bedtime. Obviously, this type of reaction to bedtime cannot be ignored by parents and makes implementing a plan
such as graduated extinction a problem.

Fortunately, an alternative approach to responding to bedtime resistance is available that may make bedtime for some children "error-
less." One strategy for getting a child to sleep at night might not have
occurred to you—keep him or her up *later* than usual. The rationale
behind what is called *bedtime fading* is to keep the child up so late that
he or she falls asleep on his or her own. For example, if bedtime is usually 9:00 P.M. but your child fights going to bed at this time, then temporarily make bedtime 11:30 P.M., a time when your child may be so
tired that bedtime is no longer a battle. If this new bedtime is successful (i.e., your child falls asleep with little resistance), then you can
begin to fade back bedtime in small increments until the bedtime at
which you want your child to fall asleep is achieved. The following
case illustrates a particularly difficult situation in which bedtime was
becoming almost a life-threatening event. My colleagues and I were
able to help this mother deal with a situation that was rapidly getting
out of hand.

> Gloria's mother called me one afternoon after hearing that I may be able
> to offer some help. Listening to her exhausted voice over the telephone
> brought back memories of my own child's bedtime difficulties and the
> point at which I became willing to try anything. She relayed to me some
> background information about her daughter and the current problems
> that she faced when trying to get Gloria to sleep.

Gloria was a very active and generally happy 12-year-old girl who had developmental delays that caused her speech to be limited. She also needed some additional help with everyday activities such as feeding herself, bathing, and schoolwork. Despite the hard work, Gloria liked school a great deal and enjoyed being with other children her age. Her teachers liked her as well, enjoyed having her in class, and never suspected the problems that her mother was experiencing with Gloria at home.

Gloria's mother described to me how each evening she felt a sense of dread come over her. She had learned to associate nightfall with the difficulty that she was having getting Gloria to go to bed. Ever since Gloria was born—which she reminded me was now more than a dozen years ago—she would cry and resist going to bed in the evening or even when her mother tried to get her to nap. In recent years, as Gloria had grown, the crying had become more intense, and she began to lash out at her mother. On one recent night, Gloria kept coming out of her room. When her mother tried to get her to go back, Gloria kicked and slapped her mother so hard that her mother fell to the floor. She told me that she was afraid of Gloria and did not know how long she could keep her at home. Her mother told me that no one else knew what was happening at night because she was too ashamed to tell anyone but that things were becoming so out of hand that she had to admit that she needed help.

Obviously, Gloria's behavior was becoming unmanageable, and helping Gloria's mother with her daughter's sleep could not include any prolonged periods of ignoring her outbursts. Her mother already was trying to ignore her tantrums at bedtime and was frightened at what might happen to her. Our plan for Gloria focused on getting Gloria to sleep at night without putting her mother at risk for getting hurt. As we already have mentioned, one option was to use bedtime fading. For this plan, we try to find a time at night when the child is so tired that he or she would go to bed without trouble. We do this because we want to establish a pattern whereby the child learns to go to bed and to fall asleep on his or her own. This should seem familiar to you if you have read Chapter 4 because it is the same rationale used in the technique known as stimulus control. The bed, the bedroom, and the bedtime routine all should signal sleep. In Gloria's case (and in the case of her mother), all of these "stimuli" signaled a terrible battle rather than soothing and restful sleep. Keeping Gloria up later could help to make her less resistant to bedtime and therefore let her see how pleasant bedtime can be.

Finding the right bedtime is one of the keys to bedtime fading. Here is where the sleep diary that you completed can come in handy. Often there are times when the family has been out late at a movie or a relative's house or has stayed up late at home watching television.

During these times, the child may have fallen asleep on his or her own. To be safe, we take this time and add 30 minutes to come up with the new bedtime. If you do not have a good idea about when your child might fall asleep, then you can experiment by staying up late. Make sure that there is little activity (i.e., make it boring), and watch for when your child seems to nod off. Again, add 30 minutes to this time and try using that as the bedtime. An important note about napping: If your child is also napping during the day, then refer to Chapter 7 as well. Sometimes bedtime resistance occurs because the child is sleeping during the day and simply is not tired at the designated bedtime. Chapter 7 describes a case like this, which first involves changing naps rather than trying to work on bedtime. If your child is also napping, then this alternative approach may help.

Once you have settled on a bedtime, use a bedtime routine for the 30 minutes or so before this new bedtime, and put your child to bed. Make sure that she stays awake prior to the new bedtime. This is important. You may be tempted to let your child fall asleep earlier than the new bedtime if she seems to be nodding off and close to sleep. Resist! Remember, you want your child to fall asleep after the bedtime routine and when she is in bed. Letting your child fall asleep on the couch in front of the television and then transferring her to bed defeats the purpose of the plan. Keep your child awake until the new bedtime. Your patience will be rewarded.

If you put your child to bed at the new bedtime and she seems wide awake after about 15 minutes, then have her get up, and extend the bedtime for one more hour. Even if your child does not resist sleep during this time, you do not want her lying in bed awake for too long. The reason you want to avoid prolonged periods in bed without sleep is that you do not want your child to begin to associate the bed with *not* sleeping. Just as we discouraged Harry in Chapter 4 from wrestling in bed at night because that might keep him up, we try to keep to a minimum the time in bed when a child is awake. Again, the bed should be a signal only for sleep.

If your child is falling asleep within about 15 minutes at the new bedtime over two consecutive nights, then you can begin to move back the bedtime. For each two nights, move back bedtime by 15 minutes. For example, if you selected 12:30 A.M. as the bedtime, then move it to 12:15 A.M. after your child falls asleep successfully for two nights. Keep moving the time back (e.g., 12:00 A.M., 11:45 P.M., 11:30 P.M.) until you reach the bedtime that you want or until your child no longer falls asleep within the first 15 minutes.

Try to remain flexible when it comes to the "ideal" bedtime. We saw in Nick's case that his parents' desired bedtime for him was 8:00 P.M., but Nick did not seem tired until about 10:00 P.M. Because

Nick was not napping during the day and he seemed to be well rested after his 9 hours of sleep (10:00 P.M. to 7:00 A.M.), we believed that 10:00 P.M. was a good bedtime for him. Part of the reason that he resisted going to sleep at 8:00 P.M. was because he simply was not ready for sleep that early in the evening. His sleep problem was therefore partly due to his parents' selection of a bedtime that was inappropriate for him. Use Figure 1.1 in Chapter 1 to give you an idea of how much sleep your child needs according to his or her age. Also keep in mind, however, that each of us has different sleep needs, so what is good for one child may not be good for a second child of the same age. If your child seems well rested during the day, then he probably is getting enough sleep. Conversely, if he seems tired even after 8 hours of sleep, then that may not be enough time.

Following are some general guidelines for designing a bedtime fading program. As with all programs, you may need to experiment a bit to determine what works best for your child.

- Select a bedtime when your child is likely to fall asleep with little difficulty and within about 15 minutes. To determine this bedtime, use the sleep diary to find a time when your child falls asleep when left alone (e.g., 1:00 A.M.), then add 30 minutes to this time (new bedtime = 1:30 A.M.).
- If your child falls asleep within 15 minutes of being put to bed at this new bedtime and without resistance for two consecutive nights, then move back bedtime 15 minutes (e.g., from 1:30 A.M. to 1:15 A.M.).
- Keep your child awake before the new bedtime even if he or she seems to want to fall asleep.
- If your child does not fall asleep within about 15 minutes after being put to bed, then have him or her leave the bedroom, and extend the bedtime for 1 more hour.
- Continue to move back the bedtime (e.g., from 1:15 A.M. to 1:00 A.M.) until the desired bedtime is reached.

Returning to Gloria's case, we found that Gloria reliably would fall asleep at around 1:00 A.M. if she were left alone. Based on this information, we selected a 1:30 A.M. bedtime for Gloria and asked her mother to begin a bedtime routine at 1:00 A.M. As often happens when using faded bedtime, Gloria would sometimes start to fall asleep as the evening progressed but before the new 1:30 A.M. bedtime. Her mother would engage her in some activity (e.g., fixing lunch for tomorrow, folding laundry) that would keep her from falling asleep but that was not too exciting and that would not keep her from falling asleep later.

Gloria's mother initially was hesitant about this program. Anything that revolved around bedtime caused her a great deal of anxiety because of the very negative history she had with her daughter and sleep. One specific concern was when she would need to tell her daughter to go to bed. Usually, her mother would wait until Gloria looked sleepy. Previously, when Gloria looked as though she was about to fall asleep on the couch, her mother would tell her to go to bed. Unfortunately, this would usually be followed by a fight, even though Gloria obviously was tired. This is when the bedtime routine is so helpful. By building up to bedtime rather than bringing it on suddenly, you avoid the abrupt transition, which can be very unpleasant for children. Gloria probably did not like to be wrenched away from her activity to be immediately put to bed. Adding the more gradual transition seemed to help her accept bedtime and helped her mother cope with this previously dreaded time of night.

## COMPARING GRADUATED EXTINCTION AND BEDTIME FADING

We have examined two very different ways to deal with disruption at bedtime. *Graduated extinction* involves letting your child get upset and waiting for progressively longer periods of time before checking on the child. *Bedtime fading* involves keeping your child up much later than usual so that the child falls asleep without incident and then gradually moving back this bedtime until it matches your expected time to sleep. The question that arises is how to decide between these two plans. "Which one is better for my child and me?"

Fortunately, both of these approaches seem to be successful in helping many families reduce or eliminate bedtime problems. Research conducted with many children with different needs indicates that either approach can achieve your ultimate goal: having a peaceful end to the day[4]. There are both pluses and minuses to each of the approaches, however, and families should take these factors into consideration when choosing between the plans (see Table 5.1). For example, many families who cannot bear to listen to even a few minutes of their child's cries may not do well with graduated extinction. In addition, some children engage in behaviors that are so disruptive that you cannot ignore them. Some of the children whom we have worked with who have ADHD, for example, have been able virtually to destroy their bedroom in a few minutes. Their parents cannot afford to wait even a few seconds during such an episode without intervening. For these families, faded bedtime becomes a good choice because they are able, in many cases, to avoid any of the disruption at bedtime. There are trade-offs, however, for families who choose faded bedtimes.

**Table 5.1.**   Comparing graduated extinction and faded bedtime

| Graduated extinction | | Faded bedtime | |
| --- | --- | --- | --- |
| Pluses | Minuses | Pluses | Minuses |
| • Can be used at the regular bedtime rather than having to wait until late at night<br>• Can check on the child for reassurance<br>• Usually works within the first week | • Requires listening to child's cries, which can be difficult for many families<br>• Can result in an increase in behavior problems<br>• Some behaviors, such as injurious ones, cannot be ignored | • Often can be "errorless," with no increase in behavior problems<br>• Often prevents long bouts of crying | • Requires that someone remain up late at night<br>• Can take several weeks before the desired bedtime is reached |

For many, the very late night or early morning schedule is too much for them. Because someone has to stay awake, sometimes until 1:00 or 2:00 in the morning, faded bedtime becomes more trouble than it is worth. Also, it often takes several weeks to fade back the bedtime until the child is going to bed at the desired time, which can be trying for many families, whereas graduated extinction sometimes can be successful within days, which can be quite appealing to many parents. As you can see, the choice between the two approaches often comes down to personal preferences (quick but disruptive in the case of graduated extinction or slower but calmer in the case of faded bedtimes), although in cases with extreme behavior outbursts, faded bedtime may be the only option.

## COMBINING PLANS WITH MEDICATION

Sometimes my colleagues and I face decisions about the use of medication and whether to recommend to families to continue the medication that their child is receiving before beginning plans that involve interventions such as graduated extinction or bedtime fading. Obviously, the decision about whether to use medication must be one that is made in consultation with your physician. Any change in medication, whether it is to use it or to discontinue its use, should be preceded by a discussion with a medical professional of the possible consequences.

Once the child's physical health is considered, another concern is evaluating the effects of your plan on your child's sleep. The concern is that if you change more than one thing at a time—such as starting some medication at about the same time that you begin a sleep plan—then you may not be sure what caused any changes in your child's sleep. You want to be able to definitively determine whether your plan worked. This is more than just something of passing interest. If you can confidently determine that your graduated extinction plan, for example, helped your daughter to go to bed at night, then you will know what to do if this problem ever comes back (which, unfortunately, can happen). If you started the plan just as you changed the use of some medication, however, then you will not know which of these to change should the problem resurface.

Sleep medications that are available and their recommended use are discussed in some detail in Chapter 12, and you should refer to that chapter if your child is currently receiving some medication or if there are plans to start. At this point, however, it is important just to remember the following: DO NOT CHANGE MORE THAN ONE THING AT A TIME. Knowing what caused sleep to improve (or to worsen) will be of tremendous value at a later time.

## WHEN SLEEP PROBLEMS REAR THEIR UGLY HEADS . . . AGAIN

It may seem very pessimistic to bring up what happens if your child's sleep problems return. Unfortunately, even with the best plans, sleep problems often return in some form during the months or years after initial success. This should not be completely surprising; many children have a difficult time sleeping because they were born that way—in other words, these children appear to be biologically predisposed to sleep problems in the first place. Their tendency to be "light sleepers" (which may have been inherited from parents or other relatives) interacts with family schedules, the way that the family responds to them, and other factors to cause many of the sleep problems described in this book. We therefore may not be "curing" their sleep difficulties in the traditional sense but simply making it easier for these children to adapt to regular sleep schedules.

My colleagues and I often see children who have done quite well with a plan such as graduated extinction, only to have their problems return after an illness, a vacation, or some other change in their lives that disrupts their sleep pattern. Dena's case is a good example. Only a few weeks after her parents had successfully implemented a graduated extinction program and her bedtime problems had subsided, a cold seemed to interrupt the newly established sleep cycle, and she was resisting bedtime again. Illnesses often can disturb sleep and can therefore be responsible for interfering with the types of plans described. Unfortunately, even after the illness is over, your child's sleep may continue to be off.

Another very common cause of the failure of a previously successful plan is the "trip to Grandma's," which is another way of saying that changes in routines can interrupt the sleep pattern that you have developed. Letting a child who has sleep problems stay up later on weekends can cause the "Sunday Night Syndrome." This is difficulty going to bed on Sunday night after being allowed to stay up later on Friday and Saturday nights. Again, trying to recover from these changes can be surprisingly difficult.

Sometimes these changes in sleep routines are inevitable. Going on vacation, sleeping at a relative's house for a weekend, a party that goes on past bedtime, and of course illnesses either should not be avoided or cannot be avoided. Therefore, if you anticipate some event that may interfere with your child's new sleep schedule, then try to lessen its impact. If you let your child stay up later on Friday night as a treat, then try to cut back on Saturday evening's bedtime so that Sunday evening is not so much of a problem. Try not to disrupt the bedtime routine even if your child is ill. You want the routine to become part of sleep, and it should be an automatic part of every night. Think ahead about how you can preserve the sleep patterns that you have established. This may prevent you from having to begin a plan completely from scratch after every unusual event.

## BEGIN AT BEDTIME

Often, children have more than one problem with sleep. Many times, children who have difficulty at bedtime also wake frequently during the night and may experience other sleep problems, such as nightmares or sleep terrors. One of the questions, then, is where to begin. Which of the sleep problems should you target first? Fortunately, some research[5] in my and my colleagues' lab points to some practical suggestions about where to begin your sleep plans.

Several years ago, one of my graduate students—now Professor Jodi Mindell—chose to use sleep problems in children as the topic of her doctoral dissertation. In designing the study, we decided to examine children who had both bedtime problems and problems waking up throughout the night. In order to be careful about how the study was conducted, she treated the bedtime problems first for half of the children and treated the night-waking problems first for the other half of the children. Once these problems were brought under control, she then helped the parents treat the second sleep problem. The study primarily relied on graduated extinction as a treatment for both sleep problems (how to use graduated extinction for night waking is discussed in Chapter 6) and was successful for all of the children. What was unexpected and surprising in this study was that it made a big difference which problem was treated first. When the children were treated for their bedtime problems first, more often than not their night waking went away on its own! No separate plan was needed for night waking for over 78% of the children for whom their bedtime problems were resolved with graduated extinction. For those children for whom night waking was treated first, achieving success with this sleep problem seemed to have no effect on bedtime problems. Parents still needed a second plan to deal with their child's disruption at bedtime.

What this study reveals is that we may be able to save a great deal of time and effort for children who have problems both at bedtime and with night waking if we first help them with their bedtime problems. The savings in parent time and anxiety can be substantial. We do not know how many people are likely to benefit from treating bedtime problems first. We also do not know whether we would achieve the same results with a plan other than graduated extinction. For example, if we helped children with bedtime by using faded bedtimes, then would their night waking be resolved as well? We do not know. Despite these unanswered questions, the findings from this study are extremely helpful in deciding how first to begin with sleep problems. "Begin at bedtime" may be the best sleep strategy.

## CONCLUSION

Bedtime problems often are complex and require different strategies for their treatment. Different families require different approaches because of the needs of the child, the needs of the family, or unusual home situations. This chapter covered several options for families so that you can design and adapt plans to fit your own individual requirements. Take the time to think through what will work best for you, and you should find a better night's sleep within a few weeks.

# 6

# Sleeping Through the Night

I have always felt that I could handle almost anything if only I could get some closure—a point at which I could say, "I've completed this," and could move on to the next challenge. No matter how ambitious the goal, getting the motivation to keep going requires some small accomplishments along the way. Without these little victories, going on can be even more difficult, and your "gumption" can drain away until you are close to giving up. This to me is one of the most insidious consequences of the type of sleep problem discussed next—night waking. After a full day of fun and play, work and demands, and even perhaps a battle at bedtime, knowing that it is over for the day can provide some comfort and the return of optimism. Unfortunately, for parents who have children who do not sleep through the night, the day never seems to end. For these families, life sometimes can seem like a never-ending struggle to catch up on all of the things that you need or want to do.

Children who do not sleep through the night often can be put into one of two categories: 1) those who wake up but are not disruptive and 2) those whose waking includes the same type of crying and tantrums discussed in Chapter 5. In some ways, helping children who wake up but do not become disruptive can be a more difficult problem. This chapter begins with a brief review of why children may not sleep through the night and then examines a number of treatment options for children who are disruptive as well as for children who are not.

## CAUSES OF NIGHT WAKING

Chapter 2 discussed how early sleep patterns may set the stage for later problems that children may experience sleeping through the night. Many infants are put to bed each evening while they are already asleep. This can happen because the parent was feeding the infant and the baby fell asleep or because the infant just fell asleep in a parent's arms. If it is close to bedtime, then the parent naturally will put the infant into his or her crib. If this is the only way that the infant can fall asleep—that is, with a parent present—then you run the risk that the infant will never learn to fall asleep independently. Couple this bedtime pattern of falling asleep only with the parent with a natural sleep phenomenon called partial waking—when we make the transition from REM, or dream, sleep to NREM, or nondream, sleep and briefly awaken—and you have the makings for nighttime disasters.

One theory about why children continue to awaken in the middle of the night and cry out involves partial waking. Although partial wakings happen to all of us several times each night, these events are very brief, and we typically have no memory of them the next morning. It is thought that infants who have not learned to fall asleep alone may more fully awaken from these partial wakings because they become frightened at the now-strange surroundings. Put yourself in the infant's place. You have fallen asleep in the comfort of your parent's arms, in a well-lit and safe environment. Some hours later, you awaken to find your parent gone, and it is dark and cold. Your first reaction is to become alarmed at this drastic change in the world, and you start to cry. If you are your parents' first child, then you are more likely to have night-waking problems, in part because of what comes next: Your parents, insecure about your care and reacting to any sign of your distress, come into your room, pick you up (which wakes you up even more), and try to provide comfort by holding you, feeding you, or even singing. Eventually you fall back asleep in their arms, and the pattern of not falling asleep alone is continued. Your parents' natural concern for your welfare may, in part, contribute to your inability to fall asleep alone.

In addition to possibly waking up infants more fully by attending to their cries at night, feeding at night also can be a contributory problem. Continuing to feed infants in the middle of the night can cause them to be hungry at that time each night, which in turn can cause them to wake up in the middle of the night. Chapter 13 discusses how to handle nighttime feedings so that your child will not awaken because he or she is hungry.

A final piece to this puzzle is a child's inborn nature or tendency to be a "light sleeper." Some children seem to be able to sleep through anything, whereas others awaken with the closing of a door on the other side of the house. We all are born with a certain propensity to sleep in a certain way, and when a child who is a light sleeper experiences partial wakings, he or she may be more likely to fully awaken from these events. That tendency, coupled with how parents respond to these awakenings, can result in a child who develops a long history of waking throughout the night.

One final consideration for people who experience night waking is the effects of smoking on sleep. During a talk that I was giving one afternoon on sleep problems, I mentioned that smoking right before bedtime could interfere with a person's ability to fall asleep at night because the nicotine in cigarettes is a stimulant. A member of the audience raised his hand, looking quite puzzled: "I often wake up in the middle of the night and can't fall back to sleep. If I get up and smoke a cigarette, however, I find that I can go back to sleep right away. Why would that happen if nicotine is a stimulant?" His question was an excellent one because it pointed out that I had failed to mention the flip side of smoking cigarettes: the addictive properties of nicotine.

Not only is nicotine an addictive drug—in fact, it is thought to be one of the most addictive of all substances—but also it is one for which people need frequent "fixes." Nicotine's effects are relatively short, only a few hours, which is why people will continue to smoke throughout the day. At night, however, a person goes for many hours without a cigarette fix. Waking in the middle of the night for some people is the result of withdrawal symptoms from nicotine, such that the brain says, "I need more." Getting up and smoking a cigarette temporarily satisfies the brain's desire for nicotine and allows the person to fall back to sleep. Obviously, under these circumstances, the best remedy is to quit smoking. This will be difficult and will be made worse by night waking caused by withdrawal symptoms. The long-term health rewards, however, are great for anyone who stops smoking, in addition to the improvement in sleep.

## WAKING WITHOUT DISRUPTION

As mentioned before, some children awaken in the middle of the night crying and screaming. This obviously can be disruptive to the whole family, causing everyone to have his or her sleep disrupted. A later section discusses this serious situation and how to deal with it. There also are children who wake up from sleep too early and who have difficulty falling back to sleep. They may lie in bed awake, read, play with toys, or even get up and wander about the house. Although this form of night waking is not as dramatic as the one that involves tantrums, it still can cause considerable daytime sleepiness for the child and can disrupt parents' sleep as well. Following is a case of a boy who experienced this problem for most of his life.

> Craig was 11 years old when he first was referred to my colleagues and me for his sleep problems. Craig had mild to moderate levels of cognitive impairments, which probably was one of the results of his having Down syndrome. He attended a general fifth-grade class in his local school and could carry out many important tasks on his own. He did have some attention problems and needed help staying on task. He also had some trouble communicating with others but was making progress in this area.
>
> Craig was not a problem at bedtime, and he would respond well to his parents' requests to go to sleep. The problem was that he would wake up most nights after having fallen asleep. During these times, he would get out of bed, turn on lights, play with toys, watch television, fix himself a snack, or get into bed with his parents. His parents explained that Craig had had night-waking problems since birth and that it was a constant concern for them. They worried that he was not getting enough sleep and that this might cause him to have more difficulty learning in school.
>
> During our assessment of Craig's sleep problem, we discovered that his bedtime was highly variable; sometimes he was put to bed before 8:00 P.M., and other times he was put to bed after 11:00 P.M. We questioned his parents about how they responded to his nightly sojourns. They reluctantly reported that they were quite inconsistent in how they handled his waking. Sometimes his parents would ignore him (because they were so tired), and this resulted in his either eventually going back to bed or getting in bed with them. On other nights, they would get up and tell him to go back to bed, which typically resulted in his going back to sleep without trouble. They thought that he might be getting up because he was hungry (because he often made himself a snack at these times) and were somewhat reluctant to prevent him from eating at night.

Craig would be characterized by sleep professionals as having difficulty maintaining sleep. Bedtime did not pose a problem either for him or for his parents, but several times each week he would wake up at any time from 1:15 A.M. to 6:00 A.M. and stay up sometimes for more than an hour. One of the first things that we try to determine in cases such as Craig's is total sleep time. In other words, is this child getting enough sleep? If the night waking lasts for 30 minutes or more, then it can begin to cut down on the amount of sleep that the child is receiving and can degrade the quality of his or her sleep. We also try to determine whether the child is napping during the day as a way to catch up on sleep because this can aggravate the sleep problem by increasing the likelihood that the child will have trouble sleeping through the night. To determine whether the child is getting sufficient sleep, refer to Figure 1.1 in Chapter 1 to determine what is typical for a child of that age, bearing in mind that there is a range of sleep needs at any age. A second factor that helps determine whether the child is getting enough sleep is daytime behavior. Does the child seem tired? Is the child irritable or cranky, and does he or she have trouble concentrating or have a low threshold for demands? All of these reactions can be signs of insufficient sleep. In Craig's case, the time spent sleeping was within the range of a child his age (about 9 hours, which is within the normal range for a child who is 11 years old), but he often seemed cranky (which sometimes included his hitting his teacher at school) during the day, and he usually had trouble concentrating on schoolwork. Either of these behaviors could be irrelevant to his sleep problem, but it was worth evaluating whether they improved along with his sleep. Craig did not nap during the day, so this was not of concern. Described later in this chapter are efforts to help children who have night waking and who nap during the day.

Once our assessment was complete, Craig's parents were instructed in how to establish a stable bedtime along with a routine leading up to bedtime (see Chapter 4). Ten o'clock was selected as Craig's bedtime because it was the time when his parents observed that he seemed tired. This bedtime would still allow him to sleep about 9½ hours per night, which was judged to be sufficient for him. At his parents' suggestion, he was given a light snack approximately 1 hour before he was to go to sleep because he seemed hungry when he got up at night. The snack also let his parents feel less guilty when they had to make him go right back to sleep after an awakening.

In addition to the changes around bedtime, we helped Craig's parents design a modified graduated extinction plan (see Chapter 5) to help them respond when he got up at night. Whenever they heard him get up at night, his father would lead him to his room and say, "It's still time to sleep. Go back to bed." Physical contact and any other conversation was to be kept to a minimum. Fortunately, this only had to occur once each night because Craig would go back to bed without difficulty and fall back to sleep. The results were quick and dramatic. Within the first week of the plan, Craig went from an average of about three nights each week with waking to only one night with waking. This progress continued. Some weeks, he would not have an instance of night waking, and on nights when he did awaken, his parents could simply call out to him to go back to bed.

Along with the improvements in Craig's sleep, his behavior at school appeared to improve. Instances of hitting other people or tantrums still occurred on occasion, but they were noticeably less frequent once he was sleeping through the night. In fact, his teachers noticed the improvement in his behavior at school even before they knew about how his sleep had improved at night, which suggested to us that his behavior must have changed considerably. Both of his parents were pleased at the improvement in Craig's sleep and his daytime behavior, and they were astounded at just how easy it had been to get him to sleep through the night.

Craig's case was a bit unusual because of the ease with which he responded to his parents' plan after such a long history of sleep problems. In some ways, however, his case was similar to many others. Often, parents have a good idea about what they should be doing with regard to their child's sleep but feel guilty about being too strict or appearing uncaring to their child. Often, the role of the sleep professional is to give them "permission" to be firm about bedtime or sleep. Craig's parents would do the right thing on some nights, but other times they would feel bad for him and let him come into their bed. This probably was contributing to his night wakings, and so when they stopped allowing it (along with a number of other changes), that was sufficient to significantly reduce the number of nights with waking.

### Sleep Restriction for Nondisruptive Waking

In Craig's case, his awakening was obvious to his parents. He appeared to immediately come out of his room after he awakened at night, and even if he did not go into their room, they could hear him walking around in the house. Other children, however, will wake up at some point at night but not cry out, come out of their room, or in any way signal that they are awake. Some children describe just being up, looking around the room, thinking about school, and so forth. Individuals who cannot talk to tell us about their disturbed sleep often have been found lying in bed awake, and these accidental discoveries have led to sleep problem referrals. In cases such as these, using the plan that we described for Craig (a version of graduated extinction whereby the parents send the child back to bed and then ignore any protests for a period of time) would not be effective because parents do not know when their children are awake. Under these circumstances, we often use a plan known as *sleep restriction* to help children sleep through the night.

At first glance, sleep restriction may seem counterintuitive as a way to help children sleep better. It involves restricting the amount of time that a child is in bed to the total amount of time that the child seems to sleep. In other words, rather than put a child to bed earlier, you may want to keep him or her up later. This procedure makes sense when you think about how you sleep after being kept awake for several days. I remember when my son was having frequent night wakings as well as waking up at 5:00 A.M. for the day. All week long, my wife and I got an average of about 4 hours of sleep each night. Fortunately, we had a baby sitter for that weekend, and we were able to get away for two nights. I remember the morning after our first night away from home, waking up close to noon and feeling as though I had slept forever. Being so sleep deprived caused us to "catch up" on some of this sleep and helped us sleep soundly. In much the same way, sleep restriction helps the child begin a pattern of sleeping through the night. Being truly tired may help the child sleep more soundly and without interruption.

Designing a sleep restriction plan first requires that you know how long your child actually sleeps each evening. The sleep diary (see Chapter 3 and Appendix D) can be useful here. Looking at the amount of sleep time across a 2-week period can give you an "average" night— say, 8 hours. It is important that you estimate how much time your child actually sleeps as opposed to just the time spent in bed. If your child takes awhile to fall asleep each night, then subtract that time from the sleep time. Also, subtract any time that your child spends awake in bed in the middle of the night during a period of awakening. For some children who do not create a problem during this time, it may be difficult to get an exact calculation of this time, so you may need to make an educated guess. The overall goal is to find out how long your child actually is sleeping each night.

Once you have an idea about how long your child sleeps each night, set up a schedule so that he or she will sleep somewhat less. Remember, the idea behind sleep restriction is to make the time in bed really count so that the person sleeps soundly through the night. In this spirit, set up a schedule that restricts sleep to about 90% of what the child actually is sleeping—say, 8 hours. Using 90% of the total amount of sleep time allows for times when the child may be awake but when it is not reported or is not known by the parents. Multiplying the number of hours asleep (8) by 0.9 will give you the new total sleep time to strive for (8 hours × 0.9 = 7.2 hours). Then you adjust either bedtime or waking time so that your child only sleeps for the new number of hours. Shifting to a later bedtime (e.g., from 10:00 P.M. to 11:00 P.M.) or waking your child earlier (e.g., from 7:30 A.M. to 6:30 A.M.) will create the new sleep time.

It is recommended, if you can handle it, that you adjust the schedule by waking your child earlier in the morning. Using bedtime to adjust the schedule may work just as well, but once you try to move the bedtime to an earlier hour, you may run into some difficulty. Recall that because of the way our biological clock works, it always is easier to stay up later than it is to fall asleep earlier. In this case, it usually is easier to let the child sleep later in the morning as you try to fade back to the previous schedule than it is to get the child to fall asleep earlier.

There may be times when your child is found lying in bed awake, even with this new schedule. If that ever happens and you believe that your child is wide awake, then have him or her leave the bed and do something quiet for 15–30 minutes. As mentioned a number of times before, we do not want the child to associate the bed with anything other than sleep. If he or she spends too much time awake in bed and possibly worried, thinking about school, or even thinking about not sleeping, then this will interfere with your efforts to help him or her sleep.

If your child goes for at least a week without waking in the middle of the night with this new schedule, then you can begin slowly to move toward the previous sleep schedule by about 15 minutes each week. Following is a summary of how to design and implement a sleep restriction plan:

- Use the sleep diary to estimate the number of hours that your child sleeps, on average, each night (e.g., 8 hours). Exclude any time that your child is in bed but is awake.
- Next, multiply the average number of hours actually asleep each night by 0.9 to get 90% of the time, or the number of hours that your child should be sleeping with this new schedule. For example, if your child is sleeping 8 hours total, then 90% of that would be a little more than 7 hours (8 hours × 0.9 = 7.2 hours). *Do not allow fewer than 4 hours when selecting a new sleep schedule.*
- Adjust your child's bedtime (e.g., from 10:00 P.M. to 11:00 P.M.) or the time when your child is awakened in the morning (e.g., from 7:30 A.M. to 6:30 A.M.) to approximate the new schedule (going from 8 hours to 7 hours of sleep).
- If bedtime is a problem, then refer to Chapter 5 and work on this sleep problem before you begin a sleep restriction plan.
- If you find your child lying in bed wide awake, then have him or her leave the bed and engage in some soothing activity until he or she appears sleepy. Then return him or her to bed.
- If night waking is eliminated or significantly diminished for 1 week, then you can readjust the bedtime or waking schedule by 15 minutes. This can be adjusted once per each successful week until the desired schedule has been reached.

Following is an illustration of how sleep restriction was implemented successfully for an adult who did not sleep through the night.

Julie was a 55-year-old woman who lived in a group home for people with mental retardation. Julie had serious daytime behavior problems, such as hitting her own head with her fist, biting her hand, screaming, and hitting other people. Despite these behavioral concerns, Julie was well liked by both the staff at the group home and her peers. She had a beautiful voice and took every opportunity to sing with groups. At times, she could be very helpful, assisting some of her housemates with bed making and cleanup after meals.

Staff were concerned for Julie because they often found her lying in bed awake in the middle of the night. Although she rarely got out of bed when she awoke and she did not cry or seem upset, the staff noticed that on days after having a waking the night before, she would have more problems at work and at home. She did not appear tired at these times; rather, she seemed very agitated and active. The group home staff were requesting help to get her to sleep better at night.

One of the first things that we noticed in our assessment of Julie's sleep was her early bedtime. She was put to bed at 8:00 P.M. as all of the other residents in the house were. The others seemed to fall asleep quickly at this time, and they appeared to sleep through the night. Julie, however, would lie in bed until 11:00 P.M. or 12:00 A.M. Again, she did not seem upset during this time, but it was clear that she was not tired. On a typical night, she would fall asleep by midnight but would awaken again sometime between 1:30 A.M. and 3:30 A.M. and would remain awake, often until the morning. There were days that the staff let her nap in the afternoon because she seemed so tired.

One of the first recommendations was to eliminate the daytime naps, which could have been interfering with her sleep. Julie's total amount of sleep time seemed to average about 5½ hours per night—not a great deal of time, but, given that she was 55 years old, it was close to the 6-hour average for someone about that age. Using the sleep restriction formula, we came up with a goal of about 5 hours of sleep to start (5.5 hours of current total sleep time × 0.9 = 4.95 hours for new schedule).

After eliminating the daytime naps, the next change involved bedtime, which we suggested they move to a more reasonable time (11:00 P.M.). The early bedtime seemed to be more of a convenience for staff than any realistic estimate of when Julie was tired, and a later bedtime would increase the likelihood that Julie would be tired at bedtime. We then asked that the staff wake her at 4:00 A.M. each morning, which, without her naps, would give her 5 hours of sleep. On the first day of the plan, Julie slept very little. She fell asleep within a reasonable amount of time (about 11:15 P.M.), but she awoke at about 2:30 A.M. and stayed up all night. The staff had her get out of bed several times so that she was not lying in bed awake all night, but this seemed to have no effect. On the day following this first night, Julie had significant behavior problems, and staff became quite discouraged. We tried to reassure them that this was not unusual and that Julie probably would do better within a few days—if they could survive!

On the second night, Julie was exhausted and fell asleep within minutes of her bedtime. In fact, the staff had their hands full trying to keep her up until 11:00 P.M. That night, she slept through until 4:00 A.M. when they woke her. The next day, her behavior was much improved. Each night thereafter, Julie had little trouble falling asleep, and with the exception of one brief waking, she slept through the night. After about a week of success with this schedule, we adjusted her morning waking from the 4:00 A.M. that we first recommended to 4:15 A.M. After a second week, it was moved to 4:30 A.M., and then to 5:00 A.M. (staff were feeling quite confident at this point, so they adjusted her schedule by 30 minutes instead of the usual 15 minutes). With her 11:00 P.M. bedtime and a 5:00 A.M. awakening, this gave Julie 6 hours of restful sleep, which exceeded the sleep that she had been receiving previously, even if you count her daytime naps. This seemed to be a good schedule for everyone, so the staff agreed to stick to it. They also noted that Julie's behavior during the day was significantly improved, which they attributed to her improved sleep.

Julie's case was typical in one respect: We had to provide quite a bit of encouragement in the early stages to keep people motivated. Sometimes the plans that we design can, at first, seem to make the situation worse, whether it is with a sleep restriction plan whereby the person has a night or two when he or she may sleep very little, or with other plans such as graduated extinction, whereby behavior problems may escalate. It is important during these early stages to keep your goal in mind and to remain confident that, within a few nights, you will see progress.

## Dangerous Behavior at Night

For some families, having a child up in the middle of the night without supervision is of great concern. These children may not cry and scream and awaken the family. In fact, parents sometimes would prefer that they did so that they would know that their children are up. Instead, the children quietly get out of bed and get into trouble. Some children will break toys, televisions, or VCRs if they are not closely monitored. For example, one boy with whom my colleagues and I worked was able to completely disassemble the VCR in his living room while his parents slept just one room away. The concern also can reach beyond family possessions. Often, my colleagues and I are asked to design plans for children who engage in dangerous activities in the middle of the night. A mother whose young son had autism told us of one night when her son left the house. He made his way down the block and into the home of a neighbor. Not knowing who this boy was, the neighbor called the police—who, fortunately, were familiar with him—and they brought him home. His mother told us that she was both humiliated (because she did not even know that he was missing) and frightened that he might have been seriously hurt.

The main issue for these parents is being aware that their children are awake and out of bed. In fact, quite a number of parents have difficulty sleeping themselves because of their anxiety over their child. They lie in bed worrying what will happen if tonight is the night that their child gets up and they do not hear it. Some parents react by locking their child's bedroom door at night so that he or she cannot get out. There is a risk in doing this, however, because should you need to leave the house quickly, as with a fire, you run the risk of losing very valuable time getting your child out. Others have installed Dutch, or half, doors, the bottom of which is locked. This type of door can keep young children in their rooms but also allows parents to hear or see in the bedroom. Other families have installed "peep holes" in their child's bedroom door so that they can monitor activity without opening the door. There are a number of alarm systems that you can set to go off when the child leaves the bed or the bedroom.* Some parents use something as simple as a bell on the child's doorknob to alert them when their child leaves the room. Any of these approaches can be used to signal parents when a child leaves the room, which in turn can help them prevent difficulties at night.

If parents know when their child leaves the room, then a graduated extinction procedure (described in Chapter 5 and in the next section) can be used. The case of Craig described in the beginning of this chapter provides a good illustration of the use of this technique. In addition, a plan called *scheduled awakening*, described in the next section, can be successful when you know the time when your child is likely to awaken at night.

---

*One company that markets these devices is Pioneer Medical Systems (800-234-0683; e-mail address: jrj@pioneermed.com).

## DISRUPTIVE NIGHT WAKING

Unfortunately—and more often than not—children who wake during the night let their parents know quite clearly that they are up. In a personal example, my infant son would begin to whine and whimper usually at about 12:30 A.M. Within minutes, this fussing would develop into full-blown crying and screaming, something extremely difficult to ignore. For the longest time, my wife and I felt guilty when we did not go into his room and check on him, even though we knew that checking on him probably was not the best thing to do. It was not until he was almost 2 years old that we mustered up the courage to try to ignore his night waking on a consistent basis. We used a graduated extinction procedure, a plan that has been successful for many parents but that, as you will see, is not without its limitations. Fortunately, three techniques are available for parents to help their children with disruptive night waking—graduated extinction, sleep restriction, and scheduled awakening. Each is described along with its strengths and weaknesses.

### Graduated Extinction

Chapter 5 described how graduated extinction—which involves slowly increasing the time between visits to the child's bedroom during a tantrum—could be used to reduce problems at bedtime. This technique also has been a successful tool for parents to help their children with disruptive night waking. Just as you would wait to respond to crying at bedtime, graduated extinction for night waking would involve waiting for progressively longer periods of time before checking on the crying child in the middle of the night after an awakening. The next case describes the use of graduated extinction for the frequent night waking of one young girl. Important for this case was that the mother's sleep also was disrupted by her daughter; efforts to help the mother sleep better are described as well.

> Marnie was 5 years old when we first met her. Several years before, she had received a diagnosis of pervasive developmental disorder (PDD). Her speech was delayed as were some of her other skills, although she was doing well in her first-grade class. Marnie's mother told us that the advertisement that my colleagues and I had placed in the newspaper offering help to parents whose children had trouble sleeping seemed like an answer to her prayers. Her daughter's pediatrician seemed to have run out of any acceptable suggestions to help Marnie, who had never in her 5 years slept through the night. Marnie's mother did not want to use the medication that her doctor had prescribed, although she had seriously considered it of late. Marnie's mother was at her wit's end because her

daughter would awaken one, two, or sometimes even three times per night, each time crying out quite plaintively. Her mother had tried everything that she could think of so that they both could get a good night's sleep, but nothing seemed to help.

Our initial discussions and assessment of Marnie's sleep seemed to point to a rather unremarkable sleep–wake cycle. She usually slept from between 10 and 11 hours each night, which was typical for someone her age. Marnie usually did not nap during the day, and her mother, as well as her first-grade teacher, reported that she did not seem tired during the day. Her mother had established a good bedtime routine and was consistent with Marnie's bedtime and the time when she was awakened in the morning. In other words, nothing was unusual about Marnie's sleep except for the night waking.

Marnie's mother told us that her daughter had never had a full night's sleep. As an infant, Marnie would awaken each evening, and her mother would feed her. This went on until Marnie was 2 years old, at which time her mother decided "enough was enough," and she stopped these nightly feedings. This change in feeding had no noticeable effect on sleep, however, and Marnie's mother would continue to get out of bed each night when Marnie cried, holding and comforting her in her bed.

The distress that Marnie's mother experienced because of her daughter's sleep problems was obvious. Not only did Marnie not sleep through the night, but also her mother was being awakened, each and every night for 5 years! Her mother believed that she was less tolerant of Marnie and everyone else because of her own lack of sleep. She even believed that her divorce from Marnie's father was partly the result of Marnie's nightly crying and her own disrupted sleep. She was quite motivated to do anything that it took to get her daughter to sleep through the night.

Based on a few discussions and the results from the assessments, we recommended that Marnie's mother implement a graduated extinction plan. Because the first step in the graduated extinction plan was to assess how long Marnie's mother could wait before responding to her daughter's crying, we were concerned that this might be a problem for her and that she might resist any plan that asked her to ignore Marnie when she was upset. She said, however, that she was committed to helping Marnie sleep through the night and that she was ready for anything. We agreed on a 5-minute wait period for the first night.

The first night of the plan, Marnie awoke at about 1:00 A.M. Her mother told us that waiting for 5 minutes the first time was not as difficult as she had expected. She went into Marnie's room, told her to go back to bed, and left the room. Waiting the second time, however, was more difficult. Marnie's mother told us that Marnie seemed stunned that her mother had left the room without comforting her, and she pleaded with her to come back. Marnie's mother told us that she got through these subsequent waiting periods by staring at her clock and counting down how many seconds were left until she could go back into her daughter's room. The second night, which we agreed would include a 7-minute wait period, seemed somehow easier. Marnie's mother told us that Marnie's cries seemed less intense, and they were not occurring continuously. The third night with 9-minute wait periods was even better; and by the fourth night, Marnie awoke only once, cried for less than a minute, and slept the rest of the night. A month after we began the plan, Marnie was sleeping through most nights; and on those now rare evenings when she awoke, she fell back to sleep within minutes.

Marnie's success was not followed by an improvement in her mother's sleep. Her mother recalled that before Marnie was born, she slept fairly well and only rarely awoke during the night. During her pregnancy with Marnie, she experienced disrupted sleep, which is common for women during this time. After Marnie's birth, she found that her sleep was interrupted only in part because of her daughter. In fact, she observed that she often awoke minutes before her daughter would wake up and did not know whether she somehow was responding to noise that her daughter was making or whether she too now had a pattern of night waking.

Looking at Marnie's mother's sleep patterns, we noticed nothing unusual other than the night wakings. When her sleep did not improve in the weeks following Marnie's success, we recommended a sleep restriction plan. Basically, we recommended that she set her alarm to wake up about an hour earlier than her usual schedule, go to bed at her usual time, and leave her bed if she awoke and felt that she would not go to sleep right away. After an inconsistent 2-week period during which sometimes she slept through the night and other times was up for several hours, Marnie's mother's sleep was much improved. She faded the hour when she awoke over another 2-week period until she was sleeping through most nights on her usual schedule.

The combination of Marnie's improved sleep as well as her own had a noticeable effect on her. She looked rested and refreshed and told us that she had renewed energy. She found that she was much more patient with her daughter's many needs and was pleased that she had more interest in a social life for herself. As just one sign of her improvement, she told us that she did something that she had wanted to do for years: sign up for a gourmet cooking class.

Marnie's case was gratifying for several reasons. First, we were able to help her mother design a plan that allowed Marnie to get a full night's sleep for the first time ever. Just as significant, however, were the changes that occurred in her mother's life. Just having Marnie sleep through the night was very important to her. Finally having her own full night's sleep seemed like a luxury to her. She told us that she felt a sense of renewed optimism both for herself and for her daughter and that she was ready to move on with their lives. A seemingly small thing like a good night's sleep was just what this family needed.

That Marnie's mother had her own sleep disrupted is common among other families as well. Also typical is that even when we are able to help a child sleep through the night, often the parents' sleep does not immediately return to normal. Sometimes there is a carryover effect such that the parents have difficulty going back to a normal sleep–wake cycle. Fortunately, the techniques described in this book for people with special needs work just as well for people without special needs. If you find that your own sleep is disrupted, then you can assess your sleep patterns through the assessment procedures described in Chapter 3 and begin a plan to correct any of these difficulties.

It is worthwhile to repeat that if you are faced with a person who has both bedtime disruption problems and night-waking problems, then begin with a plan for bedtime. My colleagues' and my research with children with both of these sleep problems points to the value of starting at bedtime because it often is the case that success at bedtime leads to a resolution of night-waking problems without any further assistance. In other words, if we are successful in helping children go to bed without disruption at bedtime, then they often begin to sleep through the night without having to develop a new plan. Again, you may want to refer to Chapter 5 if your child has both of these sleep difficulties.

Following is an outline of the basic ingredients for a successful graduated extinction plan. The steps essentially are the same as those used with graduated extinction for bedtime problems, which is outlined in detail in Chapter 5.

- Determine how long you are able to wait before checking on your child.
- Pick the night to begin the plan, assuming that no one will have a good night's sleep that evening—most people begin on a Friday night.
- On the first night, if your child awakens, then wait the agreed-on time (e.g., 3 minutes). If after 3 minutes your child is still crying, then go into the room (do not pick up your child, do not give him or her food or a drink, do not engage in extensive conversation), tell him or her to go to bed, then leave. Wait another 3 minutes, and go back into the room if your child is still crying. Continue the pattern until your child is asleep.

- On each subsequent night, extend the time between visits by 2 or 3 minutes. Continue the same procedure when entering the room.

As you can see, the only difference between using graduated extinction for bedtime problems and using this plan for night waking is that you wait for your child to cry out at night and wait the prescribed time before checking on him or her. If this plan is not right for you, then you can use several other techniques, which are described next, that are designed to help with disruptive night waking.

### Sleep Restriction

As alluded to previously in the section on wakings that are not accompanied by disruptive behavior, you can use sleep restriction to help reduce or eliminate the more disruptive wakings displayed by some children. Sleep restriction (and another technique known as *scheduled awakening*, which is described later) is particularly valuable for children who engage in very disruptive behavior when they awaken. Its value comes from the ability to help your child sleep through the night while avoiding many of the disruptive behaviors that you would experience with graduated extinction. Described next is a child who had very disruptive night waking and how her mother intervened to reduce these nighttime problems. The procedures for using sleep restriction—which formed the basis for the plan—were described previously in the section on nondisruptive night waking.

> Shontell, a 4-year-old and very active little girl with autism, first came to my colleagues' and my attention through her school. She was attending a preschool program for children with developmental disabilities, and her teachers were concerned that Shontell seemed extremely tired each day. In fact, she was so tired that school staff had a difficult time keeping her awake during the day. In a previous placement, they were not successful at all; and Shontell basically slept through most of the school day in the corner of her classroom. Her current program was more successful in keeping her awake most of the time, but it required a great deal of effort; both her mother and the school program were looking for some relief. Her teachers noted that Shontell was extremely disruptive in school, especially on days when she obviously was tired and when they tried to keep her from falling asleep.
>
> Shontell's home sleep schedule was particularly disturbed. She would nap for about 2 hours during the late afternoon, which her mother permitted because Shontell clearly was exhausted when she got home. The evening was usually uneventful, and her mother had a bedtime routine for all of her three children. Each night at about 11:00 P.M., after getting all of the children ready for sleep, she and the children would get into the one bed in their small apartment. Bedtime was so late because

Shontell's mother served dinner at around 9:00 P.M. and needed time to get homework and other chores with her children completed. Shontell's mother also told us that her other children did not seem tired either and that 11:00 P.M. seemed to work well for all of them except Shontell.

On a typical evening, the other children would fall asleep within about 15 minutes, but Shontell would remain awake. At times she would jump up and down on the bed and wake her siblings, so her mother would then move herself and Shontell into the living room to watch television until Shontell fell asleep. On most nights, Shontell would not fall asleep until 3:30 A.M. During this time, her mother had to remain awake for fear of what Shontell might do. One night, for example, her mother fell asleep in front of the television while Shontell was awake. Shontell went to the kitchen table, got a bottle of Pepsi, and poured it over her mother's head, presumably to wake her up!

Once Shontell fell asleep, she often awoke again. When she awoke at night, she would sometimes cry and scream, waking everyone else. Other times she would get out of bed and break toys, get into the refrigerator, or pull things off of the shelves. Shontell's mother was quite depressed and at a loss as to how to handle her daughter.

Shontell's situation posed a number of challenges. Because the family lived in an apartment, it would be difficult to design any plan that involved letting Shontell cry and scream for any length of time. Also, because there was only one bed for the whole family, any such disruption would disturb the sleep of everyone. It was also going to be difficult for her mother to give up the afternoon naps. When Shontell slept after school, this was literally the only time during the day when her mother could focus her attention on her other children. We posed the dilemma to her mother, basically offering a choice between a short period of time with increased disruption at night if she chose to go with a graduated extinction program or a plan that would take a longer time and be less disruptive at night but that would involve decreasing naps during the day. Her mother chose the latter option, which would involve fading into a sleep restriction program.

Evaluating the total amount of time that Shontell slept in a typical day, including all naps, Shontell's mother was surprised to see that her daughter actually slept for almost 10 hours each day, although there were days when she slept for only about 4 hours and others when she slept for 12 or more. We decided to try to achieve the goal of 9 hours (90% of her typical sleep time) by reducing nap time. We hoped that this would at first eliminate the problem night waking and then allow us to move her bedtime from 3:30 A.M. to something more manageable.

On the first day of the plan, her mother woke her up early from her afternoon nap just as we had planned. Again, the goal was to reduce the time that she slept during the day and restrict sleep to only at night in bed. Her mother told us that Shontell was cranky that night and never fell asleep, remaining awake all night. The next day at school was a disaster! Her teacher told us that Shontell spent the day crying and hitting everyone in school. To everyone's credit, however, despite the problem-filled day, everyone was still committed to making the plan work. On subsequent days, Shontell's mother continued to wake her about 30 minutes early from her nap, and Shontell began to fall asleep earlier at night. After the first week, her mother reported that Shontell had no night-waking episodes and that she was falling asleep at about 2:30 A.M., an hour earlier than usual. The plan then called for decreasing nap time by 30 minutes for each subsequent successful week—defined as no night waking and an improvement in her bedtime.

The weekend brought one more obstacle. Her mother reminded us that on Sundays she would take Shontell and her other children to her church in the afternoon for several hours. Typically, Shontell would sleep during this time because it was during her usual nap time. Her mother obviously was concerned about this. What if she did not let Shontell sleep and she disrupted services? Her mother did not want to give up one of the few things in her life that provided her with comfort—the community of friends and neighbors who gathered together each week to pray. In discussing the problem together, we decided to try to keep Shontell awake and provide her with some activity that would occupy her time. Shontell's mother did not feel that she could keep her awake, especially during the relatively quiet services that seemed to trigger Shontell's sleep. We suggested that Shontell's mother give her something that contained caffeine right before services as a way to keep her awake. Armed now with a favorite doll and a can of Coke, her mother was ready to tackle church services. Fortunately, services went well. The other members were very helpful and forgiving for any brief disruptions, and Shontell spent most of the time quietly playing on the floor.

As the weeks past, Shontell's sleep continued to improve. She rarely had a night waking any more, and her bedtime progressed to about the 11:00 P.M. time that the rest of the family used. Her teachers reported that she seemed rested when she came to school on most days and that she was much easier to work with, especially compared with before her sleep improved. Shontell's sleep occasionally was disrupted again (e.g., when she was allowed to nap on days when she seemed tired), but her mother knew how to recover from these episodes—by reinstituting the plan—and now felt that she had control over this once vexing problem.

Shontell's case provided us with a number of challenges that seem to characterize most children with special needs. Often, the most time-efficient techniques cannot be used because of practical considerations.

Shontell, for example, might have had significantly improved sleep and a better bedtime within a few nights if we had used a graduated extinction program. The noise and disruption that this would have caused, however, would have been intolerable to Shontell's family and neighbors. The needs of parents also have to be considered in these cases. Shontell's mother needed some time to get used to the idea of not having that quiet time when her daughter would nap, so rather than eliminate naps altogether, we designed a fading plan that would let both Shontell and her mother adjust to the new schedule. Again, this delayed the improvements in Shontell's sleep but seemed worth the time to her mother. Finally, attending church services was a potential major obstacle to the plan but also was a priority for Shontell's mother, so it required that we adjust our procedures accordingly. The success of this case should serve as a note of optimism to parents in similar situations. The techniques to improve sleep that are described in this book appear to be quite robust—meaning that they can be modified significantly and yet yield important results. As long as you follow the basic logic of these plans, you can change them to fit most individual needs and still expect to have some success.

### Scheduled Awakening

An additional technique that has been demonstrated through a number of studies[1] to help with night waking is called *scheduled awakening*. Scheduled awakening takes a slightly different approach to dealing with nightly waking, one that may seem odd to you at first. This plan actually involves waking your child in the period before he or she usually awakens. You gently touch or shake your child to the point that he or she seems to awaken, and then you let him or her fall back to sleep. This simple technique is often successful in completely eliminating night wakings—sometimes from the first night on.

One of the keys to the success of this plan is the regularity of the night wakings. In other words, your child must have fairly predictable times when he or she awakens (e.g., 12:30 A.M.) so that you know when to awaken him or her. Fortunately, most children who wake during the night follow a fairly regular pattern. This regularity comes from the unvarying rhythms that the brain follows in the different sleep stages described in Chapter 1. In the unlikely event that your child awakens at very different times each night (e.g., 12:00 A.M. on one night, 2:00 A.M. on a second night, 12:30 A.M. on a third), you probably should try a sleep restriction plan first. Again, using the sleep diary to uncover the patterns of waking usually is the first step in the success of this approach. Once this waking time—or times, in the case of children with multiple wakings—is determined, then you will want to awaken your child about 30 minutes prior to this time. That means that if your child typically awakens at 1:00 A.M., then you would awaken your child at 12:30 A.M.

It is important, however, that you be ready to experiment with this waking time. There is no way to pick the "perfect" time to awaken your child based simply on your observing night wakings. Sometimes 30 minutes may be too soon for it to work. How do you know whether you have picked the wrong time? One way to tell is to observe how your child reacts to being awakened. This type of plan seems to work best when the child does not awaken fully from sleep but just opens his or her eyes briefly and then immediately goes back to sleep. If you find, however, that when you awaken your child he or she wakes up fully and does not go back to sleep, then this may signal that you have picked the wrong time. If your child awakens fully, then move back your scheduled awakening time by 15 minutes for the next episode. If you had picked a 12:30 A.M. awakening and your child wakes up fully, then the next night try 12:15 A.M. "Play" with the time in this way until you discover the right time to wake your child.

Just as with sleep restriction, scheduled awakening is an "error-less" procedure because it can reduce or eliminate night waking without going through disturbing or dangerous tantrums. Even on the first night that you awaken your child, you probably will find that he or she will not wake up again at his or her usual time. This is especially valuable for families who cannot afford to have their child be so disruptive at night.

There always are trade-offs, as we have seen before, for the advantages of any particular program. In the case of scheduled awakening, one of the biggest disadvantages reported by parents is the necessity to wake themselves up in the early morning hours for their child's waking. It obviously is not a pleasant experience to be awakened by an alarm clock only an hour or so after you have fallen asleep. This may be the time when you are in a deep stage of sleep, and it may be extremely difficult to get out of bed to follow this plan. Even though the child may not be waking, the parent still must get up and carry out the scheduled waking. As mentioned before, avoiding the disruptive night waking is worth this temporary inconvenience. Described next is a family for whom this approach was successful.

Eddie was 7 years old when we first had contact with him and his family. Some time before, he had been diagnosed as having attention-deficit/ hyperactivity disorder (ADHD) because of his problems with attention, his impulsiveness, and his high energy level. He was a very likable kid, and some years of help by a therapist had proved successful in reducing some of his daytime problems, both at school and at home.

His sleep, however, was still of concern to his parents. For the most part, he would fall asleep at night with little difficulty, but several nights each week he would awaken. Usually the night waking would be signaled by his desire to get in bed with his parents. When he was younger, he had been allowed to get into their bed whenever he awakened, but his parents had decided more than a year ago that he was old enough to go back to his own bed. On a typical night, Eddie would wake up, get out of his bed, and knock on his parents' bedroom door. When they tried to ignore him, he would knock louder. When they told him to go back to bed, he would become very upset. Eddie would cry, sometimes saying that he had a nightmare, other times saying that he felt sick. His parents reported that about half of the time, they did not give in; and when they refused to let him come into their bed, he would cry and carry on for more than an hour. The other half of the time when they refused his request, he would work himself up so much that he would get sick. Then they would have to get out of bed to help him clean up.

On most nights when he awoke, Eddie's parents just let him come into bed because they could not stand these disruptions during the late evening hours. Both of his parents worked and had to be up early, and they dreaded the prospect of his outbursts disturbing their sleep. Recently, even these relatively uneventful episodes when they let him into their bed were upsetting them. On the one hand, they worried that he could never be separated from them at night if, for example, a friend invited him to sleep over. Because of the problems that came along with Eddie's ADHD, making friends already was difficult, and they wanted him to have every chance to socialize with kids his age. On the other hand, they also wanted their privacy. As Eddie was getting bigger, there was not much room in the bed when he was there. It seemed to be time to try something to help him sleep through the night.

During our assessment discussions, it seemed as though Eddie's problem was a combination of night waking plus his tendency to escalate disruption to the point that his parents would just give in to his demand to join them in bed. A graduated extinction plan did not seem feasible to Eddie's parents because they thought that they would not be able to ignore his crying, especially when he made himself sick. They also worried that he might feel abandoned if they did this and were concerned that it might have a permanent effect on their relationship with him. Of the two plans that would avoid disruption (sleep restriction and scheduled awakening), his parents seemed to prefer scheduled awakening. Eddie's night waking typically occurred at about midnight, some 2½ hours after his 9:30 P.M. bedtime but at a time when at least one of his parents was still awake; therefore, getting up and waking him at about 11:30 P.M. did not seem too difficult for them.

Eddie's parents began the scheduled awakening plan on the next Friday night, just in case things did not go well and they had to deal with his tantrum. His father went into his room at 11:30 P.M., and Eddie woke up even before his father got near the bed. His father stayed in the bedroom for about 30 minutes until Eddie fell back to sleep. That night Eddie did not wake up again until morning. On the second night, Eddie's father went into his room earlier (at 11:15 P.M.), and this time Eddie was fast asleep. We moved the time back because it was clear that Eddie was in a very light sleep at 11:30 P.M. His father touched his shoulder and called his son's name; Eddie mumbled something, rolled over, and went back to sleep. Each night that week, one of his parents would gently wake him at 11:15 P.M., and on none of the nights did Eddie wake up again.

For the second week of the plan, we told his parents to pick one night to "skip." We wanted to begin to test whether Eddie could sleep through the night without all of the scheduled awakenings. Unfortunately, on the night that they did not wake him, Eddie awoke on his own and came to his parents' bedroom. Because it was less disruptive than fighting over his coming into their bed, his father led him back to his own room and stayed there until Eddie fell asleep. The next day at dinner time, they all discussed that Eddie was getting too big to sleep in his parents' bed and that a married couple needed to sleep alone together. Eddie did not seem to fully understand why he had to sleep alone when they did not, but his parents believed that it was a mature discussion that probably would be continued in the future.

Because the skipped night led to an awakening, we recommended that they go for 2 more weeks waking him each night, and then they could try skipping a night. Fortunately, the second time that they skipped an awakening, he slept through the night. In the following weeks, we scheduled for them to skip one more night for each good week (i.e., no waking). Over several months, there were a few lapses when he woke up (once even after a scheduled awakening), but the pattern of success was established, and his parents were confident that they could continue to fade the wakings on their own. Six months after they first began the plan, they had stopped all of the scheduled awakenings; despite a few night wakings, they were pleased with Eddie's sleep.

Why did scheduled awakening work to eliminate Eddie's night waking? Unfortunately, despite a number of studies[2] that demonstrate the success of this technique in reducing night waking, sleep professionals still do not understand why it works. Some believe that the scheduled awakenings somehow interrupt a disrupted sleep–wake cycle and "kick start" a new and better cycle. Another view is that by waking a child when he or she is in one of the deeper stages of sleep and then letting him or her go back to sleep alone, you are giving the child practice in learning to fall back to sleep without someone else present. Learning to fall asleep alone when awakened from a deep sleep may carry over to times when the child awakens during a light sleep stage, such as in a partial waking. Perhaps researchers will soon find the clue to the success of scheduled awakenings in eliminating night waking.

A general summary of the steps to a successful scheduled awakening plan follows. Remember, however, that you may need to experiment with the waking time to find a point in the evening before a waking that seems to catch the child in a deep sleep.

- Use the sleep diary (see Chapter 3 and Appendix D) to determine the time or times when your child typically awakens during the night.
- On the night that you are to begin the plan, awaken your child approximately 30 minutes prior to the typical awakening time. For example, if your child usually has a night waking at 12:30 A.M., then wake your child at 12:00 A.M. If your child seems to awaken very easily, then move back the time 15 minutes the next night and on all subsequent nights (e.g., 11:45 P.M.).
- If there is a broad range in the times when your child awakens (e.g., from 12:00 A.M. to 1:30 A.M.), then awaken your child about 30 minutes prior to the earliest time (in this case, 11:30 P.M.).
- Do not fully awaken your child. Gently touch and/or talk to your child until he or she opens his or her eyes, then let him or her fall back to sleep.
- Repeat this plan each night until your child goes for a full seven nights without a waking. When your child has achieved this level of success, skip one night (i.e., no scheduled waking) per week. If your child has awakenings, then go back to every night. Slowly reduce the number of nights per week with scheduled wakings until your child is no longer waking during the night.

The three approaches to reducing night waking that have been described—graduated extinction, sleep restriction, and scheduled awakening—all have their own advantages and disadvantages. When trying to decide among them, it is important to consider what each plan entails for the family and, therefore, which one is the most likely to succeed. This is the time when you get to be selfish. Pick which one is best for *you*. You will need to carry out the plan night after night, so pick one that fits your own needs best. Obviously, if you cannot carry out the plan, then it will not work; so take some time to consider what is right for you. Table 6.1 lists some of the pluses and minuses of each plan.

**Table 6.1.** The pluses and minuses of the three approaches to reducing night waking

| Graduated extinction | | Sleep restriction | | Scheduled awakening | |
|---|---|---|---|---|---|
| Pluses | Minuses | Pluses | Minuses | Pluses | Minuses |
| • Can be used at the regular bedtime rather than having to wait until late at night<br>• Can check on the child for reassurance<br>• Usually works within the first week | • Requires listening to child's cries, which can be difficult for many families<br>• Can result in an increase in behavior problems<br>• Some behaviors, such as injurious ones, cannot be ignored | • Often can be "errorless," with no increase in behavior problems<br>• Often prevents long bouts of crying | • Requires that someone remain up late at night or wake early in the morning<br>• Can take several weeks before the desired bedtime is reached | • Often can be "errorless" with no increase in behavior problems<br>• Results often can be observed in the first night<br>• Often prevents long bouts of crying | • Requires that someone remain up late at night<br>• Requires regular and predictable waking<br>• Can take several weeks before the desired bedtime is reached |

## CONCLUSION

Keep in mind one of the "facts of life" about sleep problems: Even with the most successful plans, these problems can resurface. A bout of the flu, a weekend at a relative's house, flying across time zones, and even some particularly exciting event can cause a child who was sleeping through the night to again begin to have night wakings. The good news is that if your plan worked before, then it likely will work again, and sometimes even more quickly. Be prepared for some setbacks, and they will not make you feel discouraged. You have some good nights' sleep ahead of you!

# 7

# Sleeping at the Wrong Times

Humans, as a group, are meant to sleep at night and be awake during the day. Unlike certain nocturnal animals such as owls, which sleep during the daylight hours and are awake and mainly in search of food at night, we humans are designed to be active when the sun is up and asleep during the twilight hours. A handful of individuals, however, do not fit this pattern. They may be wide awake at midnight and not feel the urge to sleep until 3:00 A.M. When they are forced to be up in the morning, they usually have difficulty concentrating and just generally have trouble functioning until the afternoon. Although many of us have had the experience of having our sleep pattern "off" for short periods of time, this is a daily (or nightly) occurrence for some people with *delayed sleep phase syndrome*. It is as though they are "jet-lagged" but without the advantage of a pleasant trip out of town. Their sleep–wake cycle has shifted from the typical phase to one in which they stay awake longer and sleep later in the day than most people.

A second group of people does not sleep at the times when we typically expect—those whose biological clock runs on a non–24-hour cycle. People with profound visual loss or blindness are particularly vulnerable to this sleep disorder because they do not receive the usual cues about sleep and wakefulness from the light of the sun. Finally, a third group with sleeping timing problems seems to have developed poor sleeping habits, including napping during the day, and therefore has trouble falling asleep at night and/or has difficulty waking in the morning. Next is a discussion of all three of these types of sleep schedule problems and how the people who experience these difficulties may be helped.

## DELAYED SLEEP PHASE SYNDROME

*Early to bed and early to rise,*
*Makes a man healthy, wealthy, and wise.*
Benjamin Franklin, *Poor Richard's Almanac,* 1757

We have a prejudice in our society against people whose sleep schedules favor late nights and late mornings. As Benjamin Franklin so succinctly put it, we view "early risers" as more ambitious and more motivated, as though they are more likely to accomplish important things if they focus their energies the first thing in the morning. In contrast, people who sleep late are considered to be slacking off or lazy.

*Plough deep while sluggards sleep.*
Benjamin Franklin, *Poor Richard's Almanac,* 1757

In fact, several famous and successful figures in history preferred late nights, including the inventor Thomas Edison and the ancient philosopher Socrates. For most of these individuals, a slight tendency to stay awake later at night and sleep later in the morning does not interfere with conducting a satisfying and productive life.

Extreme "night owls"—those individuals who report not being tired at all until the early morning hours and who are unable to wake up until the early afternoon—fortunately are a rare breed indeed. In contrast to people who have sleep cycles that are out of sync because they are not sleeping well at night, these people seem to sleep well during the early morning hours and also report feeling rested when allowed to follow their body's desire to sleep on this unusual schedule. It is as though their sleep schedule has been pushed back, or "delayed," although in all other respects it is normal. Unfortunately, in comparison with the other sleep problems described, helping people with delayed sleep phase syndrome sometimes can be more challenging. Next, however, is the case of a young man whom my colleagues and I were able to help quite easily.

Patrick was a young man who lived at home with his mother and who was beginning a new stage in his life with the hope of earning a modest living working in a local grocery store. He had mental retardation of unknown origin but worked hard; with support from his mother, Patrick was able to graduate from high school and was hired for a job. It was a worsening problem at his new workplace that first brought Patrick to our attention. His mother was concerned that his difficulty with sleep might result in his losing the job that he so dearly loved.

Patrick's boss, who was the manager of a grocery store, was extremely supportive of Patrick and went to great lengths to provide the help and guidance that he needed to succeed. When Patrick first approached the manager for the job, the manager agreed to teach Patrick each one of the tasks that he would need to complete, including bagging groceries and helping to carry packages to customers' cars, as well as putting price tags on cans. The manager was pleased at how well Patrick would follow instruction, and after a 2-week training period in the afternoons, he offered Patrick a full-time 9-to-5 job.

His mother shared Patrick's elation at the news of his new job but also harbored grave doubts about his ability to hold down a full-time job. Her reservations had less to do with any inability he might have in carrying out the necessary tasks than with her fear that he would not show up to work on time. All through school and even before he entered school, Patrick had a great deal of difficulty waking up in the morning. When he was young, his mother literally had to drag him out of bed and into the shower; even after his shower, it would take him several hours until he was fully awake. As he got older and his mother wanted him to learn more independence, she set up an elaborate alarm system that required him to get out of his bed to turn off the alarm. In contrast, he would remain awake in the evening, past his mother's bedtime. Usually he would watch television in his room until he fell asleep, which his mother guessed was after 2:00 A.M. on most nights. Because of his unusual sleep pattern, Patrick's mother was rightly concerned that he would not succeed at his new job.

During the first week of his full-time responsibilities, Patrick seemed to have new energy in the morning. His mother told us that it was as though the anticipation of having a real job was enough to make him a little more alert in the morning, and she had less trouble getting him up and ready. Although he still looked tired in the morning, his excitement about working "revved" him up enough to get to work. After the first week, however, things seemed to go downhill. He went back to his old pattern of staying up late and being tired in the morning. Worse yet, Patrick's manager reported that he would find the young man asleep in the back of the store each morning. He felt as though Patrick was not serious about the job and felt let down, especially because he had been so flexible and accommodating. Patrick's mother was concerned that he was about to be fired.

When we discussed Patrick's sleep problem, it was clear that this was a long-standing concern. His mother told us that when he did not have school or work and when he could sleep on his own schedule, he would usually sleep from about 3:30 A.M. until about noon. When he followed that schedule, he had no difficulty waking and seemed fully rested and happy that day. He did not have night waking, nor were there any other obvious problems with his sleep. It seemed pretty clear from this long-running pattern that Patrick had delayed sleep phase syndrome.

Although there were several options available to try to help Patrick change his sleep–wake cycle with an eye toward better matching his job, it was suggested that instead they match the job to his cycle. In other words, could he work from noon until 8:00 P.M., a busy time for the store anyway, and maximize his peak time of alertness? When we suggested a shift change to the store manager, he was willing to give it a try for 2 weeks but warned that he could not monitor Patrick as closely during these times and that he would have to demonstrate a greater degree of responsibility. Fortunately, this change in his work hours worked immediately. Patrick was allowed to follow his body's need for sleeping later in the sleep cycle and was awake and alert throughout his work shift. His boss was pleased with his performance after the first 2 weeks, and the last time we checked, he had been working there quite happily for more than 1 year. His mother was relieved about his job success and also about not having to drag him out of bed in the morning. Patrick also was pleased. He felt obvious pride in his accomplishments at work, and he also felt—for the first time—that he was not "lazy" because of his sleep pattern but instead could achieve a great deal.

For many people with delayed sleep phase syndrome, the easiest approach to intervention is to arrange their lives to fit their sleep needs. Changing from the day shift to the evening shift at a job, for example, can make all the difference in the world. In fact, this sleep problem can serve as an example to all of us about how to listen to our bodies when it comes to circadian rhythms. It can be very valuable to determine the time of the day that is best for *you* to do certain activities. For example, for those of us more on the "night owl" side of sleep—those who prefer to sleep later in the morning and remain awake later at night—arranging tasks that require heightened alertness in the later morning (about 10:30 A.M.) may result in the best performance. In contrast, for those people who tend to be "larks"—those who prefer to awaken earlier in the morning and go to bed earlier at night—the optimal time may be several hours earlier (about 8:00 A.M.). In fact, if you feel particularly motivated, then you could keep a diary of your own pattern of alertness to determine the times of the day that work best for you, and then use these times for tasks that require your best efforts. In Patrick's case, we were able to change his work schedule to meet his sleep needs and found that he could perform dramatically better on the job.

What is the difference between someone like Patrick, who has delayed sleep phase syndrome, and someone else who just desires a later sleep schedule? In other words, can we distinguish between someone who just likes to watch late-night television and as a result is tired the next day from someone who cannot control this sleep schedule? Fortunately, there are ways to tell these two different sleep patterns apart. Someone with delayed sleep phase syndrome, for example, will not be able to adjust this pattern. Even when there is a reason the person may want to go to bed earlier, he or she cannot, even after trying for many weeks. Someone with a desired late sleep phase (e.g., the David Letterman addict), however, can adjust the times when there is an incentive—such as going to bed earlier the night before an important meeting. Oftentimes the weekend sleep schedule differs from the school or work week schedule, which is another sign that he or she has control over when he or she sleeps. It may take several nights to readjust this schedule, but it can be done fairly easily.

What can be done for someone who does not have control over the school or work schedule? Is it possible to change a long-established sleep pattern, one that may be seriously interfering with the way someone lives? Fortunately, there are several new approaches to helping people who do not sleep in cycles that match our typical daily school or work schedules. The development of these new techniques—discussed next—has come about as a result of the discovery of our biological clock and the way it works to help us sleep. Chapter 1 described some of what we know about this timing device in the brain, but it may be helpful to repeat some of this newly discovered information about our biological clock at this point to help put the new sleep techniques into perspective.

Recall that when people are kept away from cues about day and night time, such as in a cave, they tend to sleep in schedules somewhat longer than our 24-hour day. This suggests that the brain wants to awaken and sleep in cycles more like 25 hours per day. This is one of the reasons that it is relatively easy to stay awake an hour later than usual but is more difficult to fall asleep an hour earlier than our typical bedtime. What resets this clock so that we are in sync with nature's day and night? Remember that light plays an important role in the timing of our sleep. More specific, the decreasing amount of light in the later afternoon and early evening triggers the pineal gland in the brain to release more of the natural hormone melatonin. Melatonin reaches the biological clock (in a small structure known as the superchiasmatic nucleus) and tells it that it is time to sleep. Our tendency to want to sleep and awaken on a 25-hour cycle is regulated by sunlight (as well as by other daily cues, such as regular mealtimes) and the release of melatonin. This beginning information about sleep cycles has led to the discovery of several techniques for helping people whose schedules do not fit those of the rest of society and for whom this is a problem. One of these new techniques that rely on our natural tendency to want to sleep on a 25-hour cycle is referred to as *chronotherapy*.

## Chronotherapy

Chronotherapy essentially involves keeping the person awake later and later on successive nights until he or she achieves the desired new sleep schedule. For example, if a child's typical delayed sleep cycle is from 2:00 A.M. until noon, then you would begin a chronotherapy routine by keeping the child up until 5:00 A.M. during the first night, then until 8:00 A.M. for the second night, and then continue to shift the schedule ahead by approximately 3 hours each subsequent night. Eventually, the schedule will advance throughout the day until the desired sleep time (e.g., 10:00 P.M.) is reached. Figure 7.1 illustrates a typical chronotherapy schedule for someone with a 4:00 A.M. bedtime who desires a 10:00 P.M. bedtime. Following are general guidelines for creating a chronotherapy plan:

- Use the sleep diary (see Chapter 3 and Appendix D) to identify the typical sleep–wake schedule for your child.
- On the night when you are to begin the plan, keep your child awake approximately 3 hours after his or her typical bedtime. For example, if your child usually falls asleep at 1:00 A.M., then keep your child up until 4:00 A.M.
- Do not allow your child to sleep at times other than the scheduled ones—that is, no naps.

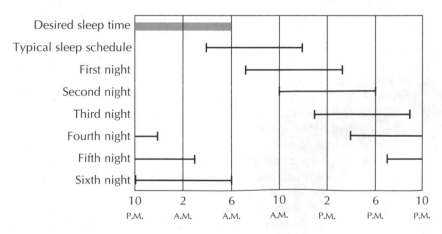

**Figure 7.1.** Sample chronotherapy schedule.

- Each successive night, you will move bedtime ahead another 3 hours (e.g., from 4:00 A.M. to 7:00 A.M.).
- Keep this schedule until your child's new bedtime approximates the desired bedtime (e.g., 10:00 P.M.).

Unfortunately, what this plan offers in terms of its simplicity is usually offset by its lack of practicality. For most families, it would be extremely difficult, if not impossible, to adhere to this type of sleep schedule. The demands of school, work, and family would prohibit following a schedule that would for a time begin having the person remain awake at night and sleep during the day. For this reason, chronotherapy is not often recommended unless all other reasonable options have been tried and have failed. Even then, implementing such a plan might have to wait until an unstructured time, such as a summer vacation, makes it possible to begin such a strategy. Fortunately, there are other options for people who experience delayed sleep phase syndrome.

## Bright Light Therapy

Whereas chronotherapy takes advantage of our non–24-hour biological clock, bright light therapy makes use of the brain's reliance on light to trigger this biological clock. Remember that decreasing light in the early evening seems to be responsible for the release of the brain hormone melatonin, which helps signal sleep. The increase in sunlight in the morning appears, in turn, to signal the decrease in production of melatonin, which corresponds to our increasing alertness. Researchers have used the connection between light and sleep to develop a technique to help "jump-start" the brain's sleep–wake cycle to better enforce the preferred schedule. Bright light therapy relies on banks of fluorescent light bulbs to provide a morning light boost, which, for some people, helps to reset their biological clock.

A typical bright light therapy plan involves having the person sit in front of a bank of lights for several hours after awaking. The lights must provide more light than is typical in a home or at school because they have to produce approximately the amount of light provided by the sun. "Light boxes" are now commercially available and usually include about six fluorescent light tubes. The person sits facing these lights and can work or carry on other activities at the same time. The use of these lights has helped some people regulate their sleep cycles toward one that better matches our sunrise and sundown awake and sleep preferences. Bright light therapy, chronotherapy, and several additional approaches, including the use of the hormone melatonin, also have been used with the group of individuals described next—those with non–24-hour sleep–wake cycles.

## NON–24-HOUR SLEEP–WAKE CYCLES

We take for granted that we sleep and are awake in cycles that correspond to the rising and setting of the sun. This type of sleep pattern has adaptive significance—it was advantageous to the survival of our species to be awake at times when it was easiest to hunt or gather food. And, it certainly makes our social and economic lives easier today that people generally are awake at similar times and feel tired and sleep at similar times. In fact, it is hard to imagine what life would be like if our sleep–wake cycle changed daily and did not necessarily correspond to those around us. This, unfortunately, is the dilemma that people who have non–24-hour sleep–wake cycles face.

The good news is that only a small proportion of people experience non–24-hour sleep–wake cycles, meaning that their sleep patterns are at odds with the day–night cycles that most of us follow. A person with a 26-hour cycle would be sleepy at 11:00 P.M. on one night, 1:00 A.M. on the second night, and on each successive night would fall asleep approximately 2 hours later. Although the good news is that this problem is relatively rare, the bad news is that it appears to disproportionately affect people with special needs. People with severe visual impairments and people with autism appear to be at greater risk for experiencing this sleep problem. Following is a case of a person with a non–24-hour sleep–wake cycle.

A colleague called me one day because he was concerned about a student who had behavior problems that seemed to follow an unusual pattern. Sixteen-year-old Mary would go for days being the ideal student, being very cooperative and motivated in school. She would have other days, however, when she would be very aggressive toward her teacher and sometimes toward other students in her class. Mary had a severe visual impairment—so severe, in fact, that her doctor was not sure whether she saw any light at all. Mary also had mental retardation, which resulted in her being very limited in her ability to communicate with others and caused her to need a great deal of help with most day-to-day activities.

Both Mary's mother and her teacher described her as going through frequent good and bad "cycles." Mary's mother told us that in addition to these fluctuating times when Mary was aggressive, her sleep also seemed disrupted. During the "bad" times, Mary might not fall asleep until the early morning hours or even not at all but then sleep at school. At these times, her teacher told us, it was difficult to keep her awake in class, and Mary would lash out at others when she was awakened early. During the "good" times, Mary slept on a normal schedule and would be quite pleasant and alert in school.

We asked Mary's mother to keep a diary of Mary's sleep each night. Over about a 4-week period, a pattern seemed to emerge. It looked as though Mary's sleep was following a pretty regular schedule for someone whose biological clock was not being reset each day. In other words, Mary seemed to follow not the regular 24-hour cycle of sleep and wakefulness but rather a 25-hour pattern. Each day, she would be tired and ready for bed about an hour later than the day before. So when on one Monday night she fell asleep at about 9:00 P.M., on Tuesday it was about 10:00 P.M., Wednesday it was close to 11:00 P.M., and by the next Monday she was up most of the night and did not fall asleep until after 4:00 A.M.

Mary's typical but orderly sleep cycle was not immediately obvious to her mother or her teacher. Her sleep pattern may have been obscured because she was not allowed to follow her desired bedtime and awake time (which would have to change each day) but instead was "squeezed into" a cycle that resembled a typical one. Therefore, on days when she probably would have preferred to sleep in the late morning and afternoon, she was still required to be awake, at least part of the time. This is what led to her having periods when she was more irritable and aggressive.

The options for helping Mary with her sleep problem were more limited than for a person with delayed sleep phase syndrome. First, it would be difficult to design a lifestyle change that could accommodate her everchanging sleep cycles and still include educational opportunities. Second, bright light therapy was ruled out as an option because her visual impairment was such that the light probably would not have been processed in her brain. Chronotherapy also was not an option because her problem was a continuing delay in her sleep phase.

Given these limitations, several other approaches were tried at the same time. First, it was recommended that Mary's daily activities, such as mealtimes, be kept constant. In other words, Mary's parents were asked to try to keep to a specific schedule for when Mary ate, when she went out for a walk, when she bathed, and so forth. Second, Mary's parents wanted to try giving her a daily dose of melatonin because of the potential for helping her reset her biological clock. In consultation with the family's physician, they purchased melatonin in their local health food store and gave Mary 3 milligrams about 30 minutes prior to the desired bedtime.

This combination of routinizing Mary's daily schedule and administering melatonin prior to bedtime seemed to significantly improve Mary's sleep. Although there were still nights when she did not seem tired and when she would remain awake for a number of hours, the number of these nights dropped significantly compared with before the plan. In addition, Mary's daytime behavior improved, which included a drop in the number and intensity of her aggressive outbursts. In an interesting development,

once Mary was less aggressive, her teachers at school were less reluctant to keep her awake during the day, and this too may have helped her
sleep better at night.

Mary's case highlights two other strategies for helping people
reset their biological clocks: consistent daily activity cues and melatonin. Our recommendation for Mary's parents to keep constant her
daily activities was based on the observation that—like sunlight—certain daily activities, such as eating, can help signal the brain about the
passage of time. Previously, because of Mary's erratic sleep–wake
schedule, her parents tended to be very flexible about bedtimes, wake
times on the weekends, mealtimes, and so forth. Unfortunately, these
changing times for important activities could have helped contribute
to Mary's sleep problems. Keeping to certain time-ordered routines
may have helped Mary regularize her sleep cycle.

Medical approaches to assisting with sleep problems are discussed
in Chapter 12. It is important, however, to briefly mention the use of
melatonin here in light of its use with Mary's sleep schedule problem.
In the 1990s, the supplemental use of melatonin has been recommended for a variety of sleep problems. These recommendations are
based on its soporific effect (the tendency of people to feel sleepy after
ingesting this substance) as well as on its potential for resetting the biological clock. Much still needs to be learned about taking melatonin in
this way. For example, although there appear to be few, if any, short-
term negative side effects, long-term studies of its effects have yet
do be conducted. It is not known, for example, whether taking melatonin night after night for months or even years will have any negative effects on sleep or on any other aspect of a person's health. As it
did with Mary, however, short-term use of melatonin (along with
other approaches) may help with problems such as non–24-hour
sleep–wake cycles.

## NAPPING AND POOR SLEEP HABITS

A final consideration for a person who does not sleep at regular times
is the voluntary type of sleep problem that results when someone has
developed poor sleep habits. Poor sleep habits were covered in some
detail in Chapter 4, along with specific recommendations for improving certain daily activities that can help people sleep better; refer to
that chapter for a more in-depth discussion of this issue. Looking at
sleep habits is important because poor sleep habits probably are the
most common explanation for sleep schedule difficulties. Delayed
sleep phase syndrome and non–24-hour sleep–wake cycles are rela-

tively rare problems; most people sleep at times that are less than desirable because of other factors.

As part of the assessment process to determine the possible causes of sleeping at the wrong times, use The Good Sleep Habits Checklist from Chapter 4. One of the more common habits that people need to address involves activities surrounding bedtime. Watching television is, for some people, counterproductive to falling asleep. Reading or another quiet activity should be substituted in the half hour or so before sleep. Eating late at night also can contribute to difficulty sleeping for some people. Delaying dessert until sometime after dinner can satisfy craving and can help people resist the urge to get up later to eat again.

Another serious concern for people sleeping at the wrong times is daytime napping. It is important to remember that short naps for some people can be very beneficial. It can help you quickly catch up on missed sleep, and it lets many people feel refreshed in the middle of the day. Naps become a problem only when they take the place of nighttime sleeping. If your child, for example, is napping during the day but is not able to fall asleep right away at night, then you may want to try to cut back on naps. Recall that Shontell's bedtime disturbance, as well as her night waking (described in Chapter 6), was helped in part by slowly fading the amount of time that she could nap and closely monitoring her nighttime sleep. Elaine's case provides another example of how napping during the day interferes with nighttime sleep and how my colleagues and I were able to help her family correct the problem.

Elaine was 14 years old when we first met her. She was participating in a research study to assess why children engage in problems such as tantrums and self-injurious behavior and to teach students how to communicate as a way to replace those behaviors. Elaine could use some words to communicate with other people, but this was limited. During the course of our research, we were approached by Elaine's teacher and asked for help with another problem in school. Elaine came to school very tired, and her teachers would let her nap for about 1½ hours just before lunch. Her teacher knew that this was not a good thing for Elaine and that her naps were cutting into the time for educational activity, but she also found it almost impossible to keep Elaine awake.

It was suggested that we meet with Elaine's mother to discuss Elaine's sleep patterns both at home and at school. During this meeting, we discovered that Elaine would remain awake at night and typically would fall asleep sometime between 1:00 A.M. and 3:00 A.M. Several times per month, Elaine would not sleep at all at night. Her mother knew that

Elaine napped at school and did not object to this because she believed that Elaine needed the rest. We had her mother chart the amount of sleep that Elaine got, on average, each day, and we found that it came to about 8 hours. We pointed out to both her mother and her teacher that her daytime naps probably were contributing to her nighttime sleep problems. Somehow Elaine started staying up later, but the naps let her compensate for this lack of sleep. As a result, Elaine was not tired on the following night, so she could stay up late again. This vicious cycle of staying up late and napping to catch up on sleep probably would not stop unless Elaine's naps were reduced or eliminated.

Together we set up a plan to help fade Elaine's daytime naps. We began by cutting into her sleep in school by about 10 minutes. The plan started slowly because Elaine's teacher was very hesitant to disturb her sleep for fear that Elaine would be more disruptive in class. When she previously tried to prevent her from sleeping, Elaine would become belligerent and more aggressive. We settled on 10 minutes because this was believed to be a short enough time to allow Elaine to get some sleep. The plan was to decrease her nap by 10 minutes each week until they were eliminated.

At the same time that we were to reduce her naps, Elaine's mother was asked to monitor Elaine's sleep at night. More specific, we wanted to make sure that Elaine was not spending a great deal of time in bed but not sleeping. If Elaine was associating the bed with not sleeping, then it would be difficult for her to fall asleep right away. Her mother monitored Elaine after she was put to bed and would have her get up when she did not seem to be falling asleep after 15 minutes.

Unfortunately, although her mother was putting in a great deal of time in an almost heroic effort to limit her time in bed to just sleeping, things at school were not going quite as well. In 2 weeks' time, her teacher had awakened her early from her nap only twice. On the second of these awakenings, Elaine had become quite upset, and this bad mood lasted for the rest of the day. After that incident, Elaine's teacher was reluctant to go through that bad experience again.

A closer look at Elaine's sleeping at school helped to provide a solution to her teacher's problem. Elaine usually was allowed to sleep from about 10:30 A.M. to noon, which was right before lunch. Because Elaine really enjoyed eating, she had no difficulty getting up and going to the cafeteria. When we had her teacher wake her up early, it meant that Elaine now had to wait at least 10 minutes before going to lunch. Not only was she grumpy after her nap, but she was also quite upset that she could not eat right away. In retrospect, the solution should have been obvious to us right away. Rather than try to wake her up earlier, we should have just delayed her nap by 10 minutes each week. This way she would still wake up from her nap right before lunch. This time her teacher had little difficulty following the plan, and, after a few months, Elaine was no longer napping in school. At the same time, we observed a change in her sleep at night. Over time, she was able to fall asleep at an earlier and earlier time. Once we reached the point at which Elaine was no longer napping in school, she was sleeping more at night and was averaging about 8½ hours of sleep, 30 minutes more than before we began the plan.

Elaine's sleep problems and the quest for a solution are typical of many efforts to help children sleep better. Often, people cannot or will not follow some parts of a plan, even though they are involved in its design. It may be that some people agree to follow certain plans only because they feel pressured. Some parents, for example, feel guilty if they do not agree to a plan for fear that others will judge them to be less dedicated to their child's welfare. Similarly, teachers sometimes find themselves in positions in which any reluctance to participate fully might be interpreted negatively. Many times, too, people agree to a plan without knowing how much work actually is involved. Parents, for example, often overestimate their ability to ignore the cries of their own child.

The strategy that my colleagues and I use in situations in which parts of a plan are not being fully carried out is to *not* place blame on the parent or teacher. Instead, we view these situations as failures on our part to adequately design the plan. As with Elaine's plan, we probably should have recognized that waking her early from her nap but not letting her go to lunch probably would cause more problems than her teacher (who had 11 other children in her class) could handle. Therefore, rather than try to pressure her teacher into carrying out the first version of the plan, we reevaluated our strategy and were able to come up with an equally effective alternative. Each obstacle is viewed as an opportunity to test the limits of our work.

## CONCLUSION

People who sleep at the "wrong times" actually could have one of several different sleep problems, including delayed sleep phase syndrome, non–24-hour sleep–wake cycles, and poor sleep habits. We examined a number of new and innovative approaches to helping these people sleep better, including chronotherapy, bright light therapy, and even the use of melatonin. Other approaches that can be useful have been borrowed from work with other sleep problems and include adapting sleep hygiene (see Chapter 4), stimulus control (see Chapter 4), and bedtime fading (see Chapter 5). There is reason to feel optimistic about helping these individuals sleep at times that are more desirable.

# 8

# Nightmares, Sleep Terrors, and Related Sleep Problems

Some of the most personally upsetting of all of the sleep problems are nightmares and sleep terrors. They are included here in the same chapter because these sleep problems are often confused with each other, yet you may be surprised to learn that in some ways they are almost mirror opposites. In addition, there are other disturbances of sleep, such as sleepwalking and sleeptalking, that occasionally can be a source of concern. This chapter discusses these different sleep problems and efforts to help people who are troubled by these nighttime events.

We all know what it is like to experience a nightmare. Children may be dreaming that someone is chasing them, that they are lost and late for an important event, or that someone about whom they care has died. If the dream is frightening enough, then the child may wake up in a sweat, crying, and often can remember much of what he or she has dreamed. The beginning of a sleep terror can resemble a nightmare. Your child may begin screaming in a terrifying way in the middle of the night, and you rush to comfort him or her. Quickly it becomes clear, however, that this is different. Whereas you are able to comfort your child after a nightmare, now your child is inconsolable. Whereas usually a nightmare ends suddenly with the person waking up, a child having a sleep terror remains asleep. What causes these two types of sleep problems, and how should we respond to them?

Discussed next are nightmares and sleep terrors and efforts to help people with special needs who are bothered by them.

## NIGHTMARES

Nightmares are a near-universal phenomenon. We all dream, and most people occasionally have bad or frightening dreams. In fact, somewhere between 5% and 10% of adults have frequent nightmares, and the proportion of children troubled by them is approximately 20%[1]. People with special needs also experience nightmares, but exact figures on just how many are bothered by excessive nightmares are not yet available. One group of individuals who seem to experience more nightmares are those individuals who have been through traumatic events, including automobile accidents and instances of abuse. It is important to recognize that having nightmares does not necessarily mean that someone has been through some traumatic event. Again, almost all of us have had nightmares from time to time. Unfortunately, often people interpret a higher incidence of frightening dreams as confirmation of abuse—but the evidence for this is lacking. It may be prudent to be cautious when looking for the origins of nightmares.

Nightmares almost always occur during REM, or dream, sleep. In fact, knowing that nightmares occur during this stage of sleep helps to explain why many people report very similar experiences during these events. For example, having a nightmare in which you are trying to run toward or away from something but are having difficulty is common. Also, being frightened during a dream but not being able to scream or call out until you wake up also is something that many people experience. The reason for these common nightmare experiences can be traced to the REM sleep stage. Recall from Chapter 1 that REM sleep is when we dream, but it also is a time when the major muscle groups in the body are virtually paralyzed. It is a good thing, too, because if we could move our muscles when we dream, then there would be a lot of running around and screaming going on each night. The muscle paralysis keeps us secure in our beds. The sensation, however, of not being able to move or speak (which also involves using muscles) that comes with this temporary paralysis seems to explain why we share these feelings of powerlessness when we have nightmares.

Unfortunately, despite the fact that nightmares are so common, very little is known about why we have them and how to help those people who are bothered by them. Stress and upsetting or traumatic events appear to increase the chance that people will have nightmares. Chapter 2 described a research study[2] on nightmares in which scientists studied the sleep of people who had gone through the emotionally upsetting experience of the 1989 San Francisco earthquake. They found that going through this hellish experience caused people to have more nightmares compared with people in other parts of the country. The people in San Francisco, however, did not report having *more frightening* nightmares than anyone else. In other words, the larger number of nightmares were not necessarily more upsetting than the ones experienced by any one of us. What does this mean? This research points out that stressful events cause more nightmares, which may be what separates most of us from people who are bothered by them. What contributes to these nightmares may be stressful events but may also include a tendency to be more anxious in general, which in turn may cause nightmares to be experienced differently by different people.

Because of the connection between stress or anxiety and nightmares, efforts to help people who are bothered by excessive nightmares have focused on decreasing their anxious feelings. The following case may help illustrate how this can be accomplished.

Quinn was his parents' first child and was the center of their lives. They had waited until their mid-40s to have a child and initially were devastated to learn that their infant son had Down syndrome. Shortly after his birth, however, it became clear that they would love their son with a depth of feeling that was unparalleled and that they could weather whatever challenges his condition might present to them. This was the family that they had always dreamed of.

Quinn generally was a very good baby, and his parents worked hard to provide him with the extra care that he required. When he was about 5 years old, he began to wake up in the early morning hours and cry. They would go into his room to find Quinn awake, sweating, and clearly upset. He usually would tell his parents that he saw a monster and was frightened that the monster might hurt him. Quinn's parents recalled that his first nightmares may have occurred shortly after they watched a video together that may have frightened him.

Quinn's nightmares did not go away, and for 9 months he awakened once per night. Because Quinn did not appear to have any other areas in his life that were unusually upsetting or stressful, we decided to try a relatively innocuous plan. The strategy was that his parents would discuss with him that the monster was only make believe and that he was much stronger than the monster. To further bolster the plan, Quinn was allowed to sleep with his toy "power sword," which he was told would kill the monster if it bothered Quinn. They told him that no one could hurt him in his sleep if he used his sword.

On the first night of the plan, Quinn awoke crying, and his parents went into his room to comfort him. They reminded him of the power of the sword, let him hold it next to him in his bed, and he fell back to sleep relatively quickly. Over the next week, he awoke only two more times, but

each time he was easy to comfort, and he fell back to sleep. In the intervening months, Quinn still had occasional nightmares, but the sword
story seemed to provide him with a safety signal that reduced his fear.
Eventually, Quinn stopped sleeping with the sword and continued to have
few nightmares.

## Using "Magic"

Quinn's case was a simple one. The "placebo effect" of the sword was
real enough; he felt that the sword protected him, and that was all that
mattered. The sword and his belief that it would help protect him
served to make him less anxious and perhaps feel more in control of
the nightmares. This type of "magic" often can be very effective for
children having nightmares. Giving them something that they believe
will protect them and that gives them back a sense of control can help
children cope with distressful dreams.

An interesting question that is unanswered in Quinn's case is
whether he incorporated the sword into his nightmare. Did he begin
to see the sword when the monster approached, and did he use the
sword to ward off or kill it? Quinn was not very clear about how the
sword helped him in these frightening dreams. Other children have,
however, reported that similar types of sleep tools (e.g., a friend's use
of a "magic wand" for his daughter) do enter into the dream itself and
serve a direct protective benefit. Again, nightmares and dreams in general still are relative mysteries to sleep professionals, and we as yet do
not know why such treatments help some children.

## Teaching Relaxation

Other children may need more or different help with their nightmare-
related sleep problems. For example, some children become so distressed over their nightmares that they are afraid to go to sleep. The
anxiety and tension (described in more detail in Chapter 10) that these
children experience can cause bedtime problems as well as night wakings. Sometimes it is necessary to teach them skills to relax at bedtime.
Like Quinn's sword, relaxation skills can serve to help children feel less
powerless over their fears. This combination of having the skill to reduce tension and having a feeling of control has been helpful for many
children who experience nightmares. Following is an outline of the
major steps necessary to teach relaxation skills, especially to children.
The goal is to have your child experience what his or her muscles feel
like tensed and, more important, how to make them more relaxed.
Often children and adults are unaware that major muscles in their
bodies are tense, and this exercise helps provide some practice at
awareness of the body.

- Have your child lie back on his or her bed. Arms and legs should be limp as well as the head. If your child is holding up his or her head, then this means that the muscles of the neck are tensing and that he or she is not completely relaxed.
- For younger children or children who seem to have a problem following the directions, a simple instruction such as "act like a wet noodle" may be enough to help them visualize what you want them to do.
- Begin with the facial muscles, asking your child to slowly and carefully tense the muscles. The tension of the muscles should last for about 5 seconds.
- Following the tension of a set of muscles, have your child relax the muscles, and give him or her 10–15 seconds to experience the good feeling of relaxation.
- As you talk to your child, use a soothing and calming voice, and take your time.
- Move from the facial muscles to the jaw (clenching and relaxing the jaw), then to the neck and shoulders, to the arms and hands, chest, stomach, thighs, legs, and feet.
- Have the child tell you whether he or she experiences any pain or discomfort. You may need to instruct him or her not to tense the muscles too tightly, or you may want to avoid certain muscle groups.
- Have the child practice until he or she can run through it alone.
- Have your child use the relaxation procedure any time he or she feels tense or anxious.

These instructions should provide you with a rough outline of how to teach your child to relax, especially at bedtime. It is important to describe the technique to your child as a very powerful one, one that should be helpful in making him or her more relaxed. This is helpful because your child's expectation for the technique can be just as important as the technique itself. This is true for relaxation as well as for any of the other techniques described in the book. Believing that something will work will help boost the power of such efforts to help children sleep.

For some children, the relaxation exercises can be made part of their bedtime routine. The last thing that he or she does before going to sleep could be practicing these exercises. This may serve two very important functions. First, it can help relieve some of the muscle tension that comes along with anxiety. Second, giving your child this task at night can help keep his or her mind off of the fearful thoughts. Remind your child, however, that this relaxation skill can be used anytime—in the middle of the night when he or she awakens and is fearful, even during the day when your child feels tense.

Another useful technique, described in more detail in Chapter 10, is *paradoxical intention*. Sometimes children become anxious about not sleeping, and these thoughts alone can contribute to their difficulty with going to sleep at night. Paradoxical intention involves informing a child (or an adult) that you want him or her to *try to stay awake*. While the child is in bed in the dark and relaxed, you give him or her permission to stay awake. For some children, taking away the demand of having to fall asleep provides enough reassurance to help them become drowsy and sleep. Again, Chapter 10 provides a more detailed description of this technique for helping children whose own thoughts seem to interfere with their ability to sleep at night.

## SLEEP TERRORS

Perhaps the most disturbing of all of the sleep disorders is a problem known as *sleep terrors*. This disorder is sometimes referred to as *night terrors*, although because it can occur during daytime naps as well, the term *sleep terrors* probably is more accurate. These episodes usually begin with a piercing scream, which parents find impossible to ignore. Along with screaming, the child appears extremely upset, usually with heart pounding and sweating. One of the characteristics of sleep terrors that is different from a nightmare is the inability to comfort the child during these events. Holding a child who is in the middle of a sleep terror usually causes him or her to push away and sometimes to become more upset. If your child has experienced this type of problem, then you know how disturbing it is not only to see your child so distraught but also to feel so powerless to help. On the positive side, when these episodes are over, the child usually falls back to sleep and does not have any memory of this upsetting night.

Sleep terrors differ from many of the other sleep problems because they occur from start to finish while the child is asleep. The screaming, which is sometimes accompanied by getting out of bed and wandering around the house, happens during NREM, or nondream, sleep, which means that this upsetting time probably does not represent a bad dream, at least in the way that we typically think of them. The fact that they occur exclusively while the child is asleep poses a problem for some of the interventions that have been described. For example, ignoring sleep terrors using a plan such as graduated extinction would be useless because the child is unaware of whether someone is present in the room.

## Sleep Longer

Our still-limited understanding about the nature of sleep terrors suggests that having a child get more sleep may help to reduce these episodes. Sleep terrors occur during the deepest stages of sleep. Recall that we go through four stages of NREM sleep: Stages 1 and 2 are a time of relatively light sleep, and Stages 3 and 4 are deeper periods of sleep. The sleep terrors that a child or an adult experiences happen while the person is in the deep Stages 3 and 4 sleep. When we are sleep deprived, we tend to have more Stage 3 and 4, or deeper, sleep. This suggests that sleep terrors may be partly the result of a child's not getting enough sleep. In contrast, sleeping more hours at night tends to decrease the amount of deep sleep. This obviously is not recommended for children who have night-waking problems because sleeping more hours will tend to produce lighter sleep and therefore can increase wakings. If a child has frequent sleep terrors but does not experience other sleep disturbances, however, then it may be helpful to have the child sleep more hours at night or take a nap during the day.

## Scheduled Awakening

Chapter 6 described the use of scheduled awakening for night waking—which involves waking the child some time prior to a typical waking. My colleagues and I have found that this technique also may be a valuable aid to children who have long-standing problems with sleep terrors. Following is a case of a child who had a many-year history of this problem whom we ultimately were able to help.

> Alfie was 11 years old when we first met, and he had a 7 year history of sleep terrors. He was born in Jamaica and was living in the United States with an aunt. His aunt told us that he had a learning disability and that his parents sent him to school here because they believed that he would receive a better education. Other than some difficulty remembering what he had read, Alfie did well in school both academically and socially. He had a number of friends in his suburban neighborhood and especially enjoyed playing street hockey.
>
> Alfie's aunt told us that he would go to bed fine at night and usually would not awaken during the night. About three nights each week, however, Alfie would cry out loudly. He would appear extremely upset, his heart would race as though he were running, and he would sweat profusely. At first his aunt thought that he was hurt or that he was getting sick; however, when it became clear that he was fine the next day, she became more concerned. She thought that because he was separated from his parents, he was having horrifying nightmares. After our initial consultation, during which I told her that the episodes did not

resemble nightmares, I asked that she contact Alfie's parents to deter-mine whether this was something new or whether he had ever had these episodes before. Alfie's aunt was surprised (and a bit annoyed) to learn that Alfie had had these episodes off and on for most of his life.

In order to try to help Alfie avoid these sleep terrors, we designed a plan for his aunt. After several weeks of charting when these sleep ter-ror episodes occurred, it became clear that it usually happened at around 12:30 A.M. Based on this information, we suggested that his aunt institute a scheduled awakening plan. She was to wake up at midnight, go into his room, and gently shake him until his eyes opened. Once he briefly opened his eyes, his aunt was to let him go back to sleep. She was to repeat this pattern each night for at least 2 weeks.

On the first night of the plan, she had a little trouble waking Alfie, who appeared to be in a very deep sleep. We told her that this was prob-ably a good sign and an indication that the midnight waking was a good idea. She repeated the waking each night for 2 weeks and did not observe Alfie having any sleep terror episodes. After the first 2 weeks, we sug-gested that she skip one night the next week, two nights the second week, and one more night each subsequent week. With the exception of one in-stance of a sleep terror, Alfie was free from these nighttime problems for the next 6 months. The intervention plan seemed to help him with sleep terrors, and it did not seem to negatively affect him in any way.

Just as we saw with night waking in Chapter 6, scheduled awak-ening was successful in helping Alfie's aunt reduce Alfie's sleep terrors. Our experience with other children such as Alfie indicates that this may be a technique that generally is useful for children with this sleep problem. The main difficulty with scheduled awakening (which is described more thoroughly in Chapter 6) is that it can be difficult for some parents to get up at night to awaken their child. Because the wakings usually can be faded out over several weeks, it does not have to be an overwhelming burden; but, depending on the timing of the waking, it still can be challenging. Following is an overview of the steps necessary to implement a scheduled awakening plan.

- Use the sleep diary (see Chapter 3 and Appendix D) to determine the time or times when your child typically experiences a sleep ter-ror during the night.
- On the night when you are to begin the plan, awaken your child approximately 30 minutes prior to the typical sleep terror time. For example, if your child usually has a sleep terror episode at 12:30 A.M., then wake your child at 12:00 A.M. If your child seems to awaken very easily, then move back the time 15 minutes the next night and on all subsequent nights (11:45 P.M.).

- If there is a broad range in the times when your child has sleep terrors (e.g., from 12:00 A.M. to 1:30 A.M.), then awaken your child about 30 minutes prior to the earliest time (in this case, 11:30 P.M.).
- Do not fully awaken your child. Gently touch and/or talk to your child until he or she opens his or her eyes, then let him or her fall back to sleep.
- Repeat this plan each night until your child goes for a full seven nights without a sleep terror. When your child has achieved this level of success, skip one night (i.e., no scheduled waking) for a week. If your child has an episode, then go back to every night. Slowly reduce the number of nights with scheduled wakings until your child is no longer having sleep terrors during the night.

Why does scheduled awakening work to reduce sleep terrors? Unfortunately, sleep professionals do not yet have an adequate answer to this question. One theory about the role of scheduled awakening in sleep terrors is that scheduled awakening during the deep stages of sleep may prevent the child from spending too much time in this part of sleep. Remember that sleep terrors seem to be more likely to occur the more time a person spends in deep sleep. The scheduled awakening may help the child sleep a "shallower" but more consistent sleep schedule, and that may account for the reduction in sleep terrors. Perhaps research over the next few years will help sleep professionals get a better understanding of this puzzling sleep problem and also will lead to more techniques to help people who experience sleep terrors.

## SLEEPWALKING AND SLEEPTALKING

Walking or talking during sleep usually does not occur during REM sleep. Sleepwalking (also called *somnambulism*) and sleeptalking are two sleep disturbances that most often occur during NREM sleep, usually within the first few hours after falling asleep at night. In children, the causes of these active sleep events have been thought to include anxiety, a lack of sleep, and fatigue. Sleepwalking and sleeptalking also have been linked to seizure disorders, and this cause should be considered for any child who experiences these sleep problems.

Sleepwalking and sleeptalking can be brief, lasting for only a few seconds, or can continue for 30 minutes or longer. For the most part, these sleep events should not be a source of concern. Contrary to some popular myths, it is not dangerous to awaken a person who is walking in his or her sleep, although it may be difficult because it occurs during a deep stage of sleep. The awakened sleepwalker may appear confused and disoriented at first but should have no trouble going back to sleep. Another myth about sleepwalking is that the person cannot be injured at that time. People who sleepwalk generally seem aware of their surroundings and tend to avoid harming themselves; however, there are occasional reports of people harming themselves or others during sleepwalking. For example, a 35-year-old man who was sleepwalking was reported to have stabbed another man[3]. In addition, the person can be hurt by bumping into objects or falling down stairs, and therefore some precautions should be taken if this is a frequent occurrence in your home.

Although my colleagues and I have not been involved in trying to help children who frequently walk in their sleep, we can suggest that you try to make sure that these individuals are fully rested and that potential sources of stress or anxiety are identified and addressed. Failing in these efforts, we would recommend a trial of scheduled awakening (see previous description), especially because of the similarity between sleep terrors and these other sleep problems.

## SLEEP EATING

There recently has been an increase in the number of reports of people taking another route to sleepwalking—right to the refrigerator! It appears that some people not only walk in their sleep but also prepare and consume snacks or even small meals. A number of people observed that they were gaining weight and only later found out that they were eating at night without knowing it. Although relatively little is known about this sleep problem, it appears to be a variation of sleepwalking. It may also be related to the use of medications such as those prescribed for depression or insomnia. The following is a case of a person who discovered after several months that she was eating while she was asleep.

> Janine was a very active and athletic 27-year-old woman. She was very concerned about fitness and was becoming increasingly frustrated because her efforts at dieting and exercise were not having the effect that she expected. Instead of losing weight, she was gaining weight! The key to her problem was discovered one night by her husband.
>
> Janine's husband, who usually was a very heavy sleeper, was awakened one night by a noise in the kitchen. He noticed that his wife was not beside him, and he got up to see whether everything was all right. He found Janine at the kitchen table, consuming the last of what appeared to have been a full box of cookies. "Giving up the diet?" he quipped to his wife with a smile on his face. Strangely, she did not look up at him, and she continued to eat. He walked over to her, touched her on the shoulder, and said, "Janine, are you OK?" With that, she stood up, walked out of the kitchen, and went to bed without ever saying a word—sending chills up her husband's spine. The next morning, he gently broached the subject of

the binge-eating episode of the night before and her strange reaction to him, but Janine just looked puzzled and denied that it ever had happened. One night, after several of these strange events—once when his wife ate several cups of sugar—they saw a television program about a woman who ate in her sleep and finally concluded that Janine had the same problem.

They approached me for some advice for this sleep problem, and we discussed her sleeping habits. Other than occasionally having trouble falling asleep at night, Janine reported having few other sleep problems. She did say that both she and her father had histories of walking in their sleep and that there were a few humorous family stories about both of them. My recommendations included having Janine eat a small snack at night before bedtime, perhaps to reduce her hunger and therefore her desire to eat at night. Her husband also agreed to institute a scheduled awakening plan whereby he would awaken Janine at about 1:15 A.M.—30 minutes before her 1:45 A.M. travels. After about 2 weeks, Janine's husband began fading the awakenings, and he reported no obvious incidents of sleep eating. Janine's weight was beginning to stabilize at an acceptable level, and they believed that she was no longer getting up at night and binging on snacks.

Janine seemed to have combined her previous history of sleep-walking with an effort to satisfy cravings for "junk" food that she was having since she had begun her diet. It is possible that increases in reports of sleep eating may be a function of increased awareness but also may be a consequence of our culture's fat-free diet craze. We await future research on sleep eating to determine just how often this occurs and who is likely to engage in this type of unusual sleep event. It may be that it disproportionately occurs among people who have a history of sleepwalking and who also have food cravings as a result of dieting. This sleep problem can be of concern if it negatively affects a person's weight. It also can cause concern because of the increased risk of injury by choking or when cooking or cutting food at a time when the person is not fully aware. Finally, these events can disrupt a person's sleep and may contribute to daytime drowsiness.

## CONCLUSION

This chapter discussed some of the more dramatic sleep problems that people experience. Nightmares, sleep terrors, sleepwalking and sleeptalking, as well as other sleep-related problems involve disturbances in different stages of sleep. As sleep professionals' knowledge of sleep stages has increased, so has their ability to provide assistance for people who experience these sleep abnormalities. Included in this chapter have been a number of suggestions that should help families address what sometimes can be rather disturbing sleep problems.

# 9

# Excessive Sleepiness

Most of us have experienced times when despite having had a reasonable number of hours of sleep, we still feel tired throughout the day. This experience of daytime sleepiness is, unfortunately for some, a chronic and obviously frustrating problem. School or work can be negatively affected, and daytime accidents are common among these individuals. Although at first it does not appear that the sleep of these people is disrupted (they usually do not have any recollection of waking during the night), often at the root of this problem is an interrupted sleep cycle. In other words, people who are excessively tired during the day after what seems to be a full night's sleep may be having their sleep interrupted without knowing it. In other cases, some individuals may have rare but very specific sleep problems that lead to daytime sleepiness or, in the extreme, involuntary attacks of sleep. This chapter covers the different types of sleep and sleep-related problems that can lead to excessive sleepiness, along with a description of treatment approaches aimed at helping people with these problems. Unfortunately, very little is known about the sleep problems associated with excessive sleepiness among people with special needs. It is hoped that more attention will focus on these individuals to determine whether they have more specific treatment needs.

## HYPERSOMNIA

If *insomnia* involves not getting enough sleep (the root word "in" means lacking or without), then *hypersomnia* is a problem of sleeping too much ("hyper" means having a great amount or abnormal excess). Despite getting a full night's sleep each evening, some people find themselves falling asleep several times each day. One young woman who I met through my teaching battled hypersomnia for many years.

Ann was a college student who came by my office during office hours to discuss her progress in class. We discussed the last exam and several questions that she had missed. As she was about to leave, she said that she never fell asleep during my class. This seemed like faint praise, but I thanked her for the feedback. "No," she said, "you don't understand. I usually fall asleep in *all* of my classes, but not in yours." Again, I didn't quite understand what she was trying to tell me, and I joked that she must be more careful picking out her professors. She laughed. "That's probably true. But I also have this problem with sleeping too much."

As we discussed her sleeping problem (this time, a little bit more seriously), Ann told me that excessive sleeping had been a problem for her since her teenage years. When she was in situations that were monotonous or boring or if she couldn't be active, she would find herself falling asleep. This could happen several times a day, depending on what she was doing. Recently, large lecture classes had become a problem for her unless the lecturer was particularly interesting or animated. Watching television and driving long distances along highways also were problems.

Ann reported that her father also had a problem with falling asleep but that his problem was different and that the symptoms were more severe. He had recently been diagnosed with narcolepsy (a sleep problem described next that can result in sudden and irresistible sleep attacks, along with disturbing sleep events such as brief paralysis and hallucinations) and was now being seen at a sleep clinic to help him deal with the problem. Both she and her brother had been diagnosed with hypersomnia. Ann had been prescribed Ritalin (a stimulant medication) about 4 years ago and said that it was only somewhat effective in keeping her awake during the day. She said that the drug helped to reduce the attacks but did not eliminate them altogether.

When I asked her how she coped with falling asleep all of the time, she became a bit embarrassed. "I think of things," she said finally. I asked her what she meant. "Well, I can pretty much control it if I keep my mind busy. I think of exciting things." I waited, and she continued. "Sometimes I fantasize that I have great intellectual powers and that I am smarter than anyone else in class. Other times I think of winning an award, or I think about sex, and for some reason I don't tend to sleep. It seems to work for me."

Ann's hypersomnia was not so disruptive as to keep her from succeeding in school, but it was a daily struggle for her to stay awake in class. The stimulant medication—Ritalin—helped her somewhat, but she still found that some classes challenged her ability to remain awake. We worked together on a plan to help her identify times when she felt herself falling asleep and fantasy scenarios that she could practice that would help her stay awake. She reported later that practicing in boring classes was working and that she was feeling more control over her sleep.

Unfortunately for Ann and for thousands of people like her, sleep professionals still do not have treatments that can completely eliminate these urges to sleep. Often stimulant medications such as Ritalin are prescribed to help keep them more alert; however, this seems to be only a partial fix. Other techniques, such as trying to become aware of when the attacks are coming on and using mental imagery to try to delay or prevent sleep, may be of some use to people who are able to use such procedures. If you suspect that your child may have hypersomnia, then contact one of the sleep centers listed in Appendix C for a possible evaluation and recommendations for treatment. Unfortunately, this is not one of the sleep problems for which the field has yet had a great deal of success in fully treating.

## NARCOLEPSY

Narcolepsy is a serious sleep problem that includes not only uncontrollable sleep attacks (such as the ones experienced by Ann) but also a number of other disturbing sleep-related symptoms associated with it. In addition to the daytime sleepiness observed in people with hypersomnia, people with narcolepsy also experience *cataplexy*, or a sudden loss of muscle tone. These are not seizures but instead are involuntary sleep attacks. The loss of muscle tone seems to occur because, unlike most of our sleep episodes, these sleep attacks involve the immediate introduction of REM sleep. This phase of sleep involves not only dreaming but also muscle paralysis. This loss of muscle tone happens while the person is awake and can be as mild as a feeling of slight weakness in the facial muscles to a complete collapse to the floor. This cataplexy can last from several seconds to several minutes and usually is preceded by some strong emotion, such as anger or happiness. Imagine that you have narcolepsy: In the middle of cheering for your favorite team, you might suddenly fall asleep; or while having an argument with a friend, you might collapse to the floor in a sound sleep.

Two other characteristics distinguish people who have narcolepsy. They commonly report *sleep paralysis*, a brief period of time upon awakening when the person cannot move or speak. This experience is often reported to be frightening by those going through it. Sleep paralysis is more common than you might think. Many individuals who otherwise have no other sleep problems—including narcolepsy—report having these frightening experiences in the morning. The last characteristic of narcolepsy is *hypnagogic hallucinations,* vivid experiences that begin at the start of sleep and are said to be unbelievably realistic because they include not only the visual aspects but also touch, hearing, and even the feeling of body movement. Examples of hypnagogic hallucinations, which, like sleep paralysis, can be quite terrifying, include the experience of being caught in a fire or flying through the air.

Narcolepsy appears to be a genetic disorder; to date, there is no totally effective treatment. Like hypersomnia, people with narcolepsy often are prescribed stimulant medications to help keep them alert during the day. Also, sometimes antidepressant medications are recommended, not because these individuals are more prone to depression but because these drugs can help prevent the onset of REM sleep. This effect of antidepressant drugs can therefore help to prevent the attacks of cataplexy.

One very simple recommendation that sometimes is helpful for people with narcolepsy is to take daytime naps. A nap in the morning and again in the afternoon can help reduce the sleep attacks that these individuals experience. In addition, making sure that the person has adequate sleep at night can be helpful. Again, if your child is having narcolepsy-like symptoms, then an evaluation at a sleep center is essential.

## BREATHING PROBLEMS

For some people, their sleepiness during the day or their disrupted sleep at night has a physical origin; namely, problems breathing while asleep. Because breathing is interrupted, it results in numerous brief arousals throughout the night, and the person does not feel rested even after 8 or 9 hours "asleep." For all of us, sleep is a time when the muscles of our upper airway relax, constricting this passageway somewhat; it therefore makes breathing a little more difficult. Unfortunately for some, breathing is constricted a great deal, and they may have very labored breathing while they sleep (*hypoventilation*). Other people experience more extreme breathing problems while asleep, and they may have short periods (10–30 seconds) when breathing stops altogether, called *sleep apnea.* Often the person affected is only minimally aware of his or her breathing difficulties and does not attribute sleep problems to breathing. A bed partner or a relative in a nearby room, however, usually will be aware of loud snoring (which is one sign of this problem) or will have witnessed the episodes of interrupted breathing, a frightening experience to observe. Other signs indicating that breathing difficulties may be responsible for disturbed sleep are sweating heavily during the night, morning headaches, and episodes of falling asleep during the day (called *sleep attacks*) but without the feeling of being rested after these episodes.

There are a number of types of breathing difficulties that can lead to sleep disruption. Specifically, three types of apnea are important to distinguish because they can have different causes, daytime complaints, and treatments—*obstructive, central,* and *mixed.* Obstructive sleep apnea (OSA) occurs when airflow stops despite the continued activity of the respiratory system. This can be caused by an airway that is too narrow or by an abnormality or damage that is obstructing or interfering with airflow. In one study[1], 100% of a group of people with OSA also reported snoring at night. Being obese sometimes is associated with OSA, as is increasing age, and OSA is more often found among males. OSA is believed to occur in about 1%–2% of the general population[2]. With the second type of apnea—central sleep apnea—respiratory activity completely ceases for brief periods of time and often is associated with certain central nervous system disorders, such as cerebral vascular disease, head trauma, and degenerative disorders[3]. Unlike people with OSA, people with central sleep apnea wake up frequently during the night, but they tend not to report excessive daytime sleepiness and often are not aware that they have a serious breathing problem. Because of the lack of daytime symptoms, people tend not to seek treatment for this problem, so relatively little is known about it. The final breathing disorder—mixed sleep apnea—is a combination of obstructive and central sleep apneas. All of these breathing difficulties interrupt sleep and result in symptoms similar to those of insomnia. One young woman with a breathing-related sleep problem who recently came to my colleagues' and my attention provides an illustration of a breathing-related sleep problem.

> I was consulting with a group of special educators one afternoon when the topic of sleep came up. One woman who worked in a group home for individuals who had mental retardation asked for help with a young woman named Linda who lived in the house and whom they were having a great deal of difficulty motivating. The worker reported that they tried everything they could think of to get her interested in the activities at home or at work, but nothing seemed to interest her except sleep. I could tell by the worker's tone of voice that she considered Linda to be lazy and was extremely frustrated with her.

    I began to ask some questions about Linda's sleep to determine whether she was having difficulties falling asleep at night or sleeping through the night and whether one of these problems was the cause of her fatigue. The worker reported that just the opposite was true. Linda would fall asleep almost immediately after she got into bed, and she never came out of her room until staff came to wake her up. In fact, she was difficult to awaken and often was cranky in the morning. Suspecting that a breathing problem might be the cause of her daytime sleepiness, I then asked whether Linda snored. "The loudest I've ever heard!" the worker exclaimed. Before she could explain any further, I followed up with a question about Linda's weight. "She's very heavy," the worker replied. Linda weighed more than 200 pounds. I recommended that they have Linda evaluated by a physician or at the local sleep center to determine whether she had a breathing-related sleep problem.

What seemed clear from our brief conversation was that Linda fit the pattern of a person with obstructed nighttime breathing. The daytime sleepiness without nighttime sleep problems was the first clue. The next indication was that Linda was described as being cranky in the morning. This could have been a result of a dry mouth and a headache that often follow a night of obstructed breathing. The answers to my questions about Linda's snoring and weight seemed to confirm my suspicions. Both are common characteristics of a person who has a breathing problem at night. The worker later told me of Linda's high blood pressure, which they thought was only because of her weight but could have been made worse by her breathing problem.

    The good news was that they were able to get Linda some help with her sleep problem, using some of the treatment suggestions described next. The sad part of the story, however, is that people for many years believed that Linda was just a lazy person. Perhaps more tragic, it will take some time to determine how much of Linda's impairment was a function of the brain damage responsible for her mental retardation and how much was a function of the cognitive difficulties that people have when they have such breathing problems at night.

    *Again, if you believe that your child has signs of a breathing difficulty, then an immediate medical evaluation is essential.* The consequences of breathing problems at night can be severe, and you should seek medical advice as soon as possible. Some of the nonmedical recommendations for these individuals include elevating the person's head with pillows at night to help ease breathing. Also, sleeping on the side instead of the back can be helpful to some people. Important recommendations for adults with breathing problems include avoiding sleeping pills and alcohol, both of which can make the breathing passages relax even more and cause increased breathing difficulty. It is also recommended to avoid smoking and to lose weight.

In severe cases, the most common recommendation is to use an instrument that provides *continuous positive airway pressure* (CPAP). A mask is attached to the person's face at night, and slightly increased air pressure provided by a compressor helps to keep the airways open and greatly improves breathing. Obviously, such a device can be used only by a cooperative individual and can take some time to get used to. As a last resort, different surgical procedures sometimes are recommended, depending on the nature of the obstruction.

## SUDDEN INFANT DEATH SYNDROME

Probably the most devastating and unthinkable event that can befall any new parents is the sudden and unexplainable death of their seemingly healthy infant. Sudden infant death syndrome, or SIDS, is the label given by medical professionals for these otherwise unexplainable deaths. Approximately 7,000 such deaths occur each year just in the United States, and this syndrome strikes families from all racial, ethnic, and socioeconomic backgrounds. The exact cause—or, more likely, causes—of this medical mystery remain unknown, and, unfortunately, there is no way to fully prevent these deaths. Because SIDS generally strikes during the night or early morning when the infant is asleep, it is believed to be a sleep-related disorder.

Although in most cases SIDS affects infants who are healthy, there is a group of infants who are identified as being more likely to be stricken by it. Such infants have experienced one or more episodes of prolonged apnea—the cessation of breathing—to the point that they are limp, have slowed heartbeats, and require resuscitation. These "near misses" are more formally referred to as *sudden aventilatory events* (S.A.V.E.). Infants who experience S.A.V.E. are at higher risk for SIDS than are other babies.

Several factors seem to be related to SIDS in infants both with and without S.A.V.E., although it is important to remember that none of these factors absolutely predicts who will experience SIDS. The research on SIDS and these potential risk factors provide for some precautionary strategies:

- Stop using illicit drugs. Research suggests that about 25% of the mothers of babies who experience SIDS had previously used illegal drugs[4].
- Stop smoking. SIDS has been found to be more prevalent in children whose mothers smoked during pregnancy, and research sug-

gests that the rate is also higher in infants whose mothers smoked after the child was born[5].

- Most infants should be placed on their back to sleep. The American Academy of Pediatrics advocates that during the first 6 months of life, healthy infants are at a lower risk for SIDS if they sleep on their back or side rather than on their stomach. Parents of infants with existing breathing problems or those who tend to spit up a great deal after feeding should consult with their pediatrician.
- Have the infant sleep with firm bedding materials. Softer bedding, such as beanbag cushions, foam pads, or waterbeds, can constrict a child's breathing and should therefore be avoided.
- Avoid overheating an infant who has a cold or an infection. Too much clothing, too heavy a blanket, or too warm a room can increase the risk of SIDS for an ill baby.
- Breast-feeding is recommended. It is possible that breast-feeding may decrease the risk of illnesses or infections, which, in turn, can decrease the risk of SIDS.

## MOVEMENT-RELATED SLEEP PROBLEMS

Most of us have had the peculiar experience of drifting off to sleep, only to be briefly awakened by a sudden start or jerking of muscles, called a "hypnic jerk." This is a perfectly normal but as yet not fully understood physical reaction to the onset of sleep. Unfortunately for some people, these types of physical movements continue throughout most of the night, and they may interrupt sleep even without the person being aware that they are occurring. Two types of movement-related sleep problems are relatively common causes of daytime sleepiness: periodic limb movements and restless legs syndrome.

### Periodic Limb Movements

Does your child wake up in the morning with his or her blankets and sheets in a pile at the foot of the bed or on the floor? Does the bed look like a wrestling match occurred there in the middle of the night? If you have observed this on frequent occasions, then it may be the result of a condition referred to as *periodic limb movements*: episodes of leg and sometimes arm movements that occur throughout sleep. Sometimes these episodes of limb movements can be as brief as a few minutes; other times, they can go on for hours. Often, people are not aware of these movements during sleep. If they occur often enough, however, then the affected person may have his or her sleep interrupted and will feel tired throughout the day.

The causes of these limb movements are not yet clear, although they sometimes have been linked to the use of certain medications.

Antidepressants, for example, can cause some people to experience periodic limb movements. If this is the case, then it may be helpful to point it out to your physician, who may be able to switch the medication and help prevent this problem. When some people *stop* taking medications such as tranquilizers or sedatives, part of the side effects can include these limb movements. Also, certain medical conditions, such as kidney disease, folic acid deficiency, poor circulation, or a metabolic disease, have been linked to periodic limb movements.

No treatment really is necessary for periodic limb movements unless they are interfering with sleep. Unfortunately, there is no cure for the more severe cases of periodic limb movements, although some treatments have been tried when sleep is significantly interrupted. When poor circulation is thought to be the cause of these problems, some professionals recommend vitamin E supplements because this can help improve circulation. The use of muscle relaxants is not recommended because they often just suppress the twitches without fully eliminating them, and these drugs can be habit forming. One medication that may be helpful is called Sinemet (a combination of two drugs: levodopa and carbidopa), which is used for people with Parkinson's disease. Other approaches include the use of vitamin and mineral supplements, although it is not yet clear whether this is an effective treatment for many people with periodic limb movements.

### Restless Legs Syndrome

Described as the feeling of crawling, pulling, or tingling beneath the skin of the legs, *restless legs syndrome* affects some 5% of the general population[6]. This physical problem often coexists with periodic limb movements such that if a person experiences periodic limb movements, then he or she usually (but not always) has restless legs syndrome as well. These extremely uncomfortable feelings usually come on when the person relaxes, so it can be extremely disruptive when the person tries to fall asleep at night. They also can occur when the person sits for any length of time, making traveling very difficult. Although this problem previously was believed to occur only in older adults, subsequent research suggests that it can affect children and adolescents as well[7].

Medical treatment usually is recommended for people with restless legs syndrome, although exercising prior to bedtime can be helpful for some people who have this problem. The same drug that has proved beneficial for some people with periodic limb movements—Sinemet—also has brought relief for about a third of the people with restless legs syndrome. Other medical approaches include the use of benzodiazepines (which are a class of medications used to induce sleep) for milder cases and opioids (which are strong pain relievers and also bring on sleep) in more resistant cases. If you suspect that your child has either periodic limb movements or restless legs syndrome, then it is recommended that a medical exam be conducted.

### Rhythmic Movement Disorder

Some of the children who are referred to my colleagues and me rock back and forth in their beds before going to sleep. Sometimes this rocking includes head banging against the wall or the side of the crib. In all of these cases, parents usually report that the rocking or head banging seems to be soothing to their child and that it helps them fall asleep. These types of behaviors are more formally referred to as *rhythmic movement disorder,* and they are fairly common (in their less-injurious forms) among infants and toddlers. There also appears to be a higher rate of this type of rocking among children with developmental disabilities. One young boy's case will help illustrate this problem and our efforts to help his parents intervene.

Vinnie was an 18-month-old boy with a diagnosis of autism. His parents contacted us because of his head banging. Vinnie occasionally would bang his head against objects such as the wall or the floor when he was left alone for long periods of time. Fortunately, he would stop this head banging if someone told him to, and he was doing it less and less during the day as he grew older. He also would bang his head against the wall next to his bed at night before falling asleep, and his parents found that when they told him to stop, he would continue as soon as they left the room. Although the head banging was not so severe as to do a great deal of harm to him, there was a spot on his head where his hair was thinning, and his parents were concerned that this would worsen if he were not helped soon.

In our initial discussions with Vinnie's parents, we tried to determine why he was banging his head at night. Our guess was that this had become a calming ritual for Vinnie and that he had learned to use it to help him fall asleep. We designed a plan for his parents that would reduce any damage he was doing with the head banging and also would help him learn to fall asleep without this ritual. His parents had at one point tried to put some padding up against the wall to protect him, but Vinnie always found ways to take it down. We suggested that they sacrifice several nights and sit in his bedroom at bedtime. When Vinnie banged his head, they were to tell him to stop, but otherwise they were instructed not to talk to him in any way. They also were to place his favorite stuffed animal in bed with him.

His parents found that on the first night, Vinnie had a great deal of trouble falling asleep. He remained awake for 2 hours past the usual time when he fell asleep, but his parents persisted with the plan. Similar results were observed on the second night, but by the third night, Vinnie fell asleep within 30 minutes. We asked that his parents continue to remain in his room at bedtime until the number of reminders for him to stop head banging was one or less. After that point, we asked them to sit just outside his room and listen for any head banging. When they heard him bang his head, they were to call to him to stop. After about 2 weeks, Vinnie was falling asleep within a reasonable amount of time on most nights without head banging, and his parents felt comfortable not monitoring his bedtime behavior.

We were able to design this type of plan for Vinnie because he was able to stop banging his head when he was asked. We prevented him from using his typical strategy for falling asleep (head banging) and made him come up with other comforting strategies that were not potentially injurious to him. His parents noted that Vinnie seemed to ball up his pillow in a certain way that was comforting to him, and this was the way he usually fell asleep. He seemed to ignore his favorite stuffed animal yet, over time, was able to fall asleep without banging his head. Other children who are not so receptive to verbal instructions to stop head banging sometimes require physical intervention, such as the parent having to place a pillow in the way or having to prompt the child to put his or her head down. It is important to note in all of these plans that parents should not speak to their child during this time and generally should try to limit interactions. This is essential because you want the child not to see this as extending bedtime or as a time to get additional attention from parents. Talking, holding, or otherwise interacting with the child during this time may make your child dependent on your being there to fall asleep—essentially substituting you for head banging as a soothing sleep inducer.

Remember, noninjurious rocking probably is not something to worry about because most children stop as they get older. If it becomes more severe, however, then interventions such as the one used with Vinnie should be helpful.

## CONCLUSION

The sleep-related problems included in the category of *excessive sleepiness* represent some of the more serious problems concerning sleep. Breathing problems at night along with disorders such as hypersomnia and narcolepsy require medical intervention, and individuals suspected of having any of these difficulties should seek a medical evaluation immediately.

# 10

# Other Nighttime Difficulties

This chapter is designed to give you a brief overview of some problems surrounding sleep or bedtime that are not known specifically as sleep problems. Children who wet their bed during sleep at night, for example, are not considered as having a sleep problem, per se, and helping these children with their problem involves very different approaches from those used with problems of sleep. Also, children who are anxious or who are depressed may have their sleep interrupted, and we need to help these children in a slightly different way. Discussed next are bedwetting, anxiety and depression, and sleep-related headaches and tooth grinding and suggestions for assisting children who experience these difficulties.

## BEDWETTING

Bedwetting (more formally referred to as *enuresis*, pronounced en-yu-ree-sis) is one of those behaviors that is considered to be a problem depending on how old the person is. When a 2-year-old wets the bed at night, for example, it is not judged to be a problem (more than 90% of 2-year-olds wet the bed[1]). It generally is thought, however, that by about age 6, children should be sleeping through the night without accidents. As a result, children age 6 and older who are still wetting the bed regularly may need some additional help to let them have dry nights. This is not a particularly unusual problem among young children, considering, for example, that at least 7% of all 8-year-old children have occasional bedwetting accidents at night[2]. Although most children eventually will stop having these nighttime problems, it can take a number of years for this problem to resolve itself on its own. Unfortunately, for some children with special needs, bedwetting may never be resolved without special help.

Professionals in this area typically break down the types of enuresis into several groups. *Diurnal enuresis* is defined as wetting that occurs while the child is awake; the child has difficulty remaining dry during the daylight hours. *Primary nocturnal enuresis* is bedwetting during sleep (nocturnal) by a child who has never successfully had bladder control at night (primary). In contrast, *secondary nocturnal enuresis* is the loss of bladder control at night after a period of time—at least 3–6 months—when the child has had dry nights. This secondary form of enuresis sometimes occurs as a result of some medical problem (e.g., a bladder infection) or because of some emotional upset, such as a pending divorce by the parents.

It traditionally has been thought that bedwetting occurs among certain children because they have small bladders and that they wet the bed because they cannot hold their urine throughout the night. This does not seem to be the case. In about 10% of cases of enuresis, however, urinary tract infections are present[3]. With proper medical treatment of these infections, many children seem to resolve their problems with bedwetting. Sometimes the reverse is true, however, and bedwetting problems may be causing the urinary tract infections instead. Either way, it is important that all children who have problems with bedwetting be evaluated for possible medical causes of their nighttime accidents.

The most recent thinking about the biological causes of bedwetting includes the child's ability to produce a hormone that makes urine more concentrated and the physical ability to keep from urinating while asleep[4]. It appears that many children with bedwetting problems may not produce enough of a hormone called *antidiuretic hormone* (ADH). ADH helps to concentrate urine during sleep so that it has less water and, therefore, makes it is easier to avoid wetting accidents. Without enough of this hormone, the child's urine has more volume and is therefore more difficult to hold in at night. At the same time, these children may be less skillful at using their body's hints that the bladder is full to prevent accidents. Putting these two factors together— the relative lack of ADH and problems picking up the body's cues—may contribute to why some children have this problem and others do not.

Psychological as well as biological factors can play a role in bed-wetting. It is rarely, if ever, the case that a child willfully wets the bed to "get back" at a parent or for other similar reasons. Psychological stress and emotional upset, however, especially for children with the secondary type of enuresis—those who previously had good control and now do not—can trigger this problem. The mother of an 8-year-old boy asked for my advice about her son who had just recently begun to wet his bed. My first question was whether there was some recent, perhaps upsetting, changes going on at home, and she told me that her husband of 12 years had just moved out and they were getting a divorce. She never thought to connect her son's bedwetting with the obvious upheaval occurring at home. Fortunately, I was able to suggest some relatively easy things to do to help her help her son through this difficult time. Other children can react with bedwetting to changes such as the birth of a new brother or sister or difficulties at school. For some as yet not fully understood reason—and especially among boys—such changes can result in a regression in their previous toileting skills.

For some 80% of children, physical problems such as bladder infections are not the cause of their bedwetting[5]. As a result, a variety of techniques have been used to help the children learn (and sometimes relearn) how to avoid wetting the bed at night. Before any specific techniques are recommended, however, it usually is suggested that parents have their child limit fluids prior to bedtime and cut down on drinks or foods with caffeine, which can cause more urination. In addition, a stop in the bathroom right before going to sleep is recommended. Punishment, in the form of yelling, nagging, or ridicule, should not be used for these accidents because they can make the problem worse. Instead, fully waking your child at night—making sure that the child is truly awake—for several weeks to go to the bathroom may be enough to help him or her sleep through the night dry. If an accident occurs, then have him or her participate in the cleanup, but, again, this should not be done in a punishing way. If these small steps are not enough, then several more formal techniques usually are presented as possible aids for bedwetting.

### The Bell and Pad

A *urine alarm,* or the "bell and pad," is one of the oldest techniques for helping children with enuresis. This commercially available device consists of a pad that goes underneath the child's sheet. When the pad gets wet, it sets off an alarm that is loud enough to wake your child (and you), and the parent can direct the child to finish urinating in the bathroom. This simple technique alone has proved helpful to up to

75% of children who participate in this type of plan[6]. Following is an outline of the bell and pad technique*:

- Hook up the alarm yourself each night. Test it by touching the sensors (it is safe) with a wet finger.
- Listen for the alarm carefully, and respond to it quickly.
- Have a night-light or flashlight nearby so that you will be able to see what you are doing when the alarm sounds.
- As soon as you hear the alarm, get out of bed, and turn off the alarm.
- Have your child go to the bathroom and finish urinating.
- Help your child clean his or her clothes and bed.
- Use the alarm every night until your child goes for 3 or 4 weeks without bedwetting. This can take 2–3 months, so be patient.

On the down side, a significant number of children who do at first succeed with the use of the bell and pad may relapse, or begin again to have bedwetting problems. For these children, additional procedures sometimes are added to this technique, two of which are described next.

### Dry Bed Training

Dry bed training includes the use of the bell and pad along with three other steps. On the first night of dry bed training, the child is awakened each hour and brought to the bathroom. There the child is encouraged to urinate and then is given something to drink and is asked to try to hold it in until he or she is awakened again. Finally, the child is allowed to return to bed. On the second night of this plan, the child is awakened only once, 3 hours after going to bed, and is again given something to drink and returned to bed. For each subsequent night that the child succeeds in staying dry, the waking time is moved back 30 minutes until it reaches 1 hour after bedtime. If the child has an accident two or more times during any 1-week period, then the waking schedule is repeated. It is thought that this type of waking schedule may interrupt the child's typical sleep pattern and may help him or her learn to remain dry at night.

---

*Information about purchasing alarms is available from these companies:
Nytone Alarm: Nytone Medical Products, 2424 S. 900 West, Salt Lake City, UT 84119; 801-973-4090.
Potty Pager Silent Alarm: Ideas for Living, 1285 N. Cedarbrook, Boulder, CO 80304; 800-497-6573.
Wet-Stop Alarm: Palco Laboratories, 8030 Soquel Avenue, Santa Cruz, CA 95062; 800-346-4488.

The second part of the plan is referred to as a "positive practice" procedure. The child is helped to practice how to delay urination. After waking with a wet bed and cleaning up, the child is asked to lie in bed and count to 50 and then to go into the bathroom to try to urinate. The child then returns to bed. This training is repeated 20 times. This practice routine of holding urination should be implemented after a wet bed and again at bedtime the next night.

After the first night of the waking schedule, the bell and pad are introduced to signal when the child has wet the bed. Each time that the alarm goes off, a "cleanliness training" plan is then followed. This basically involves having your child participate as much as possible in the cleanup after a toileting accident has occurred. The child is encouraged to take off the wet bed clothes or is prompted through it if he or she cannot do it alone and also is encouraged to change the wet bed linens. This is repeated 20 times after each instance of bedwetting before the child is allowed to go back to sleep. This type of training may serve two purposes. First, it fully awakens the child after a bedwetting incident. This seems to be important to the success of any of these programs because children can be prompted to get up and go to the bathroom while not being fully awake, and therefore he or she may not learn to interrupt sleep to go to the bathroom alone at night. The second role of cleanliness training may involve its unpleasantness. Obviously, your child will want to avoid going through these 20 trials of dressing and undressing, and this may provide more motivation to be aware of when he or she should go to the bathroom. Following is an overview of the steps involved in dry bed training:

- Establish a nightly waking schedule. Upon waking the child, the parent brings him or her to the bathroom, and the child is asked to urinate. After the bathroom trip, the child is given some fluids to drink and is asked to try to hold it in until the next waking. On the first night, the child is awakened each hour. On the second night, the child is awakened 3 hours after going to bed. If the child is dry for the remainder of that night, then the waking is moved back to $2^{1}/_{2}$ hours after bedtime. The waking time is moved back 30 minutes for each dry night until it reaches 1 hour after bedtime. If the child wets the bed two or more times in 1 week, then the schedule is restarted.
- Begin a positive practice procedure. Ask your child to lie in bed, count to 50, and then get up and go into the bathroom and try to urinate. This should be repeated 20 times in order both right after having a wet bed and again the next night at bedtime.
- Install the bell and pad. This should be started on the second night of the waking schedule.

- Introduce cleanliness training. If your child wets the bed and the alarm goes off after the first night, then have your child change out of his or her wet clothes and remove the wet sheets from the bed. Direct the child to get changed and make the bed. After each of 20 instances, this last step is repeated before the child can go back to sleep.

Research that has examined how dry bed training helps children who wet the bed suggests that dry bed training may improve the success over using the bell and pad alone[7]. The extra steps, such as positive practice and cleanliness training, may be helpful for some children who may not respond well to only being awakened after they wet the bed. There are, unfortunately, some negative aspects of dry bed training. One problem with this technique that is reported by some parents is that it can be difficult and unpleasant for both the parent and the child. Repeating the steps for cleanliness training—putting on and taking off bed clothes after an accident—can sometimes turn into middle-of-the-night struggles between parent and child. The other negative aspect is that relapse—or the recurrence of bedwetting some time after the program is completed—may be as high as it is for the bell and pad alone, which is about two of every five children. One variation of these techniques that has been used to reduce relapse in bedwetting is known as Full Spectrum Home Training.

### Full Spectrum Home Training

Full Spectrum Home Training (FSHT) includes two of the components of dry bed training: the bell and pad and cleanliness training. It adds two techniques to try to help the child stay dry once the program is completed. A "retention control training" procedure is taught to the child during the day in a manner similar to the positive practice part of dry bed training. The child is given a large amount of fluids and is asked to tell when he or she feels the need to urinate. The child is then asked to wait for 3 minutes before going to the bathroom in order to practice holding the urine. If the child is successful on the first day at 3 minutes, then the time is extended to 6 minutes on the second day. Each day, the time is increased by 3 more minutes unless the child has an accident. If that happens, then do not increase the time on the next day until the child is again successful at waiting before urinating. For each successful day, the child is given some reward to encourage his or her progress. This reward can be money or something else for which the child would be motivated to work. The general idea behind retention training is that you are helping your child gain the ability to hold urine for longer and longer periods of time in the hope that it will carry over to nighttime.

The final part of the FSHT package is an "overlearning" component. This part of the plan is specifically designed to help children with the problem of relapse and begins after the child has been dry for 14 consecutive nights. Following this 2-week success, the child is given fluids before bedtime in order to help strengthen the ability to stay dry overnight. On the first night of overlearning, the child is given 4 ounces of water to drink in the last 15 minutes before bedtime. If the child sleeps through the night with no accidents for two consecutive nights, then the amount of water is increased by 2 ounces. The amount of water that the child is given to drink before bedtime is increased this way (2 ounces for each two successful nights) until a maximum amount is reached. This maximum is calculated by taking the child's age in years and adding 2 ounces. A 7-year-old, for example, would have a maximum of 9 ounces, and a 10-year-old would stop at 12 ounces. If the child has an accident, then cut back on the fluids by 2 ounces until success again is achieved. When the child has reached the maximum and has had 14 consecutive dry nights, the overlearning portion of the plan is completed. Following is an overview of the steps involved in FSHT:

- Install the bell and pad and begin the procedure.
- Introduce cleanliness training. If your child wets the bed and the alarm goes off after the first night, then have your child change out of his or her wet clothes and remove the wet sheets from the bed. Direct the child to get dressed and make the bed. After each of 20 instances, this last step is repeated before the child can go back to sleep.
- Begin retention control training during the day. Give your child a large amount of fluids. When your child indicates that he or she has to urinate, ask him or her to hold it for 3 minutes. Give your child some tangible reward (e.g., money, some other prize) for holding urination after this time. Increase the time by 3 minutes each day until your child can hold his or her urination for 45 minutes, at which point training ends. If your child fails on one day, then do not increase the time on the next day.
- Include the overlearning component of training after 14 consecutive successful (dry) nights. Give your child 2 ounces of water in the 15 minutes before bedtime on the first night, and add 2 ounces for each two consecutive dry nights.
- If your child has an accident, then cut back on the water by 2 ounces.
- Stop adding more water when the maximum for your child is reached. The maximum number of ounces is determined by taking the child's age in years and adding 2 ounces.

- Overlearning ends when the child has had 14 consecutive dry nights while drinking the maximum fluids prior to bedtime.

One advantage of the FSHT program may be in its ability to reduce relapse among children. Research suggests that less than half of the children using this plan relapse as compared with those on the other plans discussed[8]. Again, however, it is important to remember that this plan, like dry bed training, requires a significant commitment by the family; and it can be several months before complete success is achieved.

## Medical Treatments for Bedwetting

Medical treatments have been used to help children who have difficulty with nighttime wetting. One group of these medications may surprise you—they are antidepressants, or the drugs typically used for people who experience severe bouts of depression. The success of antidepressants, such as the drug imipramine (also called Tofranil), is *not* a sign that these children are depressed. Instead, it is thought that the drug may relax muscles around the bladder, which should help it hold more fluid for a longer period of time. Also, another effect of this drug is that it suppresses REM sleep (as we saw in Chapter 9 when we discussed the REM sleep attacks of people with narcolepsy). This interruption of normal sleep also may help children with bladder control.

Drugs such as imipramine can be effective in initially reducing bedwetting, although their positive effects seem to disappear when the child stops taking the medication. Antidepressants are powerful medications (see Chapter 12 for more detail), and parents are cautioned to follow their doctor's advice closely if they decide to try a medical approach with their child.

A newer medical approach to treating bedwetting involves the use of the drug desmopressin acetate. This drug is an artificially produced form of the body's natural ADH that seems to be in short supply among many children who experience bedwetting problems. Desmopressin acetate is given to children in a nasal spray, and older children can learn to give themselves the medication when it is needed. This drug provides a substitute for natural ADH and helps the child's body make less urine, reducing the risk of nighttime accidents.

For both of these medical treatments for bedwetting, there is a concern about side-effects as well as problems with wetting returning after treatment is stopped. Sometimes parents prefer to use a combination of approaches such as a medication that stops the problem quickly along with the bell and pad or one of the other treatment packages that help the child stay dry at night once the medication is reduced and ultimately eliminated. This becomes an issue of personal preference that should be discussed frankly with your child's physician. Finally, some families turn to medication on a short-term basis to help a child who is going to an overnight camp or staying with a friend. The medication may allow the child to avoid embarrassing situations if the bedwetting problem is not yet under control.

## PROBLEMS WITH ANXIETY

Being anxious or depressed can have a direct impact on how one sleeps. It probably is not surprising to you that feeling tense can make it difficult to fall asleep. It also is true that feelings of anxiety or anxious thoughts can cause you to awaken in the middle of the night and disturb sleep in general. It is quite common for children to be anxious about everyday things in their lives. For example, many children are fearful of animals, strangers, or new situations. When it comes to sleep, fear of the dark or fear of monsters lurking in the closet or under the bed can interfere with a child's ability to fall asleep. Traumatic events also can trigger feelings of anxiety that can negatively affect a child's sleep. One such child recently came to my colleagues' and my attention.

Rickie's father called us in response to an ad in the local newspaper for children with sleep problems. Neither Rickie, who was 6 years old, nor anyone else in the family had ever had any significant sleep problems until about 18 months before. A year and a half before his father contacted us, the family was in a serious car accident. Their minivan was hit on the side by a drunk driver, and everyone in the family was hurt, although fortunately not seriously. After the accident, all of the children had trouble sleeping, including not wanting to go to bed and waking up crying. Two months or so passed, and all of the children seemed to be back to normal except for Rickie. He continued to have trouble almost every night. He would appear quite frightened about going to sleep and usually would wake up at some point and call out to his parents. At bedtime and upon waking, his parents would be in his room, spending a great deal of time talking about how there was nothing to be frightened about. It was suspected that these lengthy discussions may have helped contribute to Rickie's continued difficulties going to sleep and falling back to sleep after awakening.

Rickie's sleep problems seemed to be spilling over into his daytime behavior. His father told us that he was much more hesitant in social situations, such as playing with friends, and he cried when he had to ride in the car. Rickie's father described these changes as daytime nightmares—episodes in which he would scream and cry uncontrollably. He would go in the car only if he could sit next to his mother or father in the front seat.

Rickie's problems were most worrisome to his parents because they were so disruptive to the whole family. Rickie's parents were concerned because their other children seemed to have recovered so nicely from the accident, but Rickie had not.

We recommended that his parents teach Rickie relaxation exercises before bedtime to help him relax but also to help him keep his mind occupied and refocus his attention. Each night before sleep, his parents were instructed to have Rickie lie back on his bed and practice tensing and relaxing each of his major muscles in order. After about 15 minutes of practice, his parents would kiss him goodnight and tell him to feel his muscles tingle, which he would do until he fell asleep. The goal was for Rickie to be able to relax this way each night on his own; however, his parents enjoyed the positive routine each evening (especially because he was not getting upset anymore), so they stayed with him each night until he finished his exercises. From the very first night, Rickie stopped having trouble at bedtime. His parents were then instructed to tell him to practice his relaxation if he awoke at night. After about 1 month, Rickie was sleeping through the night on most nights and would go to bed without difficulty. His parents also encouraged Rickie to use his relaxation skills in social situations in which he felt tense and while riding in the car. This seemed to have a positive impact on his behavior during the day.

Rickie responded quite well and quite quickly to the relaxation exercises. They seemed to help him relax in situations in which he felt tense and also helped to refocus the discussions with his family to something more constructive and positive than just saying that there was nothing to be afraid of. Relaxation training is one of the most often recommended treatments for children and adults who are anxious. See Chapter 8 for some guidelines for trying out such a plan.

### Paradoxical Intention

Asking a person to do one thing but expecting him or her to do the opposite is a pop psychology concept that has been the brunt of numerous jokes. This "reverse psychology," or, more formally, *paradoxical intention,* however, does have a place when trying to help people sleep. Some children and adults become extremely concerned that they will not be able to sleep. Perhaps there is an important event coming up the next day that they feel will be ruined if they do not sleep well. These anxious thoughts can, by themselves, interfere with sleep, making them a self-fulfilling prophesy. In other words, it is as though these individuals make their fear of not sleeping come true just by worrying about it. For these individuals, using paradoxical intention sometimes can be useful. When using it for children, the parents and child should go through the usual bedtime routine, but the parents should tell the child that falling asleep is not that important. They want the child in bed, with the lights off, and with his or her eyes closed; however, they instruct the child that he or she should try to remain awake without opening his or her eyes or moving around too much. If a child is becoming anxious about not being able to sleep, then giving him or her permission to stay awake can help to relieve these fears and paradoxically help the child fall asleep.

## Other Helpful Hints for Children with Anxiety

Sometimes the solution to nighttime fears can be something as simple as providing a night light. This is helpful for children who may be frightened by the dark. In addition, sometimes "magic" is used to help children get control of their fears. The case of Quinn, for example (see Chapter 8), shows how the parents gave their child a "magic" sword that they said would slay any monsters that happened into his room. This power of suggestion can be very persuasive and can be used to a family's advantage to help a child feel more in control. Self-talk, which involves having the child repeat positive sayings, such as "I am a big girl and am not afraid," also can be helpful. Finally, providing children with some positive treat after a night without difficulty can be quite helpful. One girl who said that she was afraid at night got to spend some extra time with her father the next morning when there were no outbursts the night before. Try to match the type of assistance with your child's preference and age to give him or her several different ways to overcome these anxious feelings or thoughts.

## PROBLEMS WITH DEPRESSION

Depression—that feeling of sadness that all of us experience from time to time—can also negatively affect sleep. Some people who are depressed may awaken early in the morning and not be able to fall back asleep. Others may have the opposite problem: They cannot seem to get out of bed, and their lives are spent struggling to carry on even minimal daily activities. There is a "chicken and egg" problem when trying to understand how sleep and depression are related: Does poor sleep make you depressed, or does depression disrupt your sleep? For most people who have serious problems with depression, their condition obviously affects their sleep. Conversely, not sleeping well can make some people depressed in part because of their inability to control their own sleep and in part because they cannot function as well during the day. Although it is not yet fully understood *how* sleep and depression are related, it is essential that you recognize that they are related, at least among some people.

It also is important to point out that some of the classic signs of depression are behaviors that commonly are observed among otherwise healthy children and adolescents. In addition to changes in sleep patterns—which is normal during development—adolescents show other typical signs of depression, such as changes in eating habits and changes in their interest in activities. Observing just one of these signs in your child is not necessarily an indication that he or she is depressed. If your child shows several or all of these signs, however, then it is important to take them seriously.

Problems in school or with friends may be causing your child's difficulties. Some adolescents stay up late and sleep late to avoid school. Their "sleep problem" appears to be related to difficulties at school, a problem that was once known as *school phobia* but is now known by the more generic term *school refusal*. Unlike people with delayed sleep phase syndrome (see the case of Patrick in Chapter 7), whose sleep patterns are constant throughout their life, individuals engaging in school refusal usually begin to have sleep problems after problems in school develop. Unfortunately, it is very difficult to help these adolescents with their sleeping problems unless you simultaneously help them with their problems at school. Sometimes these students are depressed as a result of academic or social problems, and they learn to "sleep in" to temporarily avoid them. In fact, some of these students do not cooperate with attempts to change their sleep patterns because to do so would eliminate a way out of their difficulties during the day. If you suspect that your child is deliberately avoiding school by staying up late at night or cannot sleep because of problems with anxiety or depression, then it is imperative that you talk to your child about the problems and possibly seek outside professional help.

The close relationship between sleep and depression is most obvious when you notice that one treatment used for people with depression that is related to the seasons—known as the "winter blues," "cabin fever," or, more formally, *seasonal affective disorder*—also is a successful treatment for some sleep problems. The bright light therapy, discussed in Chapter 7, for people whose biological clocks are off schedule also has helped many people who get depressed mainly during the winter months, when there is less sunlight. If your child seems to have depression-related sleep problems, then using bright light therapy may prove helpful. Refer to Chapter 7 for a more detailed discussion and description of this procedure.

There are a number of different approaches for helping people who experience depression, but a comprehensive description of these techniques is beyond the scope of this book. Again, if you suspect that your child is depressed, then professional consultation is recommended.

## SLEEP-RELATED HEADACHES

Some people experience headaches when they wake up in the morning. Obviously, if this occurs on a regular basis, then these people are starting off each day in a negative mood that can set the tone for the rest of the day. There are at least three possible causes for early morning headaches—breathing difficulties, caffeine withdrawal, or sleep deprivation—each one of which can be helped fairly easily.

One cause of early morning headaches discussed previously is breathing difficulties at night. When sleep is interrupted either by difficulties breathing or, in the extreme, by stopping breathing altogether for a brief period of time (sleep apnea), the lack of oxygen during the night can cause early morning headaches. Refer to Chapter 9 for a detailed discussion of sleep-related breathing difficulties to determine whether your child's morning headaches are linked to this nighttime problem.

A common but frequently overlooked cause of early morning headaches is caffeine withdrawal. Withdrawal from any drug (the caffeine in coffee, tea, soft drinks, and other sources *is* a drug) is the body's reaction to no longer having the substance available. In a cruel twist, when the brain detects a lack of the drug that it was used to having, it sends out messages that result in unpleasant feelings—including headaches. Because caffeine leaves the system in a matter of hours, going all night without having any can trigger early morning withdrawal symptoms, usually in the form of headaches. It is more than just a little ironic that the headache medicine that you might take (e.g., aspirin) works better when it is taken with caffeine. Makers of Excedrin, for example, can claim that Excedrin works better than other headache medications simply because they include a hefty dose of caffeine with the aspirin. The only true cure for caffeine-related headaches is to wean the person off of caffeine over a period of weeks.

Sleep deprivation also can cause a person to have headaches in the morning. Not getting enough sleep restricts NREM, or nondream, sleep and increases the proportion of REM sleep. Because your brain needs REM sleep so much, it "catches up" on this type of sleep at the expense of NREM sleep when you go without sleep for a time. During REM sleep, the vessels in the brain tend to dilate (i.e., become larger), which can cause morning headaches. When you do not get enough sleep, therefore, your brain's need to recover REM sleep can cause you to have headaches in the morning. The treatment here is obvious—get more sleep. Even napping during the day, if there are pressures for your evening time, can help to eliminate sleep deprivation–related headaches.

If none of these causes of headaches seems to fit your child's case, then a medical exam may help rule out other possible causes of early morning headaches. As described next, for example, tooth grinding during sleep may be a cause of headaches, and a medical consultation may prove helpful in identifying these sources of your child's pain.

## NIGHTTIME TOOTH GRINDING

Nighttime tooth grinding, which has the formal name *sleep-related bruxism*, includes all forms of teeth clenching and grinding that occur during sleep. This does not seem to be a serious sleep concern on its own; however, the dental consequences (grinding down of the teeth) can become serious in people who frequently grind their teeth. In addition, people who grind their teeth are more likely to have jaw pain and headaches than those who do not grind their teeth. Research on adults suggests that tooth grinding can be related to daytime stress, such that having a high-stress day can lead to nighttime tooth grinding[9]. Why doesn't everyone who is stressed grind his or her teeth? It may be that people who have minor misaligned or unbalanced teeth (called *malocclusions*) are at more risk for tooth grinding and that when these people are stressed during the day, this combination of dental and psychological factors causes tooth grinding.

One group of children with special needs who are particularly susceptible to tooth grinding are those with Rett syndrome. This is a serious neurological disorder that is found almost exclusively in girls and often includes mental retardation, serious motor impairments, epileptic seizures, and difficulties with communication. This syndrome usually becomes noticeable during their second year of life and is estimated to occur in 1 of every 10,000 female births worldwide. Tooth grinding appears as a common symptom of Rett syndrome.

A number of different approaches have been suggested to help children who have serious and long-standing problems with tooth grinding, although there is no cure for this problem. The most successful treatment of tooth grinding to date, however, involves the use of dental splints. Made in consultation with a dentist, acrylic splints are constructed to fit your child's back teeth. Many children who sleep with these splints have been successful in reducing their nighttime tooth grinding. In addition, it is important to look for sources of stress for your child that may be making this problem worse, and use the relaxation exercises described in Chapter 8 to address these difficulties.

## CONCLUSION

This chapter described a variety of problems that occur at night or around sleep. Just as was found with the sleep problems of children, knowing the cause of such problems as nighttime headaches, anxiety, and depression can give hints about how to help children who experience these problems. Fortunately, the causes of these nighttime difficulties rapidly are becoming known to sleep professionals, and more effective treatments are being developed each year.

# 11

# Daytime Behavior Problems

You may be asking yourself why a chapter on daytime behavior problems is included in a book about sleep. A child who is noncompliant or who is aggressive may not have any sleep problems at all, and daytime difficulties may not be related to what happens at night. For some people, however, not sleeping well can contribute to daytime problems. Research that my colleagues and I have conducted with children having special needs demonstrates that *for people who already have behavior problems during the day,* sleep problems can make these behaviors worse[1]. The irritability that you or I may experience when our sleep is disrupted can reveal itself among people with special needs as hitting other people, refusing to follow requests, or, in extreme cases, even self-injurious behaviors such as face slapping or hand biting. It seems that poor sleep patterns do not cause daytime behavior problems, but it is clear that disrupted sleep can make these problems worse.

In addition to the possible relationship between poor sleep and daytime problems, sleep professionals often find that some "sleep problems" resemble problems that parents experience with their children at times other than at bedtime or in the middle of the night. The tantrums that children display at night may differ only in timing from tantrums that occur in other situations. For example, the tantrum that follows a request to go to bed may be no more a problem with sleep than the tantrum that occurs in school following a request to do work or the tantrum that occurs at mealtime at home. Because these difficulties actually may represent very similar problems, a good number of parents need help with their child's behavior problems both at night and during the day.

It is the possible connection between sleep and behavior problems, along with the all too common observation that children who have tantrums at night may also present challenges during other times, that prompted inclusion of this chapter. First is a brief overview focusing on *why* children might have behavior problems such as tantrums, and then are some suggestions for parents to help reduce the behavior problems of their children. Obviously, a comprehensive discussion of these issues cannot be presented in one short chapter; however, this chapter should help you get started on the road to improved behavior. A number of very good books have been written that cover the topic more thoroughly (see the Additional Readings section at the end of this book).

## WHY DO CHILDREN HAVE BEHAVIOR PROBLEMS?

The key to helping a child to stop misbehaving lies in understanding what is motivating the child at that point in time. Although there are many theories about how past events such as traumas, relationships with parents, or even problems at birth can contribute to a child's behavior problems, we often are powerless to change any of these. In other words, a past trauma may be one reason that a child has a tantrum at a relative's house or in the car, but because we are not able to wipe away the past, we must look to the present for a practical solution to the problem. As a result, we often focus on the "here and now" to determine why a boy, for example, is screaming in a supermarket or why a little girl is crying when she is asked to get dressed in the morning. I am *not* saying that past events are unimportant, only that many are difficult to identify and that most are impossible to remedy.

### Rule Out Medical Problems

As with sleep problems, physical causes for behavior problems must be ruled out. Although it is relatively rare for some medical problem to be the cause of your child's being upset, overlooking this possibility can lead you to many frustrating situations that could have been avoided. It is important to point out that, like poor sleep, medical problems can make behavior problems worse, but they usually are not the sole cause of a child's difficulties. This means that even if you find a medical problem and can cure this illness, it may not lead to the complete elimination of the behavior that is so disruptive.

What should you look for? Any illness that causes pain, for example, can be at the bottom of an increase in problems. An ear infection, a headache, or a stomachache will make your child more irritable, which in turn will make him or her more likely to have behavior problems. Children with special needs often are more prone to physical problems; therefore, we to need to be more vigilant in finding a possible medical condition contributing to misbehavior. A child in a wheelchair, for example, who cannot shift position can be extremely uncomfortable after only a few minutes, and this can cause fussiness and anger outbursts. Simply shifting the child's physical position periodically may help reduce behavior problems. In general, children who are not verbal or who do not express themselves well often cannot tell you when they are in pain, so a complete physical exam may be in order, especially if a child has a sudden increase in behavior problems. At the same time that you are having your child evaluated for a possible medical problem, you can follow the steps described in this chapter. Too many people wait for months to find the definitive medical diagnosis for their child only to find out that there is nothing that they can do about it anyway. The steps described in this chapter can be followed at the same time that you are looking for or treating a medical problem and can begin to help your child within a few weeks.

## Impulsivity

Although not technically a medical problem, some children are very impulsive by nature; this can lead to a number of difficulties. Children with attention-deficit/hyperactivity disorder (ADHD), for example, sometimes blurt out the first thing that comes to mind, stop playing a game in the middle to move on to something else, or do not finish cleaning their room because they are distracted by some other interesting activity. These types of behaviors can frustrate teachers, friends, and family members and can have some rather negative long-term consequences. Teachers may give these children only negative feedback ("Would you sit down!"), which eventually can make the child feel quite bad about him- or herself. Friends may reject such a child, and this can stunt the development of good social skills. Family members also can begin to see the child as only a bother and may feel too drained at the end of the day to give the child much "quality time." It is important to remember that these types of behaviors by the child are not intentional acts aimed at annoying people, but rather they are the result of the child's difficulty in reining in his or her impulses. We discuss later how you can help such a child get more control over these impulses.

## Attention Difficulties

One area that parents often have trouble understanding is the limit of their child's attention span. What some parents consider noncompliance sometimes can be simply a difficulty on the part of the child to remember what he or she was supposed to do. For example, asking a young child in the middle of a television program to clean his room at the next commercial is an invitation to disaster. By the time the commercial rolls around, the parent's request is "out of mind," and the fact that the child did not clean his room probably is just a difficulty in remembering rather than deliberate noncompliance. If the parent waited for the commercial to make the request ("While the commercial is on, I want you to go into your room and put your dirty clothes in the hamper"), then the child is much more likely to cooperate. Again, young children are just learning how to remember things after being distracted, and some older children with special needs also may be having trouble with this skill. Determine whether this is the cause of your child's "behavior problem," and, if so, then try to make requests 1) that are clear ("Put your shoes in your closet" versus "Clean up this mess") and 2) that can be completed immediately ("Put your dishes in the sink" versus "Put your books away when you come home from school").

## WHAT IS YOUR CHILD TRYING TO TELL YOU?

In addition to impulsivity and attention difficulties, behavior problems sometimes can serve a purpose for a child. One way to view behavior problems such as tantrums, aggression, or noncompliance is as a way for children to communicate their wants and needs. For example, crying often is the only way that infants can let us know what they want. They cry when they are hungry, when they are cold or wet, and even when they just want you near them. In fact, some parents are experts at reading the messages in their child's cries. At the same time, older children may use screaming in a store or hitting another child to communicate things that they cannot get any other way. Some exciting research in the field of behavior problems suggests that many of these difficulties can be viewed as a form of communication and that we can reduce behavior problems in children by teaching them better ways to communicate with us[2].

My colleagues' and my research[3] and that of others[4] who work with people who have special needs point to several common "messages" that children seem to communicate through their behavior problems (see Figure 11.1). Understanding what a child is communicating with his or her behavior problem is at the heart of any treatment plan designed to help a child with this difficulty.

*Attention* from others is a common desire of many children. For most children, talking to a parent or friend, getting hugs, or even just being near others is something that they work hard to achieve.

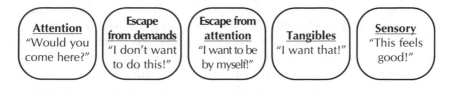

**Figure 11.1.**　Common messages of children's behavior problems.

Although some children quickly learn the ability to get attention from others in positive ways, others take a different route and use their behavior problems. Through screaming or other behavior problems, some children are very successful in focusing attention on themselves. For example, I was once walking down the hall in a school to consult in a classroom and was a little lost until one clue helped me not only to quickly pick out which classroom I needed to go in but also to know that the behavior problem of the child in question was attention getting. In one class there was a teacher yelling at the top of her lungs at a child who was misbehaving. The yelling directed me to where the classroom was, and the fact that the teacher was yelling made me believe that the child was being very successful in getting that teacher's attention. This is an important example because it should remind us that some children would prefer even something that seems unpleasant—like yelling—over being ignored.

A good portion of the "terrible twos" may be explained as attention-getting behavior. I remember a scenario when my son was almost 2, and he was being quite fussy. I asked him what he wanted and he told me, "Milk." After getting him a glass of milk, he did not look satisfied and said, "No want milk, want water!" A glass of water still did not satisfy him, and he said, "No, want milk!" Milk, water, which was it? After going through this several times, it dawned on me that he probably did not want something to drink at all but instead just wanted to spend some time with me. He did not know how to initiate and carry on a sophisticated conversation, so he used his demanding requests to engage me. I was able to avoid tantrums during future episodes by remembering what was really motivating him and using that as a cue to spend some time with him.

A second message that is seen quite frequently among children is *escape from demands*. In other words, some children misbehave to get out of doing things that they do not like. For example, one child with autism with whom I worked was hitting his teacher, and she asked for some advice on how to make him stop. During one class, I watched as his teacher asked him to point to a certain picture. Instead of pointing to it, he hit her in the face. Her response was to very calmly ask him to stand up and sit alone in the corner. In her mind, she thought that she was punishing him for hitting her, and, in fact, she felt guilty about using this "time out" program. As we later found out, however, being allowed to stop working and instead sit away from his desk was exactly what he wanted! He learned that the way to get out of doing any schoolwork was to hit his teacher.

Sometimes children act up to get out of doing things that are too difficult for them. Other times, a child may misbehave to escape the boredom of doing things that are too monotonous and mundane. Whatever the reason for wanting to escape, it is important to look for escape from demands as a message and to use that to help the child with this problem.

A different child may act out to *escape from attention* rather than (or in addition to) escape from demands. In other words, the message may not be "I don't want to do that" but instead may be "I want to be alone." Often, children with autism will hit themselves or others to be left alone. Although it is not fully understood what makes other people sometimes unpleasant to be around for these children, it is critical to know that their behavior problems are occurring for this reason. Some children without autism also will misbehave to avoid being around people whom they do not like. Knowing whether a child is acting up to get attention or to avoid attention is important for our efforts to help these children be better behaved.

Sometimes the goal of a child's misbehavior is to get some "thing." Behavior problems that occur to get things, or *tangibles,* are quite common and can be seen on almost a daily basis in any supermarket or toy store. A child's crying and flailing about on the floor in the candy aisle after being told that she cannot have a Snickers bar is an example of a tangibly motivated behavior problem. In addition to toys or foods, the "thing" that a child may want could be an activity. For example, being told that he cannot go outside because it is raining can cause a boy to become aggressive because he is being denied this favorite activity. Why do children continue to act this way? Because, like the other messages just mentioned, sometimes they work! If a child cries enough in a supermarket, then the parent is likely to give in and get the child what he or she wants. This giving in obviously will increase the chance that the child will cry again the next time he or she really wants something. The next section covers how to avoid these situations with your child.

The final message is a more private one than the messages just covered. The goal is *sensory* feedback—the child acts in a particular way because it looks, feels, tastes, or sounds good to him or her. In other words, the behavior itself is pleasant in some way to the child, and he or she keeps doing it because of the way it feels. A child who rocks back and forth for hours at a time may be doing this just because it feels good and not because of attention, escape, or tangibles. Children with severe disabilities will hit themselves lightly but constantly because of the sensory feedback that it provides them. Knowing that a behavior is occurring for sensory reasons is important because it tells us that simply ignoring it will not work. In fact, being ignored and not having anything else to occupy them can be at the heart of why children act in ways to keep themselves stimulated. Other behavior plans such as time out (e.g., removing the child to a corner of the classroom) also will be ineffective because the child is not behaving this way to get attention but rather just because of the way it feels.

## HOW DO YOU KNOW WHAT YOUR CHILD IS TRYING TO TELL YOU?

The obvious next question is, "Now that I know about these messages, how do I find out what my child is trying to tell me with his or her behavior?" Sometimes understanding the message of a behavior problem is simple and obvious. For example, a child who screams each time a certain request is made (e.g., "Say your name") but very rarely at other times may be screaming to escape from demands. Conversely, often the message is obscured, and it is difficult to figure out just what is setting off a problem. Parents should keep a record of each time the behavior occurs, what was happening at the time when it occurred (called the *antecedent*), and how they responded to it (called the *consequence*). For example, if your child hits you while you are on the phone and you say, "Stop that," and explain why it is wrong to hit, then you would write down

Antecedent:      I was on the telephone
Behavior:        Hitting
Consequence:    Told her to "stop that" and explained why hitting is
                wrong

From looking at just this one interaction, can you guess what might be motivating this girl's aggression? If the mother was on the phone and not paying attention to her daughter, then the daughter may be trying to get attention by hitting. Also, if the mother usually responds to this hitting by spending even a little bit of time with her, then the behavior is successful and the girl probably will hit again when she wants her mother's attention. When you observe these types of patterns, you can begin to make good educated guesses about what may be motivating your child's difficulty.

There are other, more formal ways of assessing the message behind behavior problems, and these usually are used by professionals in
psychology, education, or special education, although parents also
have found them to be valuable at times. One assessment technique,
called a *functional analysis,* uses the basic observation task just described, but observations of the child are in situations that are pur-
posely set up or staged. For example, if you thought that your child
was screaming to escape demands, then you might give your child an
easy task for 5 minutes, followed by a more difficult task for 5 minutes,
and then compare how often your child misbehaved in each situation.
You would have to repeat this several times in different orders to make
sure that it was the type of task and not something else that was causing differences in your child's behavior. If you thought that tangibles
were involved, then you could compare your child's behavior both
with and without his or her favorite toy. You basically test out each of
your guesses until you find something that regularly results in your
child's misbehavior.

Because of the time and disruption involved in using a functional
analysis to determine these messages, my colleagues and I developed
an alternative to help better understand behavior problems. Called the
Motivation Assessment Scale[*], this questionnaire can be used to make
more informed guesses about what might be causing a child's disruptive behavior. It is filled out by a parent for behavior problems at home
or by a teacher for school difficulties, and it provides information
about what might be motivating the problem.

## THE SEVEN "C'S" FOR CHANGING BEHAVIOR

Once you have an idea about *why* your child may be misbehaving,
there are several different steps that you can take to help reduce the
frequency of these problems. The following "seven C's" should go a
long way toward improving many behavior problems; however, more
severe problems or problems that do not improve over several months
probably should receive the attention of a professional.

### Calm Yourself

Calming yourself is most important! If you are upset, then you cannot
be an effective parent. In fact, it probably would be better not to do

---

[*]Information about the Motivation Assessment Scale can be obtained
from Monaco & Associates, Inc., 4125 Gage Center Drive, Suite 204, Topeka,
KS 66604; 913-272-5501 or 800-798-1309.

anything while you are angry than to try to work on your child's behavior problem. The mother of one of the children with whom I once worked told me how she used a time-out program on herself whenever she was getting upset. She would grab a glass of wine and close herself in the bathroom for 30 minutes until she was composed and could face the problems again. She told me that this happened only about once per week but that it really helped her not to act rashly or lash out at her child. In addition to your own version of a time out, you can use the relaxation exercises described in Chapter 8 on yourself to help you calm down when you feel yourself getting upset. Finally, if you cannot do it alone, then the support of family, friends, or other parents in similar situations can be very helpful, and you should reach out in some way when you feel out of control.

### Communication

We saw that research is uncovering the messages behind many of the behavior problems that children display. Research that my colleagues and I have worked on since the mid 1980s points to the ability to reduce even some of the most severe behavior problems by teaching a very specific form of communication[5]. What we do is find the message being communicated by the behavior problem (e.g., "I don't want to do this!") and then teach the child a better way to communicate this message—a technique referred to as Functional Communication Training. For example, if a child is screaming because his schoolwork is too difficult, then we would teach him to say, "Help me," to his teacher, who in turn would give him more assistance on the task. If another child is screaming but this child's message is, "Would you come here?" then we teach a better way to get someone's attention. It is important to point out that improving communication skills in general does not by itself lead to fewer behavior problems. It must involve teaching a better way to communicate the message being sent by the child's misbehavior. (More detail about Functional Communication Training is available in the Additional Readings section at the end of this book.)

### Choices

Giving a child a choice in important situations sometimes can be a miracle cure for behavior problems. For example, when my son was younger, he hated taking a bath. We found that when we told him, "It's time to take a bath," he would resist and find a hundred excuses to delay or avoid it. However, when we gave him the choice, "Do you want to take your bath with your He-Men or your Ninja Turtles?" he would pick one set and go off to get them to put in the bathtub. Giving him some control over the situation seemed to make taking a bath more acceptable to him, and we found much less resistance.

The example of my son's problems at bathtime is a good one because it points out how we can give children choices even in situations in which there does not seem to be room for a choice. He still had to take a bath every day, but at least he could pick the toys that he would play with. One child with whom I worked who would refuse to go on the school bus was in a similar predicament. She had to go to school and get on the bus, but we still could provide her with some options. Each day as she was getting ready for school, her mother would ask her, "Do you want to carry your blue bag or your black bag on the bus?" After the girl picked one of the bags and the bus arrived, her mother would ask, "Do you want to sit in the front or the back?" and would lead her on the bus. Giving her these choices, along with other forms of encouragement, helped to eliminate any resistance to boarding the school bus. Try to find ways to provide choices to your child, even in these seemingly non-choice situations.

### Change Preparation

Young children especially will respond better to requests when they are told what is coming next. It seems that the more stressed and harried we are, the less time we have to prepare our children for the things that they have to do. This lack of warning, even for a few seconds, can cause some children to refuse even relatively simple requests. Mealtime is a good example. Telling a child, "You have 5 more minutes and then it's time for dinner," can help the transition from playing or television watching to the family meal. In fact, sometimes children give parents a hard time about doing something that they *like* when they are rushed and not forewarned. This suggestion takes some practice. You need to plan ahead to try to avoid problems, and it takes some getting used to if you do not already do this. But for many children, a prewarning about a request can mean the difference between a smooth transition and a battle of minds and bodies!

### Consequences

There are two important issues to deal with when it comes to how you respond to your child, or the "consequences." One concern is how to react to a behavior problem at the time when it is occurring. The second concern is how to react when your child is being good. We often spend a great deal of time thinking about how to respond to the behavior problem and much less time on those good times and how to make them more frequent. The bottom line to these issues is obvious: We want to react to behavior problems in ways that make them less likely to occur again, and we also want to respond to the child who is being good in ways that makes these times more frequent. Consequences for good behavior are covered in the next section.

Understanding the message or messages that your child is trying to communicate with his or her behavior problem should help you with the consequences. For example, if a child is misbehaving to escape brushing his teeth, then a parent should make an effort to be sure that the child does not completely succeed. This does not mean wrestling the child to the ground, clamping open his mouth, and forcing him to brush! Instead, it would involve being sure that the child spends at least a few seconds brushing his teeth before you stop making the request. You can always work on increasing the amount of time brushing later, but the child must learn that he or she cannot completely escape when he or she resists. As you can see, knowing that the cries or tantrums are aimed at avoiding tooth brushing would stop you from doing something that might actually cause more trouble, such as sending him to his room—which would let the child escape. In other words, if you know what your child is communicating with his or her behavior problem, then you want to make sure that he or she is not successful at it. Your response should make it clear that behavior problems will not get you what you want.

It is quite common for children not to seem to mind some punishment that their parents may give them. This is one reason that strong punishment for behavior problems rarely, if ever, is recommended. Viewing misbehavior as communication may help explain why some children do not seem to mind being punished. In the example just described of the boy who was screaming and crying when asked to brush his teeth, his parent thought that yelling at him and sending him to his room was a pretty severe punishment. Yet, as you can now see, in this boy's eyes, this was probably the *best* thing that the parent could have done, letting the child get out of brushing his teeth. The punishment came when they instead made him brush his teeth, even if only for a few seconds. It is important to remember that what is a punishment to you may be a reward to the child. Again, understanding the message tells you what your child may like and dislike and how to respond to misbehavior.

## Constructive Feedback

How you respond to good behavior could be viewed as constructive feedback. Constructive feedback implies that not only are you encouraging good things, but also you are providing guidance for growth. Sometimes this takes the form of simple praise: "You really did a nice job on your homework!" More often when a child has a more severe behavior problem, this feedback is provided more formally. "Star charts," for example, are charts designed to give visual feedback to a child for times of good behavior. These charts frequently find a home on the refrigerator, and parents can give paste-on stars each day or activity for good behavior. Older children sometimes can benefit from a more formal "contract," whereby both parent and child sit down and write out expectations of each other.

You may need to keep your expectations modest at first. Do not expect that any plan will produce miraculous changes. Instead, set your sites on modest goals. For example, having a child who is extremely impulsive sit for even 2 minutes might be a good goal to encourage in a child. Rewarding a child for these small steps can help the child feel that change is possible and can motivate the child to strive for more.

### Consider the Next Time

Can you anticipate future problem situations and change things to prevent a problem the next time? For example, sometimes children misbehave to escape task demands. Although we can teach them how to communicate for help or for a break, we also can examine what we are asking them to do and determine whether it can be improved. Breaking down a task into smaller steps often can prevent escape-motivated behavior problems. Thinking ahead and redesigning home or school situations (e.g., getting the next day's clothes picked out to avoid the next day's rush) often can eliminate problems before they occur.

### CONCLUSION

Following these simple steps will be helpful to the majority of families who are having trouble with their child's behavior. In more difficult situations, however, outside help and assistance may be useful. Some of the techniques we described, such as finding out the message for your child's behavior and teaching alternative ways to communicate, can take considerable skill in more complicated cases. Your school or local college or university may be good places to turn for advice. Be patient and be optimistic. A great deal of information about behavior problems and their treatment has been learned since the mid-1980s, and valuable help is available.

# 12

## Sleep and Medications

Using medication probably is the first thing that people think of when it comes to sleep problems. Your local drug store has shelves of over-the-counter medicines that are marketed to help people sleep, and about 21 million orders are written each year in the United States for prescription sleeping pills[1]. Why, then, do I not spend more time in this book on these medications? The simple answer is this: Medication is not recommended as a long-term solution for the majority of sleep problems. According to most sleep professionals, medication usually is recommended only as a short-term answer to a sleep problem—usually for no more than a few weeks. Instead, the other, nonmedical, suggestions made throughout this book are what even the medical profession prefers for people who have troubled sleep. Despite the preference for nonmedical help, however, there are times when medication is suggested. This chapter describes the most common sleep medications and the issues surrounding their use.

What causes the wariness about medical treatments? One concern is *dependence*—the possibility of becoming addicted to sleep medication. Addiction to sleeping pills can happen in several different ways. People can become *tolerant* of, or used to, the sleep medication, needing more and more of it over time to be able to fall asleep. As we will see, some of the older sleep medications (called barbiturates) were more likely to cause dependence than more recently developed drugs. Another problem with some medications is *insomnia rebound*: The sleep problems do not just come back after the person stops taking the medication; they come back *worse* than before. The person tries to stop taking his or her medication, but the sleep problems return in a more severe form, so the reaction is to go back to taking medication. This vicious cycle can be extremely difficult to break once it has begun.

In addition to fears that people will become addicted to these medications and have a difficult time getting away from their use, there are concerns that the sleep problems will not be "cured" even after a period of time on medication. For the most part, the effects of sleep medication last only as long as you take it; there tends to be no lasting benefit once its use is discontinued.

There also are specific concerns with the use of sleep medications for children with special needs. What is important to note is that many, if not most, of the sleep medications tend to reduce the amount of REM, or dream, sleep. This is of particular concern for children with cognitive disabilities, such as those with mental retardation. We know that a lack of REM sleep can itself cause cognitive impairments. This means that people who already may have difficulty with skills such as learning and remembering may develop further impairment because of the use of these medications. You can see that a decision to use medication for problems surrounding sleep is not a simple one and that a number of risks come with its use.

Described next are the different classes of medications used for problems surrounding sleep (see Table 12.1 for a summary). It is important for you to be informed about the current thinking surrounding these drugs to help you judge whether they should be used with your child.

## BARBITURATES

During the early 1900s, a group of drugs—called *barbiturates*—were created to help people fall asleep. This family of drugs includes Seconal, Amytal, and Nembutal. Their discovery was important because, at the time, people regularly used alcohol and other drugs, such as opium, to help with difficulties falling asleep. By the 1930s, the barbiturates were widely prescribed by physicians; unfortunately, by the 1950s, they were among the drugs most abused by adults in the United States. Because of the strong addictive properties of this group of drugs, they no longer are regularly recommended for sleep problems. Barbiturates occasionally are recommended in cases in which other drugs are not effective and in which their use can be monitored closely.

**Table 12.1.**   Common sleep medications

| Medication[a] | Use |
|---|---|
| Barbiturates<br>　Secobarbital (Seconal)<br>　Amobarbital (Amytal)<br>　Pentobarbital (Nembutal) | An older class of "sleeping pills" that are highly addictive and that have the potential for severe harm if mixed with other medications. No longer generally recommended for sleep problems. |
| Benzodiazepines<br>　Triazolam (Halcion)<br>　Remazepam (Restoril)<br>　Estazolam (ProSom)<br>　Quazepam (Doral)<br>　Flurazepam (Dalmane) | A family of medications used to induce sleep that replaced the use of barbiturates. They tend to have fewer side effects and less potential for addiction than barbiturates. |
| Antihistamines<br>　Benadryl<br>　Over-the-counter "sleeping pills" (e.g., Sominex, Unisom, Sleep-Eze) | A class of drugs that have the effect of causing drowsiness. These drugs have been used to induce sleep, although their effectiveness is questionable. |
| Other sleep-inducing medications<br>　Chloral hydrate | A drug that helps induce sleep. No longer generally recommended because of the potential for harm if mixed with other drugs. |
| 　Zolpidem tartrate (Ambien) | A new class of "sleeping pill" that has fewer side effects compared with benzodiazepines. |
| 　Melatonin | A natural brain hormone that can help people fall asleep and may help to reset the body's biological clock. |
| Antidepressants<br>　Imipramine (Tofranil) | Used to induce sleep, especially in people who are depressed. These drugs reduce attacks of REM sleep that cause paralysis (cataplexy) in people with narcolepsy and sometimes are given to people with breathing-related sleep problems. Also used for children with enuresis (bedwetting) to help bladder control and as a substitute for stimulants for children with ADHD. |
| Stimulants<br>　Methylphenidate (Ritalin)<br>　Pemoline sodium (Cylert) | Used for people with problems of excessive sleepiness. |
| Other sleep-related medications<br>　Levodopa and carbidopa (Sinemet) | An anti-parkinsonism drug that is used to help reduce the jerky limb movements in people with periodic limb movements and for people with restless legs syndrome. |
| 　Desmopressin acetate | An artificial form of the body's natural antidiuretic hormone (ADH) that is used for children with bedwetting problems. |

[a]The drug's brand name is provided in parentheses.

## BENZODIAZEPINES

Since the 1960s, a second group of drugs—called *benzodiazepines*—have been used in place of barbiturates as the drug of choice for people who have trouble falling asleep. These drugs have a number of effects on people in addition to helping them fall asleep, including acting as a tranquilizer to calm people who are tense or anxious and acting as a muscle relaxant. You probably will recognize right away the common name of at least one of the benzodiazepines—Valium—which is used to help calm people who are feeling tense. Valium is not recommended as a sleep medication, and currently only five of the benzodiazepines are approved by the Food and Drug Administration (FDA) for use with people with insomnia—Halcion, Restoril, ProSom, Doral, and Dalmane.

Although safer and less likely to have significant side effects than barbiturates, benzodiazepines, when used improperly, can have serious consequences. When used for long periods of time (e.g., several months), benzodiazepines can be addictive. In addition, they can cause rebound insomnia; and, when taken in combination with alcohol, benzodiazepines can lead to death. Taking too much of this drug also can impair a person's memory, again a particular concern for people with special needs. Finally, benzodiazepines tend to produce "lighter" sleep, which, unlike our natural sleep rhythms, paradoxically may cause more night waking and may have as-yet-unknown negative effects when used on a long-term or chronic basis.

Benzodiazepines usually are categorized into two different groups: those that last longer in the body (long acting) and those that relatively quickly stop having an effect (short acting). Long-acting sleeping pills can cause people to feel "drugged" or "hung over" the next day because the medication is still having its sedative effect even after you want to wake up. The short-acting drugs tend to stop working at about the time or before you are ready to be awake. The down side to these short-acting drugs is that some people may experience interrupted sleep or early morning waking because the medication no longer is having an effect. One of the decisions that needs to be made when choosing a sleeping pill is whether sleeping through the night and/or waking too early are the problems and therefore a long-acting drug is necessary or whether initiating sleep and feeling refreshed the next day are the main concerns and therefore a short-acting drug is needed. The following sections highlight the five FDA-approved benzodiazepines, both long-acting and short-acting, for insomnia.

## Halcion

The benzodiazepine that stays the shortest amount of time in the body is Halcion (also called triazolam). You may recognize this drug from the negative publicity that it received in the early 1990s when charges that its use led to suicidal thoughts made headlines. Today, it generally is believed to be safe when used at its proper (lower) dosage and when it is taken for only short periods of time (several weeks to months). Because Halcion remains effective for only a few hours, it typically is recommended for people whose only sleep problem is initiating sleep.

## Restoril

Restoril (temazepam) is a long-acting benzodiazepine that takes a little more time to begin working than some of the other drugs. As a result, it usually is recommended that it be taken 30 minutes before you want to fall asleep and is therefore not useful for people who need a middle-of-the-night sleeping pill. Restoril's ability to work for a longer period of time makes it one of the medications given to people who have trouble staying asleep throughout the night.

## ProSom

ProSom (estazolam) can stay in the body for as long as 24 hours, so it can cause drowsiness in some people into the next day. Like Restoril, ProSom is used for people who have trouble remaining asleep throughout the night.

## Doral

An addition to the long-acting benzodiazepines is Doral (quazepam), which also is prescribed for people with night-waking problems. Because its effects last well into the next day, it often is recommended for people who have daytime anxiety as well as nighttime sleep problems.

## Dalmane

The longest acting of the benzodiazepines is Dalmane (flurazepam), which, like Doral, often is recommended for people who need its effects into the next day. Some individuals may experience depression, irritability, or temper problems with its use.

## ANTIHISTAMINES

If you have ever taken a cold medicine that included an antihistamine, then you know that this drug can make you drowsy. This is why

Benadryl, which is primarily an allergy medication with an antihistamine, often is recommended for children who cannot fall asleep at night. Antihistamines also are the main ingredients in the over-the-counter drugs such as Sominex, Unisom, and Sleep-Eze. These drugs generally are not recommended for use as a sleep aid. Some professionals question whether they are effective in making people fall asleep, and most agree that the side effects, such as daytime grogginess, may be worse than the prescription medications. Like the other sleep medications, these drugs lose their effectiveness when used over a long period of time.

## OTHER SLEEP-INDUCING MEDICATIONS

In addition to barbiturates, benzodiazepines, and antihistamines, other medications have been used to help induce sleep in people with insomnia. Chloral hydrate sometimes is used to help people who have difficulty initiating sleep; however, the benefits of this drug must be weighed against the risk of serious harm that can result when people mix this drug with others. For example, the "Mickey Finn cocktail," which is celebrated in movies as a knockout drink, is a combination of chloral hydrate and alcohol. Typically, chloral hydrate is used only in medically supervised settings.

### Ambien

Although it does not belong to the family of benzodiazepines, Ambien (also known as zolpidem tartrate) bears some resemblance to benzodiazepines in its effect on sleep. Like Halcion, it is a short-acting drug that leaves the body within a few hours of its ingestion. This makes it useful for people who just need help falling asleep but do not have night-waking problems and do not want the groggy feeling the next day. Initial research on this newly developed drug suggests that it may not decrease the deep sleep that is affected by other medications and that addiction to this drug may be less likely[2].

### Melatonin

Unquestionably, one of the biggest medical fads of the mid-1990s is the use of the hormone melatonin. As described previously in this book (see Chapters 1 and 7), melatonin is a natural brain hormone that appears to be related to the resetting of our biological clock. Following the discovery that melatonin may play a role in our sleep, research[3] was conducted to determine whether and how its use might affect the sleep of people who were experiencing problems. Initial positive findings brought with them a wave of unwarranted optimism about melatonin's potential not only as a cure for sleep problems but also as the answer for everything from sexual disorders to longer life. Many parents of children with autism were intrigued by the link between melatonin and its chemical relative serotonin (which often has been implicated in autism) and the potential of melatonin to help their children with sleep as well as with other difficulties that their children experienced. Now that the media excitement has subsided, what do we know about melatonin and sleep problems?

Melatonin has two apparent effects on sleep. For some people, it seems to act as a soporific, or a drug that makes you tired. In addition, it seems to reset the biological clock and help people who sleep at the wrong times. This ability to reset the brain's clock is especially important for people who are blind and who do not get light cues from the sun. One of the attractions of melatonin over the other sleep medications is that it is a natural substance that is already present in the brain. In addition, studies to date[4] indicate few, if any, side effects like the ones often found in other sleep medications.

On the surface, melatonin appears to be an ideal sleep medication with few down sides. The effects of melatonin, at least for some people, however, may be fleeting. Just as with the other sleep medications, a proportion of people seem to adjust to the levels of melatonin over time and may need to increase their dosages. This is a caution for people who are relying on melatonin as a long-term solution to a sleep problem. Be aware that because the use of melatonin every day over a long period of time has not been studied well, it is not known whether there are any long-term negative effects of using this substance over months or years. Compounding the concern is that the production of melatonin is not regulated by the FDA and is therefore not tested by the federal government for impurities. This issue is not an idle concern and became very serious when another supplement used for insomnia—L-tryptophan—was found in 1989 to cause a serious illness that included severe muscle pain. It is believed that substances used in the processing of L-tryptophan caused this illness, although, to date, no definitive evidence has surfaced. Although there have been no reports of problems with melatonin, the fact that it is not regulated opens melatonin up to similar potential problems.

Finally, several professional organizations recommend caution when it comes to using melatonin for sleep difficulties. Both the American Sleep Disorders Association (ASDA) and the National Sleep Foundation warn against self-administration, and the National Nutritional Foods Association advises against giving it to children except when it is with the guidance of a physician. Despite all of the positive signs to date, melatonin should be used only under the advice of a medical professional.

## ANTIDEPRESSANTS

In the 1950s, scientists were developing drugs for people with schizophrenia when they found that one of the compounds that they were working with—called *tricyclic antidepressants*—seemed to make people less depressed. Imipramine (also called Tofranil) is an example of one of the tricyclic antidepressant drugs. These antidepressant medications have been very helpful for some people who have long experienced serious depression. At the same time, these drugs have a number of other benefits that have proved useful for people with sleep and sleep-related problems. Because these drugs make people drowsy, they often are given to people who are dealing with both depression and insomnia. It is interesting to note that for some children with attention-deficit/hyperactivity disorder (ADHD), the tricyclic antidepressants can have the same effect as drugs such as Ritalin (which is a stimulant) and can help them focus their attention during the day. Because these drugs also help induce sleep, they sometimes are recommended for children with sleep problems *and* with ADHD in place of drugs such as Ritalin—which as stimulants can interfere with a child's ability to fall asleep.

Another effect of antidepressant medication is that it reduces the amount of REM sleep. As mentioned previously, this sometimes can be a problem because of the negative effects that reduced REM sleep has on cognitive ability. Some people with narcolepsy, however, find these drugs quite helpful. Recall that people with narcolepsy experience sleep attacks with temporary paralysis (cataplexy) during the day. These sleep attacks actually are the immediate encroachment of REM sleep into a state of wakefulness. Taking antidepressants can reduce these attacks during the day, which can significantly improve the quality of life for people with narcolepsy.

Two other groups of people also seem to benefit from this group of drugs. Chapter 10 described that children who have trouble with bedwetting sometimes are prescribed these medications because of their ability to help children hold their urine longer. Finally, antidepressant medication is used with people who have breathing-related sleep problems (see Chapter 9). The medication appears to be helpful in easing the breathing of these people, which in turn helps improve their sleep. As you can see, the tricyclic antidepressant medications have uses far beyond just reducing depression.

## STIMULANTS

A small group of people sleep too much, including those with hypersomnia and narcolepsy (discussed in Chapter 9). For these people, taking a stimulant during the day can keep them more alert. Two drugs that usually are associated with ADHD—Ritalin (methylphenidate) and Cylert (pemoline sodium)—also are prescribed for people who have a great deal of difficulty staying awake during the day.

## OTHER SLEEP-RELATED MEDICATIONS

Finally, two other medications are used for people with sleep-related problems. The combination of two drugs—levodopa and carbidopa, together called Sinemet—is used to help reduce the jerky limb movements in people with periodic limb movements and for people with restless legs syndrome. Replacing antidepressants for children with enuresis is an artificial form of the body's natural antidiuretic hormone (ADH)—called desmopressin acetate. This drug seems to reduce the volume of a child's urine, which helps prevent him or her from having nighttime toileting accidents.

## CONCLUSION

Every child and every family is different; and their needs, desires, and difficulties must be accounted for when making decisions about using medication for sleep and sleep-related problems. Clearly, there are times when a short-term use of medication can be a blessing for some individuals; however, such decisions require careful consultation in partnership with a physician. All medications have their risks and negative side effects, and informed decision making is essential prior to using medications for sleep problems. I hope that the other recommendations made throughout this book provide families with alternatives to medication that may be just as effective but more acceptable for use with children who have special needs.

# 13

# Preventing Sleep Problems

It is fitting that we end the book with a discussion of how to help parents prevent their young children from developing sleep problems. Using some of the techniques already discussed, along with important information about early child development, parents can help their children learn good sleep habits during the initial years of life. Ideally, couples who are expecting the birth of a child or who have recently gone through childbirth will use this information to inoculate their infants against potential sleep problems—much as they would inoculate their child against the measles or the mumps. A second group that may find the information in this chapter helpful are parents who already have a child with sleep problems and who are expecting the birth of another child. Preventing a repeat of the sleep problems with the next child often is high on the list of priorities. Being prepared for potential sleep problems can help ward off years of disruptive nights.

This is a good time to briefly revisit some of the previous discussion of how a child's innate bent toward having sleep problems works together with the way we react to them to cause sleep difficulties. In other words, some children will sleep well almost despite us, whereas other children are born with sleep problems and will be resistant to most efforts to help them. Children who are born with the potential for sleep problems are more likely to react negatively to changes in sleep schedules or feeding or other irregularities. They tend not to be as adaptive to variation or unpredictability around sleep as other infants and are therefore more likely to learn bad habits regarding sleep. This chapter discusses how parents can help their very young children develop good sleep habits and prevent their children from developing more serious problems regarding sleep.

## DEVELOPMENTAL CHANGES AND SLEEP

One of the mysteries of parenthood—especially for first-time parents—is what to expect of your child when it comes to sleep. At one extreme, some parents without much experience think that their newborn should fall asleep at around 8:00 P.M., sleep through the night, and awaken at 7:00 A.M. At the other extreme are parents who are frightened by stories of children who never sleep. The reality of newborns is that their sleep varies tremendously in the first weeks or months of life. Some infants miraculously sleep a solid 6–8 hours through the night almost from the day they are born. Others may awaken three or four times each night and be fully awake at 5:00 A.M. The only thing certain about the sleep of infants is its uncertainty. All of these sleep patterns are "normal."

By about 6 months of age, however, it is expected that a child generally will sleep through the night. If you look back at Figure 1.1 in Chapter 1, then you will see that the average number of hours of sleep for a child this age is about 13 per day. This may mean that your child will sleep some 10–11 hours at night and then nap for the remainder of the time. Always remember that these times are approximate—some children sleep less, and some sleep more. Whether the amount of sleep is a problem will be determined by the child's behavior during the day. If he or she sleeps only 10 hours per night but seems rested during the day, then it probably is not a problem. If, however, a child is sleeping 14 hours per night but still seems tired, then he or she may not be getting enough sleep.

What if a 6-month-old or older child is not sleeping through the night? Again, because this is approximately the age when you would expect a child to be getting a full night's sleep, a child of this age who wakes up one or more times each night could have the beginnings of a sleep problem. If your child is younger than 6 months, then you can start to develop habits that will help him or her have better sleep patterns. These habits are described later in this chapter.

In addition to developmental differences in sleep patterns—such as sleeping less as we grow older—another consideration for some sleep problems is a child's personality, which sometimes is referred to as *temperament*. Researchers (as well as most parents) have long known that children are born with different ways of dealing with the world. Some children are "easy": They sleep and eat on regular schedules, and they adapt well to new situations or people. Other children, unfortunately, are categorized as more "difficult." These children, even as infants, eat and sleep erratically; and they do not adapt well to new situations, people, or changes in routines. They may be fussy or cranky if their usual order is disrupted. Researchers who follow such children over long periods of time have found that many (but not all) children identified as difficult when they were infants were likely to have other behavior problems, even into adulthood.

When it comes to sleep, temperament or personality may play a role, especially for problems such as bedtime tantrums or disruptive night waking. The child who gives you a difficult time over meals also may protest at bedtime. The key to whether a child who may be difficult also will have problems sleeping depends on several factors. Some children, by nature of their biology, will have trouble sleeping. They may not be tired enough at bedtime to fall asleep easily, or they may be "light sleepers" and easily awakened at night. How we respond to their sleep problems also will affect sleep. As discussed previously, especially nervous parents may make sleep problems worse by giving a great deal of attention to a child who has a tantrum at bedtime or who is disruptive at night. Couple a natural tendency to sleep poorly with a difficult personality and parents who may not know how to react, and you have all of the ingredients for a child with one or more sleep problems.

In this equation

$$\text{poor sleep biology} + \text{difficult personality} + \text{parental reaction} = \text{sleep problem}$$

we can change at least one of these factors—parental reaction. We know that a good reaction strategy to sleep problems can help children sleep better, even if we cannot change their sleep biology or their personality. Following certain guidelines very early on may help children establish better sleep habits before more serious problems begin. What follows are some suggestions for helping your child develop regular patterns that can improve sleep.

## PREVENTION STRATEGIES

Helping your infant begin life with good sleep habits involves examining not only sleep patterns but also eating habits and other daily routines. For example, one of the more important factors in helping a child sleep through the night is proper fading of nighttime feedings. A child who continues to be fed in the middle of the night may continue to have disturbed sleep. In addition, the bedtime routines described in Chapter 4 can be started early to help set the stage for better sleep later in life. Responding well to bedtime problems or night waking right from the start also can help prevent more difficult episodes months or years later. Finally, some children may need help in reducing their naps; how to accomplish this and the rest of these prevention approaches are described next.

### From Birth: Establishing Good Sleep Habits

Within the first few months of life, infants should start to develop their sleep–wake patterns. At first, a child may sleep for 6- to 8-hour stretches on and off throughout the day and night. You can help your child spend more time sleeping at night in a number of ways. Daylight helps trigger our biological clock, so be sure to expose your child to morning daylight whenever possible. In contrast, a dark bedroom at night can help the natural release of melatonin, which aids the onset of sleep. Daytime activity and exercise can help children sleep better and longer at night, but activity in the few hours before bedtime should be curtailed. Daytime naps that last too long also can interfere with nighttime sleep, so limit these to no more than 3 consecutive hours.

Create a bedtime routine leading up to sleep. This should be a series of activities that you and your child share and that remain the same each evening. A bath or washing followed by getting dressed for sleep usually is a good start. Then, some quiet calm time, such as reading from a favorite book even if for only a few minutes, not only can help your child fall asleep, but also research suggests that activities such as reading to children can have significant positive effects on development[1]. Some families incorporate prayers and/or a bedtime song into their routine. Finally, hugs and kisses can be the final signal to your child that it is time to sleep.

After your nightly routine, it is important that you put your infant in the crib or bed *before* he or she is asleep. You do not want your child to associate falling asleep with being fed or even with being in your arms because this will interfere with later bedtimes. It also may cause problems when your child awakens in the middle of the night and someone is not there because now he or she has not learned to fall asleep alone. If this is already a problem, then refer to Chapters 5 or 6 for help in dealing with these sleep difficulties.

## At 3 Months: Fading Nighttime Feedings

A major contributor to early awakening or bedtime problems in very young children is nighttime feedings. Infants who are used to being fed at night likely will have their sleep disrupted and also may have problems going to sleep on their own. This can occur for several reasons. First, infants who are fed right before bedtime often come to associate feeding with sleep. This often very pleasant time for both child and parent—feeding followed by sleep—can become a habit that is difficult for the child to break once the feedings are discontinued. The infant may not be able to fall asleep without first being fed. Second, the child's diaper may become overly wet in the middle of the night, and this can wake some children. Finally, feeding affects the body's timing and rhythm, and late-night feeding can change it enough to disrupt sleep. Being used to these late feedings can cause the child to become hungry several hours after falling asleep, and this can awaken the child in the middle of the night.

Typically, children should be able to go without being fed at bedtime or in the middle of the night by the age of 3 months. At about this age, then, you can start to teach your child to not feel hungry at night by increasing the time between feedings. Richard Ferber, a specialist in children's sleep problems, recommends a fading schedule that parents can follow to help eliminate extra feedings around sleep times[2]. The goal is not to stop these nighttime feedings all at once but instead to reduce the time or amount of fluids that the child receives each night and increase the time between feedings until you can eliminate bedtime and middle-of-the-night feedings.

On the first night of this fading schedule, limit the number of ounces of liquid that your child receives to 7 if he or she is bottle-fed, or reduce the number of minutes fed to 7 if your child is breast-fed. The amount of time between feedings should be at least 2 hours. On each night afterward, reduce the number of ounces of fluid or minutes breast-fed by 1, and increase the time between feedings by 30 minutes. This continues on each subsequent night until the eighth night when the child should no longer be fed at bedtime or in the middle of the night. It is important to remember that a child who is 3 months of age or older no longer needs these feedings to be properly nourished and that any discomfort should fade within a few days. If your child fusses at bedtime or awakens crying at night, then refer to the section later in this chapter that provides help with these situations. Again, proper fading of nighttime feeding may help prevent later sleep problems. Following is an outline of the procedure for fading nighttime feedings:

- On the first night, give your child 7 ounces (if bottle-fed), or feed him or her for 7 minutes (if breast-fed) with 2 hours between feedings.
- On each subsequent night, reduce ounces or minutes by 1 (e.g., the second night would be 6 ounces or minutes), and increase the time between feedings by 30 minutes (e.g., from 2 hours to 2½ hours).
- A crying child may be hungry, but he or she does not *need* the nourishment.
- By the eighth night, the child should no longer be fed at bedtime or in the middle of the night.
- Any nighttime disruption can be handled as described in the next section.

### At 6 Months: Sleeping Through the Night

Most infants can sleep through the night without awakening when they are 6 months of age. This is important for parents to know because many parents believe that it is normal when their child does not sleep through the night at this age. In fact, my colleagues and I often find that telling parents this information gives them "permission" to begin to change the nighttime problems. If your child continues to awaken one or more times at night after having fallen asleep and he or she is at least 6 months old, then refer to Chapters 5 and 6 for help in dealing with this problem.

### The Preschool Years: Reducing Naps

By age 2, children should be able to have an active morning without a nap. Sometime between the ages of 3 and 6, most children no longer need an afternoon nap. Remember that we all are different when it comes to sleep needs. Some children and adults can nap during the day without it negatively affecting their sleep. In contrast, other individuals who nap, even for a short period of time, can have trouble falling asleep at night or may awaken earlier than desired. If your child's napping is interfering with sleep, then it may be time to fade back on this daytime sleeping. Chapter 7 discusses the procedures to use when naps are a problem for your child's sleep.

### CONCLUSION

You can make a difference in your child's sleep. Following the guidelines outlined in this book should help you to help your child sleep better at night and feel better during the day. But, obviously, it takes patience and persistence to get through the rough spots—the nights of feeling that your and your child's disrupted sleep will never end. My colleagues' and my experience with hundreds of families tells us that if you stick with it and invest your time and energy in your child's sleep now, then your efforts will pay off a thousandfold in the weeks and months to come. My own son, who had most of the sleep problems described in this book, now has little trouble falling asleep most nights and almost never wakes up again before morning. In fact, as his teen years approach, he is beginning to "sleep in" on weekends, a phenomenon that my wife and I would never have expected from the 2-year-old who would wake up for the day at 5:00 A.M. I wish you luck in your efforts, and I hope that you and your family sleep better soon!

# A

# Support Groups
and Associations

## BEDWETTING

**National Enuresis Society**
7777 Forest Lane
Suite C-737
Dallas, TX 75230-2518
Telephone: 800-NES-8080

## GENERAL SLEEP PROBLEMS

**American Sleep Disorders Association/Sleep Research Society**
1610 14th Street, N.W.
Suite 300
Rochester, MN 55901
Telephone: 507-287-6006
Fax: 507-287-6008

**National Heart, Lung, and Blood Institute Information Center/National Center on Sleep Disorders Research**
P.O. Box 30105
Bethesda, MD 20824-0105
Telephone: 301-251-1222
Fax: 301-251-1223

**National Sleep Foundation**
729 15th Street, N.W.
Fourth Floor
Washington, DC 20005
Telephone: 202-347-3471
Fax: 202-347-3472

**Sleep Diagnostics Center**
2617 W. Peterson
Suite 104
Chicago, IL 60659
Telephone: 773-262-4110
Fax: 773-465-5576

**Society of Light Treatment and Biological Rhythms**
Executive Office
10200 W. 44th Avenue
Suite 304
Wheat Ridge, CO 80033
Telephone: 303-424-3697
Fax: 303-422-8894

## LIMB MOVEMENT PROBLEMS

**Restless Legs Syndrome Foundation**
4410 19th Street, N.W.
Suite 201
Rochester, MN 55901
Telephone: 507-287-6465
Fax: 507-287-6312

## NARCOLEPSY

**American Narcolepsy Association**
P.O. Box 1187
San Carlos, CA 94305
Telephone: 800-222-6086 in California; 800-222-6085 from elsewhere

**Center for Narcolepsy Research**
845 S. Damen Avenue M/C 802
University of Illinois at Chicago
Chicago, IL 60612-7350
Telephone: 312-996-5176
Fax: 312-996-7008

**Narcolepsy Institute at Montesiore Medical Center**
111 E. 210th Street
Bronx, NY 10467
Telephone: 718-920-6799
Fax: 718-654-9580

**Narcolepsy Network**
P.O. Box 1365
FDR Station
New York, NY 10150
Telephone: 914-834-2855
Fax: 914-834-0957
or
P.O. Box 42460
Cincinnati, OH 45242
Telephone: 513-891-3522
Fax: 513-891-9936

## SLEEP APNEA

**American Sleep Apnea Association A.W.A.K.E.**
(Network of support groups)
2025 Pennsylvania Avenue, N.W.
Suite 905
Washington, DC 20006
Telephone: 202-293-3650
Fax: 202-293-3656

# SPECIAL NEEDS–
# RELATED ORGANIZATIONS

**National Attention Deficit
Disorder Association (ADDA)**
P.O. Box 972
Mentor, OH 44061
Telephone: 216-350-9595;
800-487-2282
Fax: 216-350-0223

**American Association on Mental
Retardation (AAMR)**
444 N. Capitol Street, N.W.
Suite 846
Washington, DC 20001-1512
Telephone: 202-387-1968
Fax: 202-387-2193

**American Council of the Blind**
1155 15th Street, N.W.
Suite 720
Washington, DC 20005
Telephone: 202-467-5081;
800-424-8666
Fax: 202-467-5085

**The Arc of the United States**
500 E. Border Street
Suite 300
Arlington, TX 76010
Telephone: 817-261 6003
Fax: 817-277-3491
TDD: 817-277-0553

**Autism Society of America**
7910 Woodmont Avenue
Suite 650
Bethesda, MD 20814-3015
Telephone: 301-657-0881;
800-3AUTISM
Fax: 301-657-0869

**CAN (Cure Autism Now)**
5225 Wilshire Boulevard
Suite 503
Los Angeles, CA 90036
Telephone: 213-549-0500
Fax: 213-549-0547

**DB-LINK
The National Information
Clearinghouse on Children
Who Are Deaf-Blind**
Teaching Research
345 N. Monmouth Avenue

Monmouth, OR 97361
Telephone: 800-438-9376
Fax: 503-838-8150
TTY: 800-854-7013
For further information, call Gail
Leslie: 503-838-8756

**Hydrocephalus Support Group,
Inc.**
Debby Buffa, Chairperson
P.O. Box 4236
Chesterfield, MO 63006-4236
Telephone: 314-532-8228

**National Center for PTSD**
(Post-Traumatic Stress Disorder)
VA Medical Center (116D)
215 N. Main Street
White River Junction, VT 05009
Telephone: 802-296-5132
Fax: 802-296-5135

**The National Easter Seal Society**
230 W. Monroe Street
Suite 1800
Chicago, IL 60606-4802
Telephone: 312-726-6200;
800-221-6827
Fax: 312-726-1494
TDD: 312-726-4258

**Spina Bifida Association of
America**
4590 MacArthur Boulevard, N.W.
Suite 250
Washington, DC 20007-4226
Telephone: 202-944-3285;
800-621-3141
Fax: 202-944-3295

**The Association for Persons with
Severe Handicaps (TASH)**
29 W. Susquehanna Avenue
Suite 210
Baltimore, MD 21204
Telephone: 410-828-8274
Fax: 410-828-6706

**Tourette Syndrome Association**
42–40 Bell Boulevard
Bayside, NY 11361
Telephone: 718-224-2999
Fax: 718-279-9596

# B

## Sleep Pages on
## the World Wide Web

## GENERAL SLEEP PAGES

### Accredited Sleep Disorders Centers

**http://www.sleepnet.com/asda.htm**

This site provides a roster of American Sleep Disorders Association Accredited Member Centers and Laboratories.

### Diagnosing and Treating Sleep Disorders

**http://www.njc.org/Diagnostic_Services/diag.htm**

This site lists the diagnostic services of the National Jewish Center for Immunology and Respiratory Medicine (which provides information to physicians about its clinical and research programs in allergic, respiratory, and immune system disorders). Visit its Nocturnal Asthma Research Center and Sleep Lab.

### Phantom Sleep Page (apnea, snoring, and more)

**http://www.newtechpub.com/phantom/**

The Phantom Sleep Page presents useful information about sleep and sleep disorders, including snoring and sleep apnea, for the public, patients, and professionals. It contains articles, bibliographies, connections to research and support groups, and newsletters from patient education and support groups worldwide.

### Searle healthNet

**http://www.searlehealthnet.com/sleep/dateline/**

This site provides highlights of recent sleep news as reported in newspapers around the country.

### Sleep Home Pages: Brain Information Service

**http://bisleep.medsch.ucla.edu/default.html**

The Sleep Home Pages provide a comprehensive resource for individuals who are involved in the research or treatment of sleep and sleep-related disorders. They include discussion forums and links to other research-related information.

---

Because addresses to web sites change frequently, some of these addresses may no longer be valid. You can find an updated list at http://www.albany.edu/psy/fac_vmd.html.

## Sleep Medicine Home Page

**http://www.cloud9.net/~thorpy/**

This home page lists resources regarding all aspects of sleep, including the physiology of sleep, clinical sleep medicine, sleep research, federal and state information, patient information, and business-related groups.

## The Sleep Well

**http://www-leland.stanford.edu/~dement/**

The Sleep Well was created as a reservoir of information on sleep and sleep disorders. It is also a wish that everyone may "sleep well" and obtain the wisdom to do so from these pages. It provides a calendar of important sleep events and meetings, information on sleep disorders, and a way to search Mental HealthNet for more information on sleep disorders.

## SPECIFIC SLEEP-RELATED DISORDERS

### A.W.A.K.E. New York's Home Page

**http://www.bway.net/~marlene/awake.html**

A.W.A.K.E. New York is a local support group designed to help people with sleep apnea. Their goal is to educate patients, physicians, and the general public on diagnosis and treatment of sleep apnea.

### Center for Narcolepsy Research at UIC Home page

**http://www.uic.edu/depts/cnr/index.html**

In December 1986, the Center for Narcolepsy Research (CNR) at the College of Nursing was established with private funds along with overhead support from the University of Illinois at Chicago (UIC) to help increase knowledge about narcolepsy, a disorder of excessive sleepiness. This web site provides information about narcolepsy, as well as links to other sites.

### Children's Sleep Problems

**http://www.psych.med.umich.edu/web/aacap/factsFam/sleep.htm**

The American Academy of Child and Adolescent Psychiatry provides this Facts for Families page as a public service to assist parents and families in their most important roles. It provides a very brief overview of sleep problems in children.

## Cure Narcolepsy Now

**http://www.cloud9.net/~thorpy/NARCO.HTML**

The goal of this site is to encourage communication among researchers for the exchange of information, biological material, ideas, and concepts that will lead to appropriate research to find the gene responsible for narcolepsy and ultimately lead to a cure.

## Frequently Asked Questions About Coffee and Caffeine

**http://daisy.uwaterloo.ca/~alopez-o/caffaq.html**

This site provides information about all beverages and products that contain caffeine, including tea, coffee, chocolate, caffeinated soft drinks, caffeinated pills, coffee beans, and so forth.

## Laser Surgery for Snoring and Sleep Apnea

**http://www.islandnet.com/~sreid/laser.html**

This site provides an overview of one-step laser surgery for snoring by Otolaryngology Associates Dr. R.I. Dickson and Dr. D.R. Mintz.

## Melatonin Information and References

**http://www.aeiveos.com/diet/melatonin/index.html**

Because of the widespread press regarding melatonin and the popularity of melatonin reviews, this web site has organized a comprehensive set of references about melatonin on the World Wide Web. Although not a complete list, it serves as a good jumping-off point for people investigating melatonin.

## Obstructive Sleep Apnea

**http://www.med.upenn.edu/penntoday/vol06n01/article/sleep.html**

This site provides information (and pictures!) about obstructed sleep apnea from the Penn Center for Sleep Disorders.

## Restless Legs Syndrome

**http://www.rls.org/**

This site provides information on restless legs syndrome and periodic limb movement disorder. This site also provides information on the Restless Legs Syndrome Foundation, Inc.

## SIDS Network

**http://sids-network.org/**

This site provides a great deal of information about sudden infant death syndrome, discussion groups, references, and downloadable brochures.

## Sleep, Dreams, and Wakefulness

**http://ura1195-6.univ-lyon1.fr/home.html**

The Jouvet Sleep Lab in France (which also is an interchangeable French/English language site) provides both clinical and basic sleep researchers with an admirable place to join in their community of interest. This site provides comprehensive resources for those involved in sleep research and the treatment of sleep-related disorders.

## Stanford University Center for Narcolepsy

**http://www.hia.com/hia/narcoctr/**

This site provides a great deal of information about narcolepsy from the Stanford University Center for Narcolepsy, including information about the center and its research.

## The Treatment of Sleep Disorders of Older People

**http://text.nlm.nih.gov/nih/cdc/www/78txt.html**

The National Institutes of Health Consensus Development Conference on the Treatment of Sleep Disorders of Older People brought together clinical specialists in pulmonology, psychiatry, psychology, geriatrics, and internal medicine; other health care providers; and the public to address the cause, diagnosis, assessment, and specific treatments of sleep disorders of older people. Following $1\frac{1}{2}$ days of presentations by experts and discussion by the audience, a consensus panel weighed the scientific evidence and prepared this consensus statement.

# C

# Accredited Sleep Disorders Centers

## WHAT CAN I EXPECT FROM A VISIT TO
## AN ACCREDITED SLEEP DISORDERS CENTER?

The first goal of a sleep disorders center is to find out as much as possible about your child's sleep history. An interview will be conducted, and you will be asked to fill out forms like the ones in this book to give the sleep professionals a good picture of your child's sleep and sleep-related behaviors. The sleep professionals then will determine whether an overnight evaluation is needed. If they suspect, for example, that breathing problems may be a cause of the sleep problems, then they likely will recommend a more complete evaluation. A warning: Several parents have reported that some centers will not evaluate children who have severe disabilities, such as mental retardation or autism, because these children can be too disruptive during nighttime evaluations.

An overnight evaluation typically includes a *polysomnographic (PSG) evaluation.* The person spends one or more nights sleeping in a "sleep laboratory" while being monitored on a number of measures, including respiration and oxygen desaturation (a measure of your airflow); leg movements; brain wave activity, measured by *electroencephalograph* (EEG); eye movements, measured by an *electrooculograph* (EOG); muscle movements, measured by an *electromyograph* (EMG); and heart activity, measured by an *electrocardiogram.* The child will need to be able to sleep in this laboratory while attached to wires or electrodes to help monitor sleep activity. From these measures, the sleep professionals can make recommendations for treatment based on the nature of your child's sleep problems.

Following is a list of American Sleep Disorders Association Accredited Member Centers and Laboratories across the United States (an updated list can be found on the World Wide Web at the following address: http://www.sleepnet.com/asda.htm. You can also obtain a current listing and additional information by sending e-mail to Gregory G. Mader [gmader@millcomm.com] at the American Sleep Disorders Association [1610 14th Street, N.W., Suite 300, Rochester, MN 55901-2200]).

An asterisk (*) following the name of a center indicates that it is accredited as a Specialty Laboratory for Breathing-Related Sleep Disorders. All other programs are accredited, full-service sleep disorders centers.

## ALABAMA

Brookwood Sleep Disorders Center
Brookwood Medical Center
2010 Brookwood Medical Center
  Drive
Birmingham, AL 35209
Robert C. Doekel, M.D.
205-877-2486

Sleep Disorders Center of Alabama,
  Inc.
790 Montclair Road
Suite 200
Birmingham, AL 35213
Vernon Pegram, Ph.D.
Robert C. Doekel, M.D.
205-599-1020

Sleep–Wake Disorders Center
University of Alabama at
  Birmingham
1713 Sixth Avenue South
CPM Building, Room 270
Birmingham, AL 35233-0018
Vernon Pegram, Ph.D.
Susan Harding, M.D.
205-934-7110

Sleep–Wake Disorders Center
Flowers Hospital
4370 W. Main Street
P.O. Box 6907
Dothan, AL 36302
Craig Kornegay, RPSGT
Chris Speigner, PSGT
Ann B. McDowell, M.D.
Alan Purvis, M.D.
David Davis, M.D.
334-793-5000 x1685

Columbia Center for Sleep Disorders
250 Chateau Drive
Suite 235
Huntsville, AL 35801
Thomas H. Arrington, RPSGT
Alan H. Arrington, M.D.
205-880-6451

Huntsville Hospital Sleep Disorders
  Center
911 Big Cove Road
Huntsville, AL 35801
Paul LeGrand, M.D.
Debra J. Collier, RRT, RPSGT
205-517-8553

Sleep Disorders Center
Mobile Infirmary Medical Center
P.O. Box 2144
Mobile, AL 36652
Robert Dawkins, Ph.D., M.P.H.
334-431-5559

Southeast Regional Center for
  Sleep/Wake Disorders
Springhill Memorial Hospital
3719 Dauphin Street
Mobile, AL 36608
Lawrence S. Schoen, Ph.D.
334-460-5319

USA Knollwood Sleep Disorders
  Center
University of South Alabama
Knollwood Park Hospital
5600 Girby Road
Mobile, AL 36693-3398
William A. Broughton, M.D.
334-660-5757

Baptist Sleep Disorders Center
Baptist Medical Center
2105 E. South Boulevard
Montgomery, AL 36116-2498
David P. Franco, M.D.
Tammy Taylor, RPSGT
334-286-3252

Tuscaloosa Clinic Sleep Lab*
701 University Boulevard East
Suite 711
Tuscaloosa, AL 35401
Richard M. Snow, M.D., FCCP
205-349-4043

## ALASKA

Sleep Disorders Center
Providence Alaska Medical Center
P.O. Box 196604
Anchorage, AK 99519-6604
Anne H. Morris, M.D., Medical
  Director
Colleen Bridge, Assistant
  Administrator
Katie Boyle-Colborn, RPSGT,
  Clinical Supervisor
907-261-3650

## ARIZONA

Desert Samaritan Sleep Disorders
   Center
Desert Samaritan Medical Center
1400 S. Dobson Road
Mesa, AZ 85202
Paul Barnard, M.D.
Tom Munzlinger, RPSGT
602-835-3620

Samaritan Regional Sleep Disorders
   Program
Good Samaritan Regional Medical
   Center
1111 E. McDowell Road
Phoenix, AZ 85006
Connie Boker, RPSGT
Bernard Levine, M.D.
602-239-5815

Sleep Disorders Center
Scottsdale Memorial Hospital–North
9003 E. Shea Boulevard
Scottsdale, AZ 85260
Jeffrey Gitt, M.D.
Sharon E. Cichocki, RPSGT
602-860-3200

Sleep Disorders Center
University of Arizona
1501 N. Campbell Avenue
Tucson, AZ 85724
Stuart F. Quan, M.D.
520-694-6112

## ARKANSAS

Sleep Disorders Center
Washington Regional Medical
   Center
1125 N. College Avenue
Fayetteville, AR 72703
David L. Brown, M.D., Director
William A. Rivers, RPSGT,
   Coordinator
501-442-1272

Pediatric Sleep Disorders
Arkansas Children's Hospital
800 Marshall Street
Little Rock, AR 72202-3591
May Griebel, M.D.
Linda Rhodes, E.M.T., RPSGT
501-320-1893

Sleep Disorders Center
Baptist Medical Center
9601 I-630, Exit 7
Little Rock, AR 72205-7299
David Davila, M.D.
501-227-1902

## CALIFORNIA

WestMed Sleep Disorders Center
1101 S. Anaheim Boulevard
Anaheim, CA 92805
Clyde Dossantos, M.D.
Deborah Strangio
714-491-1159

Mercy Sleep Laboratory*
Mercy San Juan Hospital
6401 Coyle Avenue
Suite 109
Carmichael, CA 95608
Janice K. Herrmann, RPSGT, MA
Richard Stack, M.D.
916-966-5552

Downey Community Hospital Sleep
   Disorders Center
Rio Hondo Foundation Hospital
8300 E. Telegraph Road
Downey, CA 90240
Louis McNabb, M.D.
562-806-6523

Palomar Medical Center Sleep
   Disorders Lab*
Palomar Medical Center
555 E. Valley Parkway
Escondido, CA 92025
Toni Flemmer, Coordinator
Benjamin Kanter, M.D., FCCP
619-739-3457

Sleep Disorders Institute
St. Jude Medical Center
1915 Sunny Crest Drive
Fullerton, CA 92835
Louis McNabb, M.D.
Justine Petrie, M.D.
Robert Roethe, M.D.
Rose Ann Zumstein, Director
714-992-3981

Glendale Adventist Medical Center
Sleep Disorders Center
1509 Wilson Terrace
Glendale, CA 91206
David A. Thompson, M.D.
Kathy Cavander
818-409-8323

Division of Neurology
Scripps Clinic
10666 N. Torrey Pines Road
La Jolla, CA 92037
Milton Erman, M.D.
Steven Poceta, M.D.
619-554-9924

Sleep Disorders Center
Grossmont District Hospital
P.O. Box 158
La Mesa, CA 92044-0300
Ellie Hoey
619-644-4488

Memorial Sleep Disorders Center
Long Beach Memorial Medical
  Center
2801 Atlantic Avenue
P.O. Box 1428
Long Beach, CA 90801-1428
Stephen E. Brown, M.D.
562-933-0208

Sleep Disorders Center
Cedars-Sinai Medical Center
Pulmonary Division
8700 Beverly Boulevard, Room 6732
Los Angeles, CA 90048-1869
Warren Botnick, M.D.
310-855-4682

UCLA Sleep Disorders Center
710 Westwood Plaza
Los Angeles, CA 90095
Frisca Yan-Go, M.D.
Jerald Simmons, M.D.
310-206-8005

Sleep Disorders Center
55 Knowles Drive
Los Gatos, CA 95030
Augustin de la Pena, Ph.D.
408-341-2080

Sleep Disorders Center
Hoag Memorial Hospital Presbyterian
One Hoag Drive
P.O. Box 6100
Newport Beach, CA 92658-6100
Paul A. Selecky, M.D.
714-760-2070

Sleep Evaluation Center
Northridge Hospital Medical Center
18300 Roscoe Boulevard
Northridge, CA 91328
Liz Norman
818-885-5344

California Center for Sleep Disorders
3012 Summit Street
Fifth Floor, South Building
Oakland, CA 94609
510-834-8333

St. Joseph Hospital Sleep Disorders
  Center
1310 W. Stewart Drive
Suite 403
Orange, CA 92668
Sarah Mosko, Ph.D.
714-771-8950

Sleep Disorders Center
UC Irvine Medical Center
101 City Drive South, Route 23
Orange, CA 92868
Peter A. Fotinakes, M.D.
714-456-5105

Sleep Disorders Center
Huntington Memorial Hospital
100 W. California Boulevard
P.O. Box 7013
Pasadena, CA 91109-7013
Robert S. Eisenberg, M.D.
818-397-3061

Sleep Disorders Center
Doctors Hospital–Pinole
2151 Appian Way
Pinole, CA 94564-2578
Frederick Nachtwey, M.D.
Richard Sankary, M.D.
510-741-2525
800-640-9440 (in California)

Pomona Valley Hospital Medical
   Center
Sleep Disorders Center
1798 N. Garey Avenue
Pomona, CA 91767
Dennis Nicholson, M.D.
Fares Elghazi, M.D.
Robert Jones, M.D., FCCP
909-865-9587

Sleep Disorders Center
Sequoia Hospital
170 Alameda de las Pulgas
Redwood City, CA 94062-2799
J. Al Reichert
415-367-5137

Sleep Disorders Center at Riverside
Riverside Community Hospital
4445 Magnolia, E1
Riverside, CA 92501
Joe DeLeon, RPSGT
Steven P. James, M.D.
909-788-3377

Sutter Sleep Disorders Center
650 Howe Avenue
Suite 910
Sacramento, CA 95825
Sue Van Duyn, RPSGT, RCP, BA
Lydia Wytrzes, M.D.
916-646-3300

Mercy Sleep Disorders Center
Mercy Health Care San Diego
4077 Fifth Avenue
San Diego, CA 92103-2180
Cheryl L. Spinweber, Ph.D.
619-260-7378

San Diego Sleep Disorders Center
1842 Third Avenue
San Diego, CA 92101
Renata Shafor, M.D.
619-235-0248

Sleep Disorders Center
California Pacific Medical Center
2340 Clay Street
Suite 237
San Francisco, CA 94155
Jon F. Sassin, M.D.
Bruce T. Adornato, M.D.
415-923-3336

The Sleep Disorders Center of Santa
   Barbara
2410 Fletcher Avenue
Suite 201
Santa Barbara, CA 93105
Andrew S. Binder, M.D.
Laurie Laatsch, RPSGT
805-898-8845

Sleep Disorders Clinic
Stanford University
401 Quarry Road
Stanford, CA 94305
Alex Adu Clerk, M.D.
415-723-6601

Southern California Sleep Apnea
   Center*
Lombard Medical Group
2230 Lynn Road
Thousand Oaks, CA 91360
Ronald A. Popper, M.D.
805-495-1066

Torrance Memorial Medical Center
Sleep Disorders Center
3330 W. Lomita Boulevard
Torrance, CA 90505
Lawrence W. Kneisley, M.D.
310-517-4617

Sleep Disorders Laboratory*
Kaweah Delta District Hospital
400 W. Mineral King Avenue
Visalia, CA 93291
William R. Winn, M.D.
Gregory C. Warner, M.D.
209-625-7338

West Hills Sleep Disorder Center
23101 Sherman Place
Suite 108
West Hills, CA 91307
Gordon Dowds, M.D
Pamela Pierce
818-715-0096

## COLORADO

National Jewish/University of
   Colorado Sleep Disorders Center
1400 Jackson Street, A200
Denver, CO 80206
Robert D. Ballard, M.D.
303-398-1523

Sleep Disorders Center
Presbyterian/St. Luke's Medical
  Center
1719 E. 19th Avenue
Denver, CO 80218
John R. Ruddy, M.D.
Timothy C. Kennedy, M.D.
303-839-6447

## CONNECTICUT

New Haven Sleep Disorders Center
University Towers
100 York Street
New Haven, CT 06511
Robert K. Watson, Ph.D.
Alan J. Sholomskas, M.D.
203-776-9578

Gaylord-Yale Sleep Laboratory*
Gaylord Hospital
Gaylord Farms Road
Wallingford, CT 06492
Vahid Mohsenin, M.D.
Thomas Whelan, RPSGT
203-284-2853 or
  203-284-2800 x3355

## DELAWARE

No accredited members

## DISTRICT OF COLUMBIA

Sibley Memorial Hospital
  Sleep Disorders Center
5255 Loughboro Road, N.W.
Washington, DC 20016
Samuel J. Potolicchio, M.D.
David N.F. Fairbanks, M.D.
Bryan P. Larson, RRT
202-364-7676

Sleep Disorders Center
Georgetown University Hospital
3800 Reservoir Road, N.W.
Washington, DC 20007-2197
Richard E. Waldhorn, M.D.
Marilyn L. Faucette, RPSGT
202-784-3610

## FLORIDA

Boca Raton Sleep Disorders Center
899 Meadows Road
Suite 101
Boca Raton, FL 33486
Natalio Chediak, M.D.
Sheila R. Shafer, CMA
561-750-9881

Sleep Disorder Laboratory*
Broward General Medical Center
1600 S. Andrews Avenue
Fort Lauderdale, FL 33316
Glenn R. Singer, M.D.
954-355-5534

Center for Sleep Disordered
  Breathing*
P.O. Box 2982
Jacksonville, FL 32203
Daniel S. Wyzan, M.D.
904-387-7300 x8743

Mayo Sleep Disorders Center
Mayo Clinic Jacksonville
4500 San Pablo Road
Jacksonville, FL 32224
Paul Fredrickson, M.D.
Joseph Kaplan, M.D.
904-953-7287

Watson Clinic Sleep Disorders
  Center
1600 Lakeland Hills Boulevard
P.O. Box 95000
Lakeland, FL 33804
Eberto Pineiro, M.D.
941-680-7627

Atlantic Sleep Disorders Center
1401 S. Apollo Boulevard
Melbourne, FL 32901
Dennis K. King, M.D.
407-952-5191

Sleep Disorders Center
Miami Children's Hospital
3100 S.W. 62nd Avenue
Miami, FL 33155
Marcel J. Deray, M.D.
Belen P. Penaranda
305-662-8330

University of Miami School of
  Medicine, JMH and VA Medical
  Center Sleep Disorders Center
Department of Neurology (D4-5)
P.O. Box 016960
Miami, FL 33101
Bruce Nolan, M.D.
305-324-3371

Sleep Disorders Center
Mt. Sinai Medical Center
4300 Alton Road
Miami Beach, FL 33140
Alejandro D. Chediak, M.D.
305-674-2613

Florida Hospital Sleep Disorders
  Center
601 E. Rollins Avenue
Orlando, FL 32803
Morris T. Bird, M.D.
Robert S. Thornton, M.D.
407-897-1558

Health First Sleep Disorders Center
Palm Bay Community Hospital
1425 Malabar Road, N.E.
Suite 255
Palm Bay, FL 32907
Michael Miller, M.D.
Larry Bedwell, CRH, RPSGT
407-728-5387

St. Petersburg Sleep Disorders Center
2525 Pasadena Avenue South
Suite S
St. Petersburg, FL 33707
Neil T. Feldman, M.D.
813-360-0853
800-242-3244 (in Florida)

Sleep Disorders Center
Sarasota Memorial Hospital
1700 S. Tamiami Trail
Sarasota, FL 34239
G. Duncan Finlay, M.D.
James R. Jackson, RRT
941-917-2525

Laboratory for Sleep-Related
  Breathing Disorders*
University Community Hospital
3100 E. Fletcher Avenue
Tampa, FL 33613
Daniel J. Schwartz, M.D.
John Borden, CPFT
813-971-6000 x7410

## GEORGIA

Atlanta Center for Sleep Disorders
303 Parkway Drive
Box 44
Atlanta, GA 30312
Gail McBride-Storbeck
Francis Buda, M.D.
Jonne Walter, M.D.
Robert Schnapper, M.D.
404-265-3722

Sleep Disorders Center
Northside Hospital
5780 Peachtree Dunwoody Road
Suite 150
Atlanta, GA 30342
Russell Rosenberg, Ph.D.
404-851-8135

Sleep Disorders Center of Georgia
5505 Peachtree Dunwoody Road
Suite 370
Atlanta, GA 30342
D. Alan Lankford, Ph.D.
James J. Wellman, M.D.
404-257-0080

Sleep Disorders Center
Promina Kennestone Hospital
677 Church Street
Marietta, GA 30060
William Dowdell, M.D.
David Lesch, M.D.
Sherry Haynes, RPSGT, Program
  Coordinator
770-793-5353

Department of Sleep Disorders
  Medicine
Candler Hospital
5353 Reynolds Street
Savannah, GA 31405
Andy Williams
Pamela Rockett
912-692-6531

Savannah Sleep Disorders Center
Saint Joseph's Hospital
#6 St. Joseph's Professional Plaza
11706 Mercy Boulevard
Savannah, GA 31419
Anthony M. Costrini, M.D.
Paul Donnellan, RPSGT
912-927-5141

Sleep Disorders Center
Memorial Medical Center, Inc.
4700 Waters Avenue
Savannah, GA 31403
Herbert F. Sanders, M.D.
Stephen L. Morris, M.D.
912-350-8327

## HAWAII

Pulmonary Sleep Disorders Center*
Kuakini Medical Center
347 N. Kuakini Street
Honolulu, HI 96817
Edward J. Morgan, M.D.
Sonia Lee-Gushi, RPSGT, CRTT
808-547-9119

Sleep Disorders Center of the Pacific
Straub Clinic & Hospital
888 S. King Street
Honolulu, HI 96813
James W. Pearce, M.D.
Linda Kapuniai, Dr.P.H.
808-522-4448

## IDAHO

No accredited members

## ILLINOIS

Neurological Testing Center's
Sleep Disorders Center
Northwestern Memorial Hospital
303 E. Superior, Passavant 1044
Chicago, IL 60611
Phyllis C. Zee, M.D., Ph.D.
312-908-8120

Sleep Disorders Center
University of Chicago Hospitals
5758 S. Maryland Avenue
Room 4602, MC9019
Chicago, IL 60637
Jean-Paul Spire, M.D.
773-702-1782

Sleep Disorder Service and Research
Center
Rush-Presbyterian-St. Luke's
Medical Center
1653 W. Congress Parkway
Chicago, IL 60612
Rosalind Cartwright, Ph.D.
312-942-5440

Sleep Disorders Center
Evanston Hospital
2650 Ridge Avenue
Evanston, IL 60201
Richard S. Rosenberg, Ph.D.
847-570-2570

C. Duane Morgan Sleep Disorders
Center
Methodist Medical Center of Illinois
221 N.E. Glen Oak Avenue
Peoria, IL 61636
Ginny Elam, R.N.
309-672-4966S

Sleep Disorders Center
SIU School of Medicine/Memorial
Medical Center
800 N. Rutledge Street
Springfield, IL 62781
Joseph Henkle, M.D.
Steven Todd, RRT, RPSGT
217-788-4269

Carle Regional Sleep Disorders
Center
Carle Foundation Hospital
611 W. Park Street
Urbana, IL 61801-2595
Daniel Picchietti, M.D.
Donald A. Greeley, M.D.
217-383-3364

## INDIANA

St. Mary's Sleep Disorders Center*
St. Mary's Medical Center
3700 Washington Avenue
Evansville, IN 47750
David Cocanower, M.D.
Rebecca N. Dicus, RRT
812-485-4960

St. Joseph Sleep Disorders Center
St. Joseph Medical Center
700 Broadway
Fort Wayne, IN 46802
James C. Stevens, M.D.
Thomandram Sekar, M.D.
219-425-3552

Sleep/Wake Disorders Center
Community Hospitals of Indianapolis
1500 N. Ritter Avenue
Indianapolis, IN 46219
Marvin E. Vollmer, M.D.
317-355-4275

Sleep/Wake Disorders Center
Winona Memorial Hospital
3232 N. Meridian Street
Indianapolis, IN 46208
Kenneth N. Wiesert, M.D.
317-927-2100

Sleep Alertness Center
Lafayette Home Hospital
2400 South Street
Lafayette, IN 47904
Frederick Robinson, M.D.
765-447-6811

Sleep Disorders Center
Good Samaritan Hospital
520 S. Seventh Street
Vincennes, IN 47591
Henry J. Matick, D.O.
812-885-3877

## IOWA

Sleep Disorders Center
Genesis Medical Center
1401 W. Central Park
Davenport, IA 52804
Carol Everson, RPSGT
Michael H. Laws, M.D.
Akshay Mahadevia, M.D.
319-421-1525

Sleep Disorders Center
The Department of Neurology
The University of Iowa Hospitals and
    Clinics
200 Hawkins Drive
Iowa City, IA 52242
Mark Eric Dyken, M.D.
319-356-3813

## KANSAS

Sleep Disorders Center
St. Francis Hospital and Medical Center
1700 S.W. Seventh Street
Topeka, KS 66606-1690
Ted W. Daughety, M.D.
David D. Miller, RPSGT
913-295-7900

Sleep Disorders Center
Wesley Medical Center
550 N. Hillside
Wichita, KS 67214-4976
Pam Dickey, RCT, REEG/EPT
316-688-2663

## KENTUCKY

Bluegrass Outpatient Services Sleep
    Lab*
1110 Wilkinson Trace
Bowling Green, KY 42103
Mike Howard
Walter Warren, M.D.
502-796-6852

Sleep Diagnostics Lab*
Columbia Greenview Regional
    Hospital
1801 Ashley Circle
Bowling Green, KY 42104
Jim Sexton
Steve Zeller
502-793-1000

The Sleep Disorder Center of
    St. Luke Hospital
St. Luke Hospital, Inc.
85 N. Grand Avenue
Fort Thomas, KY 41075
Bruce Corser, M.D.
Michael Fletcher, RPSGT
606-572-3535

Sleep Apnea Center*
Columbia Hospital Lexington
310 S. Limestone Street
Lexington, KY 40508
Barbara Phillips, M.D., MSPH,
    FCCP
Tracey L. McGaughey, CPA, Director
606-252-6612 x7331

Sleep Disorders Center
St. Joseph's Hospital
One St. Joseph Drive
Lexington, KY 40504
Kathryn Hansen
606-278-0444

Sleep Disorders Center
Audubon Regional Medical Center
One Audubon Plaza Drive
Louisville, KY 40217
David Winslow, M.D.
502-636-7459

Sleep Disorders Center
University of Louisville Hospital
530 S. Jackson Street
Louisville, KY 40202
Barbara J. Rigdon, REEGT
Vasudeva G. Iyer, M.D.
Eugene C. Fletcher, M.D.
502-562-3792

Regional Medical Center
Lab for Sleep-Related Breathing
   Disorders*
900 Hospital Drive
Madisonville, KY 42431
Thomas Gallo, M.D.
Frank Taylor, M.D.
502-825-5918

## LOUISIANA

Memorial Medical Center
Baptist Campus
Sleep Disorders Center
2700 Napoleon Avenue
New Orleans, LA 70115
Gregory S. Ferriss, M.D.
Lynn Causey, REEGT
504-896-5439

Tulane Sleep Disorders Center
Tulane University Hospital and
   Clinic
1415 Tulane Avenue
New Orleans, LA 70112
Mark McCarthy, M.D.
504-584-3592

LSU Sleep Disorders Center
Louisiana State University Medical
   Center
P.O. Box 33932
Shreveport, LA 71130-3932
Andrew L. Chesson, Jr., M.D.
318-675-5365

The Neurology and Sleep Clinic
2205 E. 70th Street
Shreveport, LA 71105
Nabil A. Moufarrej, M.D.
Annette Berry
318-797-1585

## MAINE

Sleep Laboratory*
Maine Medical Center
930 Congress Street
Portland, ME 04102
George E. Bokinsky, Jr., M.D.
207-871-2279

## MARYLAND

The Johns Hopkins University Sleep
   Disorders Center
Asthma and Allergy Building, Room
   4B50
5501 Hopkins Bayview Circle
Baltimore, MD 21224
Philip L. Smith, M.D.
410-550-0571

Maryland Sleep Disorders Center,
   Inc.
6701 N. Charles Street
Unit 41
Towson, MD 21204
Thomas E. Hobbins, M.D.
410-494-9773

Shady Grove Sleep Disorders Center
14915 Broschart Road
Suite 102
Rockville, MD 20850
Jean Neuenkirch, RPSGT
Marc Raphaelson, M.D.
301-251-5905

## MASSACHUSETTS

Sleep Disorders Center
Beth Israel Deaconess Hospital
330 Brookline Avenue KS430
Boston, MA 02215
J. Woodrow Weiss, M.D.
Jean K. Matheson, M.D.
617-667-3237

Sleep Disorders Center
Lahey-Hitchcock Clinic
41 Mall Road
Burlington, MA 01805
Paul T. Gross, M.D.
Susan M. Dignan, RPSGT
617-273-8251

Sleep Disorders Institute of Central
  New England
St. Vincent Hospital
25-A Winthrop Street
Worcester, MA 01604
Jayant Phadke, M.D.
Linda Lentz
508-798-6212

## MICHIGAN

Sleep Disorders Center
St. Joseph Mercy Hospital
P.O. Box 995
Ann Arbor, MI 48106
William T. Allen, M.D.
Doris M. Fortier, RRT, RPSGT
313-712-4651

Sleep Disorders Center
University of Michigan Hospitals
1500 E. Medical Center Drive
Med Inn C433, Box 0842
Ann Arbor, MI 48109-0115
Brenda Livingston, Coordinator
Michael S. Aldrich, M.D.
Ronald Chervin, M.D.
Beth Malow, M.D.
Alan Douglass, M.D.
313-936-9068

Sleep Disorders Clinic
Bay Medical Center
1900 Columbus Avenue
Bay City, MI 48708
John M. Buday, M.D.
Mary K. Taylor, RPSGT
517-894-3332

Sleep Disorders Clinic
Henry Ford Hospital
2921 W. Grand Boulevard
Detroit, MI 48202
Leon Rosenthal, M.D.
313-876-4417

Sleep/Wake Disorders Laboratory
  (127B)
VA Medical Center
4646 John Road
Detroit, MI 48201
Sheldon Kapen, M.D.
Greg Koshorek
313-576-1000

Sleep Disorders Center
Butterworth Hospital
100 Michigan Street, N.E.
Grand Rapids, MI 49503
Lee Marmion, M.D.
Ronald Van Drunen, RPSGT
616-391-3759

Sleep Disorders Center
W.A. Foote Memorial Hospital, Inc.
205 N. East Avenue
Jackson, MI 49201
Cynthia D. Nichols, Ph.D.
517-788-4750

Borgess Sleep Disorders Center
Borgess Medical Center
1521 Gull Road
Kalamazoo, MI 49001
Tom Wittenberg, RRT
Gary R. Wilson, M.A., RRT
616-226-7081

Michigan Capital Healthcare
Sleep/Wake Center
2025 S. Washington Avenue
Suite 300
Lansing, MI 48910-0817
Pamela Minkley, RRT, RPSGT
Gauresh Kashyap, M.D.
517-334-2510

Sparrow Sleep Center
Sparrow Hospital
1215 E. Michigan Avenue
P.O. Box 30480
Lansing, MI 48909-7980
Alan M. Atkinson, D.O.
517-483-2946

Sleep Disorders Center
Oakwood Downriver Medical Center
25750 W. Outer Drive
Lincoln Park, MI 48146-1599
Lyle D. Victor, M.D.
Michael A. Middleton
313-382-6165

Sleep & Respiratory Associates of
  Michigan
28200 Franklin Road
Southfield, MI 48034
Harvey W. Organek, M.D.
810-350-2722

Munson Sleep Disorders Center
Munson Medical Center
1105 Sixth Street
MPB Suite 307
Traverse City, MI 49684-2386
David A. Walker, D.O., Medical
  Director
Leon R. Olewinski, RRT, Director
Marcia Rinal, CRTT, RPSGT,
  Manager
800-358-9641 or 616-935-6600

Sleep and Attention Disorders
  Institute
44199 Dequindre
Suite 311
Troy, MI 48098
R. Bart Sangal, M.D.
810-879-0707

## MINNESOTA

Duluth Regional Sleep Disorders
  Center
St. Mary's Medical Center
407 E Third Street
Duluth, MN 55805
Peter K. Franklin, M.D.
218-726-4692

Minnesota Regional Sleep Disorders
  Center, #867B
Hennepin County Medical Center
701 Park Avenue, South
Minneapolis, MN 55415
Mark Mahowald, M.D.
612-347-6288

Sleep Disorders Center
Abbott Northwestern Hospital
800 E. 28th Street at Chicago
  Avenue
304 Piper Building
Minneapolis, MN 55407
Wilfred A. Corson, M.D.
612-863-4516

Mayo Sleep Disorders Center
Mayo Clinic
200 First Street, S.W.
Rochester, MN 55905
Peter Hauri, Ph.D.
John W. Shepard, Jr., M.D.
507-266-8900

Sleep Disorders Center
Methodist Hospital
6500 Excelsior Boulevard
St. Louis Park, MN 55426
Barb Feider
Ted Berman, M.D.
612-993-6083

St. Joseph's Sleep Diagnostic Center
St. Joseph's Hospital
69 W. Exchange Street
St. Paul, MN 55102
Thomas Mulrooney, M.D.
612-232-3682

## MISSISSIPPI

Sleep Disorders Center
Memorial Hospital at Gulfport
P.O. Box 1810
Gulfport, MS 39502
Sydney Smith, M.D.
601-865-3152

Sleep Disorders Center
Forrest General Hospital
P.O. Box 16389
6051 Highway 49
Hattiesburg, MS 39404
Geoffrey B. Hartwig, M.D.
601-288-4790 or 800-280-8520

Sleep Disorders Center
University of Mississippi Medical
  Center
2500 N. State Street
Jackson, MS 39216-4505
Jeanetta Rains, Ph D.
Howard Roffwarg, M.D.
601-984-4820

## MISSOURI

Sleep Medicine and Research Center
St. Luke's Hospital
232 S. Woods Mill Road
Chesterfield, MO 63017
James K. Walsh, Ph.D.
Gihan Kader, M.D.
314-851-6030

University of Missouri Sleep
  Disorders Center
M-741 Neurology
University Hospital and Clinics
One Hospital Drive
Columbia, MO 65212
Pradeep Sahota, M.D.
314-884-SLEEP or 800-ADD-SLEEP

Sleep Disorders Center
Research Medical Center
2316 E. Meyer Boulevard
Kansas City, MO 64132-1199
Jon D. Magee, Ph.D.
816-276-4334

Sleep Disorders Center
St. Luke's Hospital
4400 Wornall Road
Kansas City, MO 64111
Ann Romaker, M.D.
816-932-3207

Sleep Disorders Center
St. Louis University Medical Center
1221 S. Grand Boulevard
St. Louis, MO 63104
314-577-8705

Sleep Disorders & Research Center
Deaconess Medical Center
6150 Oakland Avenue
St. Louis, MO 63139
Sidney D. Nau, Ph.D.
Korgi V. Hegde, M.D.
314-768-3100

Cox Regional Sleep Disorders Center
3800 S. National Avenue
Suite LL 150
Springfield, MO 65807
Edward Gwin, M.D.
417-269-5575

## MONTANA

No accredited members

## NEBRASKA

Great Plains Regional Sleep
  Physiology Center
Lincoln General Hospital
2300 S. 16th Street
Lincoln, NE 68502
Timothy R. Lieske, M.D.
402-473-5338

Sleep Disorders Center
Clarkson Hospital
4350 Dewey Avenue
Omaha, NE 68105-1018
Stephen B. Smith, M.D.
402-552-2286

Sleep Disorders Center
Methodist/Richard Young Hospital
2566 St. Mary's Avenue
Omaha, NE 68105
Robert Ellingson, Ph.D., M.D.
John D. Roehrs, M.D.
402-536-6305

## NEVADA

Regional Center for Sleep Disorders
Sunrise Hospital and Medical Center
3131 La Canada
Suite 107
Las Vegas, NV 89109
Paul Saskin, Ph.D.
Dory Markling, RPSGT
702-731-8365

The Sleep Clinic of Nevada
1012 E. Sahara Avenue
Las Vegas, NV 89104
Darlene Steljes
702-893-0020

Washoe Sleep Disorders Center and
  Sleep Laboratory
Washoe Professional Building and
  Washoe Medical Center
75 Pringle Way
Suite 701
Reno, NV 89502
William C. Torch, M.D., M.S.
John T. Zimmerman, Ph.D.
702-328-4700 or 702-328-4701

## NEW HAMPSHIRE

Sleep–Wake Disorders Center
Hampstead Hospital
218 East Road
Hampstead, NH 03841
Deborah E. Sewitch, Ph.D.
Jeffrey S. Shapiro, M.D., MPH
603-329-5311 x240

Sleep Disorders Center
Dartmouth-Hitchcock Medical
  Center
One Medical Center Drive
Lebanon, NH 03756
Michael Sateia, M.D.
603-650-7534

## NEW JERSEY

Institute for Sleep/Wake Disorders
Hackensack Medical Center
385 Prospect Avenue
Hackensack, NJ 07601
Hormoz Ashtyani, M.D.
Sue Zafarlotfi, Ph.D.
201-996-2366

Sleep Disorder Center of
  Morristown Memorial Hospital
95 Mount Kemble Avenue
Fifth Floor
Morristown, NJ 07962
Robert A. Capone, M.D., FCCP
Pamela Wolfsie, RPSGT
201-971-4567

Comprehensive Sleep Disorders
  Center
Robert Wood Johnson University
  Hospital/UMDNJ–Robert Wood
  Johnson Medical School
One Robert Wood Johnson Place
P.O. Box 2601
New Brunswick, NJ 08903-2601
Raymond Rosen, Ph.D.
Richard A. Parisi, M.D.
908-937-8683

Sleep Disorders Center
Newark Beth Israel Medical Center
201 Lyons Avenue
Newark, NJ 07112
Monroe S. Karetzky, M.D.
201-926-7163

Mercer Medical Center Sleep
  Disorders Center
Mercer Medical Center
446 Bellevue Avenue
P.O. Box 1658
Trenton, NJ 08618
Debra DeLuca, M.D.
Robert Perro, M.D.
609-394-4167

## NEW MEXICO

University Hospital Sleep Disorders
  Center
University of New Mexico Hospital
4775 Indian School Road, N.E.
Suite 307
Albuquerque, NM 87110
Wolfgang W. Schmidt-Nowara, M.D.
505-272-6110

## NEW YORK

Capital Region Sleep/Wake Disorders
  Center
St. Peter's Hospital and Albany
  Medical Center
25 Hackett Boulevard
Albany, NY 12208
Aaron E. Sher, M.D.
Paul B. Glovinsky, Ph.D.
518-436-9253

Sleep–Wake Disorders Center
Montefiore Medical Center
3411 Wayne Avenue
Bronx, NY 10467
Michael J. Thorpy, M.D.
718-920-4841

St. Joseph's Hospital Sleep Disorders
  Center
St. Joseph's Hospital
555 E. Market Street
Elmira, NY 14901
Kathleen R. Reilly, B.S., RRT
Paula Cook, RRT
607-733-6541 x7008

Sleep Disorders Center
Winthrop-University Hospital
222 Station Plaza North
Mineola, NY 11501
Steven Feinsilver, M.D.
516-663-3907

Sleep–Wake Disorders Center
Long Island Jewish Medical Center
270-05 76th Avenue
New Hyde Park, NY 11040
Harly Greenberg, M.D.
Gershon Ney, M.D.
Jane Luchsinger, M.S.
718-470-7058

The Sleep Disorders Center
Columbia Presbyterian Medical
  Center
161 Fort Washington Avenue
New York, NY 10032
Neil B. Kavey, M.D.
212-305-1860

Sleep Disorders Institute at St. Luke's/
  Roosevelt Hospital Center
Amsterdam Avenue at 114th Street
New York, NY 10025
Gary K. Zammit, Ph.D.
212-523-1700

Sleep Disorders Center of Rochester
2110 Clinton Avenue South
Rochester, NY 14618
Donald W. Greenblatt, M.D.
716-442-4141

Sleep Disorders Center
State University of New York at
    Stony Brook University Hospital
MR 120 A
Stony Brook, NY 11794-7139
Marta Maczaj, M.D.
516-444-2916

The Sleep Center
Community General Hospital
Broad Road
Syracuse, NY 13215
Robert E. Westlake, M.D.
Bruce B. Hall, RPSGT
315-492-5877

The Sleep Laboratory*
945 E. Genesee Street
Suite 300
Syracuse, NY 13210
Edward T. Downing, M.D.
Stephen F. Swierczek, RPSGT
315-475-3379

Sleep–Wake Disorders Center
New York Hospital-Cornell Medical
    Center
21 Bloomingdale Road
White Plains, NY 10605
Dir. Daniel R. Wagner, M.D.
Arlene Estberg, RPSGT
914-997-5751

## NORTH CAROLINA

Sleep Medicine Center of Asheville
1091 Hendersonville Road
Asheville, NC 28803
Dennis L. Hill, M.D.
704-277-7533

Sleep Center
University Hospital
P.O. Box 560727
Charlotte, NC 28256
Mindy B. Cetel, M.D.
Paul D. Knowles, M.D.
704-548-6848

Sleep Disorders Center
The Moses H. Cone Memorial
    Hospital
1200 N. Elm Street
Greensboro, NC 27401-1020
Clinton D. Young, M.D.
Reggie Whitsett
910-574-7406

Sleep Disorders Center
North Carolina Baptist Hospital
Bowman Gray School of Medicine
Medical Center Boulevard
Winston-Salem, NC 27157
W. Vaughn McCall, M.D.
Linda Quinlivan
910-716-5288

Summit Sleep Disorders Center
160 Charlois Boulevard
Winston-Salem, NC 27103
J. Baldwin Smith, III, M.D.
Richard Doud Bey, M.D.
910-765-9431

## NORTH DAKOTA

Sleep Disorders Center
MeritCare Hospital
720 Fourth Street North
Fargo, ND 58122
Joseph M. Cullen, M.D.
701-234-5673

## OHIO

The Center for Research in Sleep
    Disorders
1275 E. Kemper Road
Cincinnati, OH 45246
Martin B. Scharf, Ph.D.
513-671-3101

Sleep Disorders Center
Bethesda Oak Hospital
619 Oak Street
Cincinnati, OH 45206
Milton Kramer, M.D.
513-569-6320

Sleep Disorders Center
The Cleveland Clinic Foundation
9500 Euclid Avenue
Desk S-51
Cleveland, OH 44195
Dudley Dinner, M.D., Director
216-444-2165

Sleep Disorders Center
Rainbow Babies Children's Hospital
Case Western Reserve University
11100 Euclid Avenue
Cleveland, OH 44106
Lee Brooks, M.D.
Susan M. Koziol, RN
216-844-1301

Sleep Disorders Center
The Ohio State University Medical
  Center
Rhodes Hall, S1039
410 W. 10th Avenue
Columbus, OH 43210-1228
Charles P. Pollak, M.D.
Greg Landholt, RPSGT
614-293-8296

The Center for Sleep & Wake
  Disorders
Miami Valley Hospital
One Wyoming Street
Suite G-200
Dayton, OH 45409
James Graham, M.D.
Kevin Huban, Psy.D.
937-208-2515

Ohio Sleep Medicine Institute
4975 Bradenton Avenue
Dublin, OH 43017
Helmut S. Schmidt, M.D.
Laura Arnold, RNBSN, RPSGT
614-766-0773

Sleep Disorders Center
Kettering Medical Center
3535 Southern Boulevard
Kettering, OH 45429-1298
Donna Arand, Ph.D.
513-296-7805

Northwest Ohio Sleep Disorders
  Center
The Toledo Hospital
Harris-McIntosh Tower
Second Floor
212 Hughes
Toledo, OH 43606
Pam Lang, RPSGT, CRTT
Frank O. Horton, III, M.D.
419-471-5629

Sleep Disorders Center
St. Vincent Medical Center
2213 Cherry Street
Toledo, OH 43608-2691
Joseph I. Shaffer, Ph.D.
419-321-4980

Sleep Disorders Center
Good Samaritan Medical Center
800 Forest Avenue
Zanesville, OH 43701
Roger J. Balogh, M.D.
Thomas E. Rojewski, M.D.
Robert J. Thompson, M.D.
614-454-5855

## OKLAHOMA

Sleep Disorders Center of Oklahoma
Southwest Medical Center of
  Oklahoma
4401 S. Western Avenue
Oklahoma City, OK 73109
Jonathan R.L. Schwartz, M.D.
Chris A. Veit, M.S.W., RPSGT
405-636-7700

## OREGON

Sleep Disorders Center
Sacred Heart Medical Center
1255 Hilyard Street
P.O. Box 10905
Eugene, OR 97440
Rodney Roth, RRT, RCP
Robert Tearse, M.D.
541-686-7224

Sleep Disorders Center
Rogue Valley Medical Center
2825 E. Barnett Road
Medford, OR 97504
Michael E. Schwartz, RPSGT
Eric Overland, M.D.
Nic Butkov, RPSGT
541-770-4320

Pacific Northwest Sleep Disorders
  Program
1849 N.W. Kearney Street
Suite 202
Portland, OR 97209
Gerald B. Rich, M.D.
503-228-4414

Sleep Disorders Laboratory*
Providence Medical Center
4805 N.E. Glisan Street
Portland, OR 97213
Louis Libby, M.D.
503-215-6552

Salem Hospital Sleep Disorders
  Center
Salem Hospital
P.O. Box 14001
Salem, OR 97309
Mark T. Gabr, M.D.
Stephen J. Baughman, RRT, RPSGT
503-370-5170


## PENNSYLVANIA

Sleep Disorders Center
Abington Memorial Hospital
1200 Old York Road
Second Floor
Rorer Building
Abington, PA 19001
B. Franklin Diamond, M.D.
Albert D. Wagman, M.D.
215-576-2226

Sleep Disorders Center
Lower Bucks Hospital
501 Bath Road
Bristol, PA 19007
Howard J. Lee, M.D.
215-785-9752

Sleep Disorders Center*
The Good Samaritan Medical Center
1020 Franklin Street
Johnstown, PA 15905
Eugene Friedman, CRTT, CPFT
Brian Ahlstrom, M.D.
814-533-1661

Sleep Disorders Center of Lancaster
Lancaster General Hospital
555 N. Duke Street
Lancaster, PA 17604-3555
Harshadkumar B. Patel, M.D.
James M. O'Connor, RPSGT
717-290-5910

Penn Center for Sleep Disorders
Hospital of the University of
  Pennsylvania
3400 Spruce Street
11 West Gates Building
Philadelphia, PA 19104
Allan I. Pack, M.D., Ph.D.
Richard J. Schwab, M.D.
Louis F. Metzger
215-662-7772

Sleep Disorders Center
The Medical College of Pennsylvania
3200 Henry Avenue
Philadelphia, PA 19129
June M. Fry, M.D., Ph.D.
215-842-4250

Sleep Disorders Center
Thomas Jefferson University
1025 Walnut Street
Suite 316
Philadelphia, PA 19107
Karl Doghramji, M.D.
215-955-6175

Pulmonary Sleep Evaluation Center*
University of Pittsburgh Medical
  Center
Montefiore University Hospital
3459 Fifth Avenue, S639
Pittsburgh, PA 15213
Nancy Kern, CRTT, RPSGT
Mark H. Sanders, M.D.
Patrick J. Strollo, M.D.
412-692-2880

Sleep and Chronobiology Center
Western Psychiatric Institute and
  Clinic
3811 O'Hara Street
Pittsburgh, PA 15213
Charles F. Reynolds III, M.D.
412-624-2246

Sleep Disorders Center
Community Medical Center
1822 Mulberry Street
Scranton, PA 18510
S. Ramakrishna, M.D., FCCP
717-969-8931

Sleep Disorders Center
Crozer-Chester Medical Center
One Medical Center Boulevard
Upland, PA 19013-3975
Calvin Stafford, M.D.
610-447-2689

Sleep Disorders Center
The Lankenau Hospital
100 Lancaster Avenue
Suite 120
Wynnewood, PA 19096
Mark R. Pressman, Ph.D.
Donald D. Peterson, M.D.
610-645-3400

## RHODE ISLAND

Sleep Disorders Center
Rhode Island Hospital
593 Eddy Street, APC-301
Providence, RI 02903
Richard P. Millman, M.D.
Naomi R. Kramer, M.D.
401-444-4269

## SOUTH CAROLINA

Roper Sleep/Wake Disorders Center
Roper Hospital
316 Calhoun Street
Charleston, SC 29401-1125
William T. Dawson, Jr., M.D.
Wayne C. Vial, M.D.
Graham C. Scott, M.D.
Tim Fultz, M.S., RRT, RPSGT
803-724-2246

Sleep Disorders Center of South
  Carolina
Baptist Medical Center
Taylor at Marion Streets
Columbia, SC 29220
Richard Bogan, M.D., FCCP
Sharon S. Ellis, M.D.
803-771-5847

Sleep Disorders Center
Greenville Memorial Hospital
701 Grove Road
Greenville, SC 29605
Don McMahan
803-455-8916

Children's Sleep Disorders Center*
Self Memorial Hospital
1325 Spring Street
Greenwood, SC 29646
Terry A. Marshall, M.D.
803-227-4449 or 803-227-4489

Sleep Disorders Center
Spartanburg Regional Medical
  Center
101 E. Wood Street
Spartanburg, SC 29303
Shari Angel Newman, RPSGT
803-560-6904

## SOUTH DAKOTA

The Sleep Center
Rapid City Regional Hospital
353 Fairmont Boulevard
P.O. Box 6000
Rapid City, SD 57709
K. Alan Kelts, M.D., Ph.D.
605-341-8037

Sleep Disorders Center
Sioux Valley Hospital
1100 S. Euclid
Sioux Falls, SD 57117-5039
Liz Grav
605-333-6302

## TENNESSEE

Sleep Disorders Laboratory*
Columbia Regional Hospital
367 Hospital Boulevard
Jackson, TN 38305
Thomas W. Ellis, M.D.
David M. Larsen, M.D.
Jim Carruth, M.D.
Charlie Carroll, RPSGT
901-661-2000

Sleep Disorders Center
Ft. Sanders Regional Medical Center
1901 Clinch Avenue
Knoxville, TN 37916
Thomas G. Higgins, M.D.
Bert A. Hampton, M.D.
C. Keith Hulse, Ph.D.
423-541-1375

Sleep Disorders Center
St. Mary's Medical Center
900 E. Oak Hill Avenue
Knoxville, TN 37917-4556
William Finley, Ph.D.
423-545-6746

BMH Sleep Disorders Center
Baptist Memorial Hospital
899 Madison Avenue
Memphis, TN 38146
Helio Lemmi, M.D.
901-227-5337

Methodist Sleep Disorders Center
Methodist Hospital of Memphis
1265 Union Avenue (12 Thomas)
Memphis, TN 38104
Kristin W. Lester
Neal Aguillard, M.D.
901-726-7378

Sleep Disorders Center
Centennial Medical Center
2300 Patterson Street
Nashville, TN 37203
David A. Jarvis, M.D.
Marcie T. Poe
615-342-1670

Sleep Disorders Center
Saint Thomas Hospital
P.O. Box 380
Nashville, TN 37202
J. Brevard Haynes, Jr., M.D.
Rose Hall
615-222-2068

## TEXAS

NWTH Sleep Disorders Center
Northwest Texas Hospital
P.O. Box 1110
Amarillo, TX 79175
Michael Westmoreland, M.D.
John Moss, CRTT
806-354-1954

Sleep Disorders Center for Children
Children's Medical Center of Dallas
1935 Motor Street
Dallas, TX 75235
John Herman, Ph.D.
Joel Steinberg, M.D.
214-640-2793

Sleep Medicine Institute
Presbyterian Hospital of Dallas
8200 Walnut Hill Lane
Dallas, TX 75231
Philip M. Becker, M.D.
Andrew O. Jamieson, M.D.
214-345-8563

Sleep Disorders Center
Columbia Medical Center West
1801 N. Oregon
El Paso, TX 79902
Gonzalo Diaz, M.D., FCCP
Elizabeth Baird, RPSGT
915-521-1257

Sleep Disorders Center
Providence Memorial Hospital
2001 N. Oregon
El Paso, TX 79902
Gonzalo Diaz, M.D., FCCP
Joseph Arteaga, RPSGT
915-577-6152

Sleep Consultants
1521 Cooper Street
Fort Worth, TX 76104
Edgar Lucas, Ph.D.
817-927-5337

Sleep Disorders Center
Baylor College of Medicine
MS 710D
One Baylor Plaza
Houston, TX 77030
Max Hirshkowitz, Ph.D.
Constance Moore, M.D.
713-798-4886

Sleep Disorders Center
Spring Branch Medical Center
8850 Long Point Road
Suite 420 S
Houston, TX 77055
Todd Swick, M.D.
Kristyne M. Hartse, Ph.D.
713-973-6483 or 713-794-7563

Sleep Disorders Center
Scott and White Clinic
2401 S. 31st Street
Temple, TX 76508
Francisco Perez-Guerra, M.D.
817-724-2554

## UTAH

Intermountain Sleep Disorders
  Center
LDS Hospital
325 Eighth Avenue and C Street
Salt Lake City, UT 84143
James M. Walker, Ph.D.
Robert J. Farney, M.D.
801-321-3617

University Health Sciences Center
Sleep Disorders Center
50 N. Medical Drive
Salt Lake City, UT 84132
Laura Czajkowski, Ph.D.
Christopher R. Jones, M.D., Ph.D.,
  Medical Director
801-581-2016

## VERMONT

No accredited members

## VIRGINIA

Fairfax Sleep Disorders Center
3289 Woodburn Road
Suite 360
Annandale, VA 22003
Konrad W. Bakker, M.D.
Marc Raphaelson, M.D.
703-876-9871

Sleep Disorders Center
Eastern Virginia Medical School
Sentara Norfolk General Hospital
600 Gresham Drive
Norfolk, VA 23507
Reuben H. McBrayer, M.D.
J. Catesby Ware, Ph.D.
Virgil Wooten, M.D.
Tom Bond, Psy.D.
757-668-3322

Sleep Disorders Center
Medical College of Virginia
P.O. Box 980710
Richmond, VA 23298-0710
Rakesh K. Sood, M.D.
804-828-1490

Sleep Disorders Center
Carilion Roanoke Community
  Hospital
P.O. Box 12946
Roanoke, VA 24029
William S. Elias, M.D., Specialist
540-985-8526

## WASHINGTON

St. Clare Sleep Related Breathing
  Disorders Clinic*
St. Clare Hospital
11315 Bridgeport Way, S.W.
Lakewood, WA 98499
Arthur Knodel, M.D.
206-581-6951

Sleep Disorders Center for
  Southwest Washington
St. Peter Hospital
413 N. Lilly Road
Olympia, WA 98506
Kim A. Chase, RPSGT
John L. Brottem, M.D.
360-493-7436

Richland Sleep Laboratory*
800 Swift Boulevard
Suite 260
Richland, WA 99352
A. Pat Hamner, Jr., M.D.
509-946-4632

Providence Sleep Disorders Center
Jefferson Tower
Suite 203
1600 E. Jefferson
Seattle, WA 98122
Ralph A. Pascualy, M.D.
206-320-2575

Seattle Sleep Disorders Center
Swedish Medical Center/Ballard
P.O. Box 70707
Seattle, WA 98107-1507
Gary A. DeAndrea, M.D.
Noel T. Johnson, D.O.
Richard P. Swanson, RPSGT, CRTT
206-781-6359

Sleep Disorders Center
Sacred Heart Doctors Building
105 W. Eighth Avenue
Suite 418
Spokane, WA 99204
Elizabeth Hurd, RPSGT
Jeffrey C. Elmer, M.D.
509-455-4895

## WEST VIRGINIA

Sleep Disorders Center
Charleston Area Medical Center
501 Morris Street
P.O. Box 1393
Charleston, WV 25325
George Zaldivar, M.D., FCCP
Karen Stewart, RRT, Manager
304-348-7507

## WISCONSIN

Regional Sleep Disorders Center
Appleton Medical Center
1818 N. Meade Street
Appleton, WI 54911
Kevin C. Garrett, M.D.
414-738-6460

Luther/Midelfort Sleep Disorders
  Center
Luther Hospital/Midelfort Clinic
1221 Whipple Street
Box 4105
Eau Claire, WI 54702-4105
Donn Dexter, Jr., M.D.
David Nye, M.D.
715-838-3165

St. Vincent Hospital Sleep Disorders
  Center
P.O. Box 13508
Green Bay, WI 54307-3508
John Stevenson, M.D.
Paula Van Ert, RPSGT
414-431-3041

Wisconsin Sleep Disorders Center
Gundersen Clinic, Ltd.
1836 South Avenue
La Crosse, WI 54601
Alan D. Pratt, M.D.
608-782-7300 x2870

Comprehensive Sleep Disorders
  Center
University of Wisconsin Hospitals
  and Clinics
600 Highland Avenue, B6/579
Madison, WI 53792
Steven M. Weber, Ph.D.
608-263-2387

Marshfield Sleep Disorders Center
Marshfield Clinic
1000 N. Oak Avenue
Marshfield, WI 54449
Jody Scherr, RPSGT/REEGT
Kevin Ruggles, M.D.
715-387-5397

Milwaukee Regional Sleep Disorders
  Center
Columbia Hospital
2025 E. Newport Avenue
Milwaukee, WI 53211
Marvin Wooten, M.D.
414-961-4650

St. Luke's Sleep Disorders Center
St. Luke's Medical Center
2900 W. Oklahoma Avenue
Milwaukee, WI 53201-2901
David Arnold
Michael N. Katzoff, M.D.
414-649-5288

Sleep/Wake Disorders Center
St. Mary's Hospital
2320 N. Lake Drive
P.O. Box 503
Milwaukee, WI 53201-4565
Steve Hartmann
414-291-1275

## WYOMING

No accredited members

D

Sleep Diary
and Behavior Log

SLEEP DIARY

Child: _____                                    Week of: _____

| Day | Time put to bed | Time fell asleep | Nighttime waking (time/how long) | Describe nighttime waking | Time awoke | Describe any naps |
|-----|-----|-----|-----|-----|-----|-----|
| Sun | | | | | | |
| Mon | | | | | | |
| Tue | | | | | | |
| Wed | | | | | | |
| Thu | | | | | | |
| Fri | | | | | | |
| Sat | | | | | | |

BEHAVIOR LOG

Name: _____

| Date | Time | Behavior at bedtime | What did you do to handle the problem? | Behavior during awakenings | What did you do to handle the problem? |
|------|------|---------------------|----------------------------------------|----------------------------|----------------------------------------|
|  |  |  |  |  |  |
|  |  |  |  |  |  |
|  |  |  |  |  |  |
|  |  |  |  |  |  |
|  |  |  |  |  |  |

Fill out this log each time your child has difficulty going to sleep or wakes during the night.

E

Albany Sleep Problems Scale

## ALBANY SLEEP PROBLEMS SCALE
## (ASPS)

| Name: | Date of birth: |
|---|---|
| Diagnoses: | Sex: |
| Name of respondent: | Date adm: |

Instructions: Circle *one* number that best represents the frequency of the behavior (0 = never; 1 = less than once per week; 2 = one to two times per week; 3 = three to six times per week; 4 = nightly).

| | | | | | | |
|---|---|---|---|---|---|---|
| 1. | Does this person have a fairly regular bedtime and time when he or she awakens? | 0 | 1 | 2 | 3 | 4 |
| 2. | Does this person have a bedtime routine that is the same each evening? | 0 | 1 | 2 | 3 | 4 |
| 3. | Does this person work or play in bed, often right up to the time when he or she goes to bed? | 0 | 1 | 2 | 3 | 4 |
| 4. | Does this person sleep poorly in his or her own bed but better away from it? | Yes | | | No | |
| 5. | Does this person smoke, drink alcohol, or consume caffeine in any form? | 0 | 1 | 2 | 3 | 4 |
| 6. | Does this person engage in vigorous activity in the hours before bedtime? | 0 | 1 | 2 | 3 | 4 |
| 7. | Does this person resist going to bed? | 0 | 1 | 2 | 3 | 4 |
| 8. | Does this person take more than an hour to fall asleep but does not resist? | 0 | 1 | 2 | 3 | 4 |
| 9. | Does this person awaken during the night but remain quiet and in bed? | 0 | 1 | 2 | 3 | 4 |
| 10. | Does this person awaken during the night and become disruptive (e.g., tantrums, oppositional)? | 0 | 1 | 2 | 3 | 4 |
| 11. | Does this person take naps during the day? | 0 | 1 | 2 | 3 | 4 |
| 12. | Does this person often feel exhausted during the day because of lack of sleep? | 0 | 1 | 2 | 3 | 4 |
| 13. | Has this person ever had an accident or near accident because of sleepiness from not being able to sleep the night before? | Yes | | | No | |
| 14. | Does this person ever use prescription drugs or over-the-counter medications to help him or her sleep? | 0 | 1 | 2 | 3 | 4 |
| 15. | Has this person found that sleep medication does not work as well as it did when he or she first started taking it? | Yes | | | No/NA | |

| 16. | If this person takes sleep medication, then does he or she find that he or she cannot sleep on nights without it? | Yes | | No/NA | |
|-----|---|:---:|:---:|:---:|:---:|
| 17. | Does this person fall asleep early in the evening and awaken too early in the morning? | 0 | 1 | 2 | 3 | 4 |
| 18. | Does this person have difficulty falling asleep until a very late hour and difficulty awakening early in the morning? | 0 | 1 | 2 | 3 | 4 |
| 19. | Does this person wake up in the middle of the night upset? | 0 | 1 | 2 | 3 | 4 |
| 20. | Is this person relatively easy to comfort from these episodes? | Yes | | No/NA | |
| 21. | Does this person have episodes during sleep in which he or she screams loudly for several minutes but is not fully awake? | 0 | 1 | 2 | 3 | 4 |
| 22. | Is this person difficult to comfort during these episodes? | Yes | | No/NA | |
| 23. | Does this person experience sleep attacks (falling asleep almost immediately and without warning) during the day? | 0 | 1 | 2 | 3 | 4 |
| 24. | Does this person experience excessive daytime sleepiness that is not accounted for by an inadequate amount of sleep? | 0 | 1 | 2 | 3 | 4 |
| 25. | Does this person snore when asleep? | 0 | 1 | 2 | 3 | 4 |
| 26. | Does this person sometimes stop breathing for a few seconds during sleep? | 0 | 1 | 2 | 3 | 4 |
| 27. | Does this person have trouble breathing? | 0 | 1 | 2 | 3 | 4 |
| 28. | Is this person overweight? | Yes | | No | |
| 29. | Has this person often walked while asleep? | 0 | 1 | 2 | 3 | 4 |
| 30. | Does this person talk while asleep? | 0 | 1 | 2 | 3 | 4 |
| 31. | Are this person's sheets and blankets in extreme disarray in the morning when he or she wakes up? | 0 | 1 | 2 | 3 | 4 |
| 32. | Does this person wake up at night because of kicking legs? | 0 | 1 | 2 | 3 | 4 |
| 33. | While lying down, does this person ever experience unpleasant sensations in the legs? | Yes | | No | |
| 34. | Does this person rock back and forth or bang a body part (e.g., head) to fall asleep? | 0 | 1 | 2 | 3 | 4 |
| 35. | Does this person wet the bed? | 0 | 1 | 2 | 3 | 4 |

| | | | | | | |
|---|---|---|---|---|---|---|
| 36. | Does this person grind his or her teeth at night? | 0 | 1 | 2 | 3 | 4 |
| 37. | Does this person sleep well when it doesn't matter, such as on weekends, but sleep poorly when he or she "must" sleep well, such as when a busy day at school is ahead? | Yes | | | No | |
| 38. | Does this person often have feelings of apprehension, anxiety, or dread when he or she is getting ready for bed? | 0 | 1 | 2 | 3 | 4 |
| 39. | Does this person worry in bed? | 0 | 1 | 2 | 3 | 4 |
| 40. | Does this person often have depressing thoughts, or do tomorrow's worries or plans buzz through his or her mind when he or she wants to go to sleep? | 0 | 1 | 2 | 3 | 4 |
| 41. | Does this person have feelings of frustration when he or she can't sleep? | 0 | 1 | 2 | 3 | 4 |
| 42. | Has this person experienced a relatively recent change in eating habits? | Yes | | | No | |
| 43. | Does this person have behavior problems at times other than bedtime or upon awakening? | Yes | | | No | |
| 44. | When did this person's primary difficulty with sleep begin? | | | | | |
| 45. | What was happening in this person's life at that time or a few months before? | | | | | |
| 46. | Is this person under a physician's care for any medical condition? (If yes, then indicate condition below.) | Yes | | | No | |

OTHER COMMENTS:

# Endnotes

## CHAPTER 1

1. Lavie (1996).
2. Lamberg (1994).
3. Ibid.
4. Ibid.
5. Ibid.
6. Dement (1960).
7. Hoddes, Zarcone, Smythe, Phillips, & Dement (1973).
8. Espie & Tweedie (1991); Shibagaki, Kiyono, & Takeuchi (1987a, 1987b); Shibagaki, Kiyono, & Watanabe (1980).
9. Jan, Espezel, & Appleton (1994).
10. Lamberg (1994).

## CHAPTER 2

1. DeMyer (1979).
2. Quine (1992).
3. Barkley (1995).
4. Ball & Koloian (1995).
5. Keener, Zeanah, & Anders (1988); Zuckerman, Stevenson, & Bailey (1987).
6. Durand, Gernert-Dott, & Mapstone (1996); Kennedy & Meyer (1996); O'Reilly (1995).
7. Seligman (1975).
8. Parkes & Block (1989).
9. Spanos, Cross, Dickson, & DuBreuil (1993).
10. Ibid, p. 627.
11. Mindell (1993).
12. Wood, Bootzin, Rosenhan, Nolen-Hoeksema, & Jourden (1992).
13. Mindell (1993).
14. Ibid.
15. Ovuga (1992).
16. Thorpy & Glovinsky (1987).
17. Bootzin, Manber, Perlis, Salvio, & Wyatt (1993).
18. Anch, Browman, Mitler, & Walsh (1988).
19. Kales et al. (1980).
20. Barclay & Houts (1995).

## CHAPTER 4

1. Singh, Clements, & Fiatarone (1997).
2. Flaxman (1991).

## CHAPTER 5

1. Durand & Carr (1988); Gilberg (1984); Lovaas (1987); Rutter (1978).
2. Ferber (1985).
3. Durand & Mindell (1990); Rolider & Van Houten (1984).
4. Piazza & Fisher (1991a, 1991b).
5. Mindell & Durand (1993).

## CHAPTER 6

1. Johnson, Bradley-Johnson, & Stack (1981); Johnson & Learner (1985); Rickert & Johnson (1988).
2. Ibid.

## CHAPTER 8

1. Buysse, Reynolds, & Kupfer (1993).
2. Wood, Bootzin, Rosenhan, Nolen-Hoeksema, & Jourden (1992).
3. Ovuga (1992).

## CHAPTER 9

1. Guilleminault (1989).
2. American Sleep Disorders Association (1990).
3. Wooten (1990).
4. Data available through the Sudden Infant Death Syndrome Network, 9 Gonch Farm Road, Ledyard, CT 06399.
5. Data available from the American Sleep Disorders Association, 1610 14th Street, N.W., Suite 300, Rochester, MN 55901.
6. Ibid.
7. Ibid.

## CHAPTER 10

1. Barclay & Houts (1995).
2. Ibid.
3. Ibid.
4. Norgaard, Rittig, & Djurhuus (1989).
5. Barclay & Houts (1995).
6. Houts, Berman, & Abramson (1994).
7. Azrin, Thienes-Hontos, & Besalel-Azrin (1979).
8. Barclay & Houts (1995).
9. Lofland, Cassisi, & Drabman (1995).

## CHAPTER 11

1.  Durand, Gernert-Dott, & Mapstone (1996).
2.  Durand (1990).
3.  Durand & Carr (1991).
4.  Wacker et al. (1990).
5.  Durand & Carr (1991); Wacker et al. (1990).

## CHAPTER 12

1.  Data available from the American Sleep Disorders Association, 1610 14th Street, N.W., Suite 300, Rochester, MN 55901.
2.  Mendelson, Thompson, & Franko (1996).
3.  Jan, Espezel, & Appleton (1994).
4.  Ibid.

## CHAPTER 13

1.  Hart & Risley (1992).
2.  Ferber (1985).

# References

American Sleep Disorders Association. (1990). *The international classification of sleep disorders: Diagnostic and coding manual.* Rochester, MN: Author.

Anch, A.M., Browman, C.P., Mitler, M.M., & Walsh, J.K. (1988). *Sleep: A scientific perspective.* Englewood Cliffs, NJ: Prentice Hall.

Azrin, N.H., Thienes-Hontos, P., & Besalel-Azrin, V. (1979). Elimination of enuresis without a conditioning apparatus: An extension by office instruction of the child and parents. *Behavior Therapy, 10,* 14–19,

Ball, J.D., & Koloian, B. (1995). Sleep patterns among ADHD children. *Clinical Psychology Review, 15,* 681–691.

Barclay, D.R., & Houts, A.C. (1995). Childhood enuresis. In C.E. Schaefer (Ed.), *Clinical handbook of sleep disorders in children* (pp. 223–252). Northvale, NJ: Jason Aronson Inc.

Barkley, R.A. (1995). *Taking charge of ADHD: The complete, authoritative guide for parents.* New York: Guilford Press.

Bootzin, R.R., Manber, R., Perlis, M.L., Salvio, M., & Wyatt, J.K. (1993). Sleep disorders. In P.B. Sutker & H.E. Adams (Eds.), *Comprehensive handbook of psychopathology* (2nd ed., pp. 531–561). New York: Plenum.

Buysse, D.J., Reynolds, C.F., & Kupfer, D.J, (1993). Classification of sleep disorders: A preview of DSM-IV. In D.L. Dunner (Ed.), *Current psychiatric therapy* (pp. 360–361). Philadelphia: W.B. Saunders.

Dement, W. (1960). The effect of dream deprivation. *Science, 131,* 1705–1707.

DeMyer, M. (1979). *Parents and children: Autism.* New York: John Wiley & Sons.

Durand, V.M. (1990). *Severe behavior problems: A functional communication training approach.* New York: Guilford Press.

Durand, V.M., & Carr, E.G. (1988). Autism. In V.B. VanHasselt, P.S. Strain, & M. Hersen (Eds.), *Handbook of developmental and physical disabilities* (pp. 195–214). New York: Pergamon Press.

Durand, V.M., & Carr, E.G. (1991). Functional communication training to reduce challenging behavior: Maintenance and application in new settings. *Journal of Applied Behavior Analysis, 24,* 251–264.

Durand, V.M., Gernert-Dott, P., & Mapstone, E. (1996). Treatment of sleep disorders in children with developmental disabilities. *Journal of The Association for Persons with Severe Handicaps, 21,* 114–122.

Durand, V.M., & Mindell, J.A. (1990). Behavioral treatment of multiple childhood sleep disorders. *Behavior Modification, 14,* 37–49.

Espie, C.A., & Tweedie, F.M. (1991). Sleep patterns and sleep problems amongst people with mental handicap. *Journal of Mental Deficiency Research, 35,* 25–36.

Ferber, R. (1985). *Solve your child's sleep problems.* New York: Simon & Schuster.

Flaxman, J. (1991). Insomnia in the older adult. In P. Hauri (Ed.), *Case studies in insomnia* (pp. 237–247). New York: Plenum Medical Book Company.

Gillberg, C. (1984). Infantile autism and other childhood psychoses in a Swedish urban region: Epidemiological aspects. *Journal of Child Psychology and Psychiatry, 25,* 35–43.

Guilleminault, C. (1989). Clinical features of obstructive sleep apnea. In M.H. Kryger, T. Roth, & W.C. Dement (Eds.), *Principles and practice of sleep medicine* (pp. 552–558). Philadelphia: W.B. Saunders.

Hart, B., & Risley, T.R. (1992). American parenting of language-learning children: Persisting differences in family–child interactions observed in natural home environments. *Developmental Psychology, 28,* 1096–1105.

Hoddes, E., Zarcone, V., Smythe, H., Phillips, R., & Dement, W.C. (1973). Quantification of sleepiness: A new approach. *Psychopharmacology, 10,* 431–436.

Houts, A.C., Berman, J.S., & Abramson, H.A. (1994). The effectiveness of psychological and pharmacological treatments for nocturnal enuresis. *Journal of Consulting and Clinical Psychology, 62,* 737–745.

Jan, J.E., Espezel, H., & Appleton, R.E. (1994). The treatment of sleep disorders with melatonin. *Developmental Medicine and Child Neurology, 36,* 97–107.

Johnson, C.M., Bradley-Johnson, S., & Stack, J.M. (1981). Decreasing the frequency of infants' nocturnal crying with the use of scheduled awakenings. *Family Practice Research Journal, 1,* 98–104.

Johnson, C.M., & Learner, M. (1985). Amelioration of infants' sleep disturbances: II. Effects of scheduled awakenings by compliant parents. *Infant Mental Health Journal, 6,* 21–30.

Kales, A., Soldatos, C.R., Bixler, E.O., Ladda, R.L., Charney, D.S., Weber, G., & Schweitzer, P.K. (1980). Hereditary factors in sleepwalking and night terrors. *British Journal of Psychiatry, 137,* 111–118.

Keener, M.A., Zeanah, C.H., & Anders, T.F. (1988). Infant temperament, sleep organization, and nighttime parental interventions. *Pediatrics, 81,* 762–771.

Kennedy, C.H., & Meyer, K.A. (1996). Sleep deprivation, allergy symptoms, and negatively reinforced problem behavior. *Journal of Applied Behavior Analysis, 29,* 133–135.

Lamberg, L. (1994). *Bodyrhythms: Chronobiology and peak performance.* New York: William Morrow & Company.

Lavie, P. (1996). *The enchanted world of sleep.* New Haven, CT: Yale University Press.

Lofland, K.R., Cassisi, J.E., & Drabman, R.S. (1995). Nocturnal bruxism in children. In C.E. Schaefer (Ed.), *Clinical handbook of sleep disorders in children* (pp. 203–222). Northvale, NJ: Jason Aronson Inc.

Lovaas, O.I. (1987). Behavioral treatment and normal educational and intellectual functioning in young autistic children. *Journal of Consulting and Clinical Psychology, 55,* 3–9.

Mendelson, W.B., Thompson, C., & Franko, T. (1996). Adverse reactions to sedative/hypnotics: Three years' experience. *Sleep, 19,* 702–706.

Mindell, J.A. (1993). Sleep disorders in children. *Health Psychology, 12,* 151–162.

Mindell, J.A., & Durand, V.M. (1993). Treatment of childhood sleep disorders: Generalization across disorders and effects on family members. *Journal of Pediatric Psychology, 18,* 731–750.

Norgaard, J.P., Rittig, S., & Djurhuus, J.C. (1989). Nocturnal enuresis: An approach to treatment based on pathogenesis. *Pediatrics, 14,* 705–710.

O'Reilly, M.F. (1995). Functional analysis and treatment of escape-maintained aggression correlated with sleep deprivation. *Journal of Applied Behavior Analysis, 28,* 225–226.

Ovuga, E.B.L. (1992). Murder during sleep-walking. *East Africa Medical Journal, 69,* 533–534.

Parkes, J.D., & Block, C. (1989). Genetic factors in sleep disorders. *Journal of Neurology, Neurosurgery, and Psychiatry, 52,* 101–108.

Pennington, J.A.T. (1994). *Bowes' and Church's food values of portions commonly used* (16th ed.). Phildelphia: Lippincott-Raven Publishers.

Piazza, C.C., & Fisher, W.W. (1991a). A faded bedtime with response cost protocol for treatment of multiple sleep problems in children. *Journal of Applied Behavior Analysis, 24,* 129–140.

Piazza, C.C., & Fisher, W.W. (1991b). Bedtime fading in the treatment of pediatric insomnia. *Journal of Behavior Therapy & Experimental Psychiatry, 22,* 53–56.

Quine, L. (1992). Severity of sleep problems in children with severe learning difficulties: Description and correlates. *Journal of Community & Applied Social Psychology, 2,* 247–268.

Rickert, V.I., & Johnson, C.M. (1988). Reducing nocturnal awakening and crying episodes in infants and young children: A comparison between scheduled awakenings and systematic ignoring. *Pediatrics, 81,* 203–212.

Roffwarg, H.P., Muzio, J.N., & Dement, W.C. (1966). Ontogenetic development of the human sleep-dream cycle. *Science, 152,* 604–619.

Rolider, A., & Van Houten, R. (1984). Training parents to use extinction to eliminate nighttime crying by gradually increasing the criteria for ignoring crying. *Education and Treatment of Children, 7,* 119–124.

Rutter, M. (1978). Diagnosis and definition of childhood autism. *Journal of Autism and Childhood Schizophrenia, 8,* 139–161.

Seligman, M.E.P. (1975). *Helplessness: On depression, development and death.* San Francisco: W.H. Freeman.

Shibagaki, M., Kiyono, S., & Takeuchi, T. (1987a). Developmental disorders of skin potential responses in mentally retarded children during nocturnal sleep. *Electroencephalography and Clinical Neurophysiology, 67,* 32–39.

Shibagaki, M., Kiyono, S., & Takeuchi, T. (1987b). REM sleep latency during nocturnal sleep in mentally retarded infants. *Electroencephalography and Clinical Neurophysiology, 66,* 512–514.

Shibagaki, M., Kiyono, S., & Watanabe, K. (1980). Nocturnal sleep in mentally retarded children: Abnormal EEG patterns in sleep cycle. *Electroencephalography and Clinical Neurophysiology, 49,* 337–344.

Singh, N.A., Clements, K.M., & Fiatarone, M.A. (1997). A randomized controlled trial of the effect of exercise on sleep. *Sleep, 20,* 95–101.

Spanos, N.P., Cross, P.A., Dickson, K., & DuBreuil, S.C. (1993). Close encounters: An examination of UFO experiences. *Journal of Abnormal Psychology, 102,* 624–632.

Stevenson, R.L. (1991). *The strange case of Dr. Jekyll and Mr. Hyde.* Lincoln: University of Nebraska Press.

Thorpy, M., & Glovinsky, P. (1987). Parasomnias. *Psychiatric Clinics of North America, 10,* 623–639.

Wacker, D.P., Steege, M.W., Northup, J., Sasso, G., Berg, W., Reimers, T., Cooper, L., Cigrand, K., & Donn, L. (1990). A component analysis of functional communication training across three topographies of severe behavior problems. *Journal of Applied Behavior Analysis, 23,* 417–429.

Wood, J.M., Bootzin, R.R., Rosenhan, D., Nolen-Hoeksema, S., & Jourden, F. (1992). Effects of the 1989 San Francisco earthquake on frequency and content of nightmares. *Journal of Abnormal Psychology, 101,* 219–224.

Wooten, V. (1990). Evaluation and management of sleep disorders in the elderly. *Psychiatric Annals, 20,* 466–473.

Zuckerman, B., Stevenson, J., & Bailey, V. (1987). Sleep problems in early childhood: Continuities, predictive factors, and behavioral correlates. *Pediatrics, 80,* 664–671.

# Additional Readings

## CHAPTER 1

Blakeslee, S. (1993, August 3). Mystery of sleep yields as studies reveal immune tie. *New York Times*, C1.

Carskadon, M.A., & Dement, W.C. (1989). Normal human sleep: An overview. In M.H. Kryer, T. Roth, & W.C. Dement (Eds.), *Principles and practice of sleep medicine* (pp. 3–13). Philadelphia: W.B. Saunders.

Hobson, J.A. (1988). *The dreaming brain*. New York: Basic Books.

## CHAPTER 2

American Sleep Disorders Association. (1990). *The international classification of sleep disorders: Diagnostic and coding manual*. Rochester, MN: Author.

Bartlett, L.B., Rooney, V., & Spedding, S. (1985). Nocturnal difficulties in a population of mentally handicapped children. *British Journal of Mental Subnormality, 31*, 54–59.

Batshaw, M.L. (Ed.). (1997). *Children with disabilities* (4th ed.). Baltimore: Paul H. Brookes Publishing Co.

Durand, V.M., & Barlow, D.H. (1997). *Abnormal psychology: An introduction*. Pacific Grove, CA: Brooks/Cole.

Giles, D.E., & Buysse, D.J. (1993). Parasomnias. In D.L. Dunner (Ed.), *Current psychiatric therapy* (pp. 361–372). Philadelphia: W.B. Saunders.

Hauri, P. (1982). *The sleep disorders* (2nd ed.). Kalamazoo, MI: Upjohn Company.

Kales, A., Soldatos, C.R., & Kales, J.D. (1987). Sleep disorders: Insomnia, sleepwalking, night terrors, nightmares, and enuresis. *Annals of Internal Medicine, 106*, 582–592.

Morin, C.M. (1993). *Insomnia: Psychological assessment and management*. New York: Guilford Press.

Piazza, C.C., Fisher, W., Kiesewetter, B.S., Bowman, L., & Moser, H. (1990). Aberrant sleep patterns in children with Rett syndrome. *Brain & Development, 12*, 488–493.

Van de Castle, R.L. (1994). *Our dreaming mind*. New York: Ballantine Books.

## CHAPTER 3

Hauri, P. (Ed.). (1991). *Case studies in insomnia*. New York: Plenum Medical Book Company.

Hauri, P., & Linde, S. (1990). *No more sleepless nights.* New York: John Wiley & Sons.

Morin, C.M. (1993). *Insomnia: Psychological assessment and management.* New York: Guilford Press.

Perl, J. (1993). *Sleep right in five nights.* New York: William Morrow & Company.

Sadeh, A. (1994). Assessment of intervention for infant night waking: Parental reports and activity-based home monitoring. *Journal of Consulting and Clinical Psychology, 62,* 63–68.

## CHAPTER 4

Adams, L., & Rickert, V. (1989). Reducing bedtime tantrums: Comparison between positive routines and graduated extinction. *Pediatrics, 84,* 756–761.

Bootzin, R.R., Epstein, D., & Wood, J.M. (1991). Stimulus control instructions. In P. Hauri (Ed.), *Case studies in insomnia* (pp. 19–28). New York: Plenum Medical Book Company.

Hauri, P.J. (1991). Sleep hygiene, relaxation therapy, and cognitive interventions. In P. Hauri (Ed.), *Case studies in insomnia* (pp. 65–84). New York: Plenum Medical Book Company.

Milan, M.A., Mitchell, Z.P., Berger, M.I., & Pierson, D.F. (1981). Positive routines: A rapid alternative to extinction for elimination of bedtime tantrum behavior. *Child Behavior Therapy, 3,* 13–25.

Perl, J. (1993). *Sleep right in five nights.* New York: William Morrow & Company.

## CHAPTER 5

Durand, V.M., Mindell, J.A., Mapstone, E., & Gernert-Dott, P. (1995). Treatment of multiple sleep disorders in children. In C.E. Schaefer (Ed.), *Clinical handbook of sleep disorders in children* (pp. 311–333). Northvale, NJ: Jason Aronson Inc.

Piazza, C.C., Fisher, W., & Moser, H. (1991). Behavioral treatment of sleep dysfunction in patients with Rett syndrome. *Brain & Development, 13,* 232–236.

## CHAPTER 6

Ferber, R. (1985). *Solve your child's sleep problems.* New York: Simon & Schuster.

Friedman, L., Bliwise, D.L., Yesave, J.A., & Salom, S.R. (1990). A preliminary study comparing sleep restriction and relaxation treatments for insomnia in older adults. *Journal of Gerontology: Psychological Sciences, 46,* 1–8.

Glovinsky, P.B., & Spielman, A.J. (1991). Sleep restriction therapy. In P. Hauri (Ed.), *Case studies in insomnia* (pp. 49–63). New York: Plenum Medical Book Company.

Johnson, C.M., Bradley-Johnson, S., & Stack, J.M. (1981). Decreasing the frequency of infants' nocturnal crying with the use of scheduled awakenings. *Family Practice Research Journal, 1,* 98–104.

Johnson, C.M., & Lerner, M. (1985). Amelioration of infants' sleep disturbances: II. Effects of scheduled awakenings by compliant parents. *Infant Mental Health Journal, 6,* 21–30.

Morin, C., Kowatch, R., & O'Shanick, G. (1990). Sleep restriction for the in-patient treatment of insomnia. *Sleep, 13,* 182–186.

Spielman, A.J., Saskin, P., & Thorpy, M.J. (1987). Treatment of chronic insomnia by restriction of time in bed. *Sleep, 10,* 45–56.

Williams, C.D. (1959). The elimination of tantrum behavior by extinction procedures. *Journal of Abnormal Social Psychology, 59,* 269–273.

## CHAPTER 7

Allen, R.P. (1991). Early morning awakening insomnia: Bright-light treatment. In P. Hauri (Ed.), *Case studies in insomnia* (pp. 207–220). New York: Plenum Medical Book Company.

Czeisler, C.A., Richardson, G.S., Coleman, R.M., Zimmerman, J.C., Moore-Ede, M.C., Dement, W.C., & Weitzman, E.D. (1981). Chronotherapy: Resetting the circadian clocks of patients with delayed sleep phase insomnia. *Sleep, 4,* 1–21.

Morris, M., Lack, L., & Dawson, D. (1990). Sleep onset insomniacs have delayed temperature rhythms *Sleep, 13,* 1 14.

Rosenberg, R. (1991). Assessment and treatment of delayed sleep phase syndrome. In P. Hauri (Ed.), *Case studies in insomnia* (pp. 193–205). New York: Plenum Medical Book Company.

## CHAPTER 8

Abe, K., Oda, N., Ikenaga, K., & Yamada, T. (1993). Twin study on night terrors, fears and some physiological and behavioural characteristics in children. *Psychiatric Genetics, 3,* 39–43.

Halliday, G. (1987). Direct psychological therapies for nightmares: A review. *Clinical Psychology Review, 7,* 501–523.

Halliday, G. (1995). Treating nightmares in children. In C.E. Schaefer (Ed.), *Clinical handbook of sleep disorders in children* (pp. 149–175). Northvale, NJ: Jason Aronson Inc.

Kales, A., Soldatos, C.R., Cadwell, A., Kales, J., Humphrey, F., Charney, D., & Schweitzer, P. (1980). Somnambulism: Clinical characteristics and personality patterns. *Archives of General Psychiatry, 37,* 1406–1410.

Koe, G.G. (1989). Hypnotic treatment of sleep terror disorder: A case report. *American Journal of Clinical Hypnosis, 32,* 36–40.

Kohen, D.P., Mahowald, M.W., & Rosen, G.M. (1992). Sleep-terror disorder in children: The role of self-hypnosis in management. *American Journal of Clinical Hypnosis, 34,* 233–244.

Lask, B. (1988). Novel and non-toxic treatment for night terrors. *British Medical Journal, 297,* 592.

Llorente, M.D., Currier, M.B., Norman, S.E., & Mellman, T.A. (1992). Night terrors in adults: Phenomenology and relationship to psychopathology. *Journal of Clinical Psychiatry, 53,* 392–394.

Maskey, S. (1993). Simple treatment for night terrors. *British Medical Journal, 306,* 1477.

Mindell, J.A. (1993). Sleep disorders in children. *Health Psychology, 12,* 151–162.

Standards of Practice Committee of the American Sleep Disorders Association. (1994). Practice parameters for the use of stimulants in the treatment of narcolepsy. *Sleep, 17,* 348–351.

Thorpy, M., & Glovinsky, P. (1987). Parasomniacs. *Psychiatric Clinics of North America, 10,* 623–639.

## CHAPTER 9

Bootzin, R.R., Manber, R., Perlis, M.L., Salvio, M., & Wyatt, J.K. (1993). Sleep disorders. In P.B. Sutker & H.E. Adams (Eds.), *Comprehensive handbook of psychopathology* (pp. 531–561). New York: Plenum Medical Book Company.

Cornwell, A.C. (1995). Sleep and sudden infant death syndrome. In C.E. Schaefer (Ed.), *Clinical handbook of sleep disorders in children* (pp. 15–47). Northvale, NJ: Jason Aronson Inc.

Gibbons, V.P., & Kotagal, S. (1995). Narcolepsy in children. In C.E. Schaefer (Ed.), *Clinical handbook of sleep disorders in children* (pp. 267–284). Northvale, NJ: Jason Aronson Inc.

Palasti, S., & Potsic, W.P. (1995). Managing the child with obstructive sleep apnea. In C.E. Schaefer (Ed.), *Clinical handbook of sleep disorders in children* (pp. 253–266). Northvale, NJ: Jason Aronson Inc.

Standards of Practice Committee of the American Sleep Disorders Association. (1995). Practice parameters for the treatment of snoring and obstructive sleep apnea with oral appliances. *Sleep, 18,* 511–513.

Walters, A.S., Picchietti, D.L., Ehrenberg, B.L., & Wagner, M.L. (1994). Restless legs syndrome in childhood and adolescence. *Pediatric Neurology, 11,* 241–245.

Wooten, V. (1990). Evaluation and management of sleep disorders in the elderly. *Psychiatric Annals, 20,* 466–473.

## CHAPTER 10

Azrin, N.H., & Foxx, R.M. (1974). *Toilet training in less than a day.* New York: Pocket Books.

Garland, E.J. (1995). The relationship of sleep disturbances to childhood panic disorder. In C.E. Schaefer (Ed.), *Clinical handbook of sleep disorders in children* (pp. 285–310). Northvale, NJ: Jason Aronson Inc.

Hauri, P.J. (1991). Sleep hygiene, relaxation therapy, and cognitive interventions. In P. Hauri (Ed.), *Case studies in insomnia* (pp. 65–84). New York: Plenum Medical Book Company.

## CHAPTER 11

Barkley, R.A. (1995). *Taking charge of ADHD: The complete, authoritative guide for parents.* New York: Guilford Press.

Durand, V.M. (1990). *Severe behavior problems: A functional communication training approach.* New York: Guilford Press.

Durand, V.M., & Carr, E.G. (1991). Functional communication training to reduce challenging behavior: Maintenance and application in new settings. *Journal of Applied Behavior Analysis, 24,* 251–264.

Durand, V.M., & Crimmins, D.B. (1988). Identifying the variables maintaining self-injurious behavior. *Journal of Autism and Developmental Disorders, 18,* 99–117.

Durand, V.M., & Crimmins, D.B. (1992). *The Motivation Assessment Scale (MAS) administration guide.* Topeka, KS: Monaco & Associates.

Miltenberger, R. (1997). *Behavior modification: Principles and procedures.* Pacific Grove, CA: Brooks/Cole.

O'Neill, R.E., Horner, R.H., Albin, R.W., Sprague, J.R., Storey, K., & Newton, J.S. (1997). *Functional assessment and program development for problem behavior: A practical handbook.* Pacific Grove, CA: Brooks/Cole.

## CHAPTER 12

Kales, A., Bixler, E.O., Tan, T.L., Scharf, M.B., & Kales, J.D. (1974). Chronic hypnotic drug use: Ineffectiveness, drug withdrawal insomnia, and dependence. *Journal of the American Medical Association, 5,* 573–577.

Kales, A., Scharf, M.B., Kales, J.D., & Soldatos, C.R. (1979). Rebound insomnia: A potential hazard following withdrawal of certain benzodiazepines. *Journal of the American Medical Association, 241,* 1691–1695.

Richman, N. (1985). A double-blind drug trial of treatment in young children with waking problems. *Journal of Child Psychology and Psychiatry, 26,* 591–598.

## CHAPTER 13

Mindell, J.A. (1997). *Sleeping through the night: How infants, toddlers, and their parents can get a good night's sleep.* New York: HarperCollins.

Perl, J. (1993). *Sleep right in five nights.* New York: William Morrow & Company.

# Index